Older Adult Friendship

SOME OTHER VOLUMES IN THE
SAGE FOCUS EDITIONS

Older Adult Friendship

Structure and Process

EDITED BY
Rebecca G. Adams
Rosemary Blieszner

SAGE PUBLICATIONS
The Publishers of Professional Social Science
Newbury Park   London   New Delhi

For information address:

SAGE Publications, Inc.
2111 West Hillcrest Drive
Newbury Park, California 91320

SAGE Publications Ltd.
28 Banner Street
London EC1Y 8QE
England

SAGE Publications India Pvt. Ltd.
M-32 Market
Greater Kailash I
New Delhi 110 048 India

Printed in the United States of America

Library of Congress Cataloging-in-Publication Data

Main entry under title:

Older adult friendship : structure and process / co-edited by Rebecca
   G. Adams and Rosemary Blieszner.
          p.   cm. — (Sage focus editions ; v. 103)
       Bibliography: p.
       Includes index.
       ISBN 0-8039-3143-3.   ISBN 0-8039-3144-1 (pbk.)
       1. Aged—United States—Attitudes.   2. Friendship—United States.
   I. Adams, Rebecca G.   II. Blieszner, Rosemary.
   HQ1064.U50415   1989
   305.2′6—dc19   88-28287
                                                            CIP

FIRST PRINTING 1989

Contents

Foreword

I am deeply honored to have been asked by the editors to offer a few prefatory comments, even though an invitation to write a foreword is a clear signal that one's own work has been outstripped. Happily so, as this volume bountifully attests. My work on friendship began over two decades ago, when I was a graduate student and research assistant to Matilda White Riley who was then engaged in compiling the material for her monumental inventory of research findings (Volume I of *Aging and Society*, 1968). Following a pattern that many of you will recognize, the choice of a dissertation topic—friendship, in this case—was due less to its intrinsic attractiveness than to the fact that it was relatively unexplored. Indeed, from a sociological perspective there was primarily Georg Simmel among the old masters and a few small-scale empirical studies by sociologists interested in primary groups in general.

Having thus staked out a partial claim on the subject matter, and also being immersed in the gerontological literature, it was but a short step to integrating the two areas of interest into an examination of friendship patterns across the life course. The result was an extended essay that I suspected would remain long buried in a book that was pretty heavy going, on a relatively obscure topic, and hideously expensive, to boot (*Aging and Society*, Volume III, 1972). What ultimately happened was that I received a free ride when the entire volume (subtitled "A Theory of Age Stratification") became widely known for its contribution to the emerging sociology of age.

The publication of an article on "Sex Roles, Friendship, and the Life Course," in 1979, ended my active involvement in friendship studies. I all too readily accepted the going wisdom that informal relationships were sociologically marginal (indeed, at one point in the 1972 essay I contrasted friendship with "major" roles). Over the next decade and a half I continued to receive a few papers each year on friendship among the elderly to review for various publications, but there was little here to excite the soul—the statistical techniques typically overwhelmed the data base, and a literature review was tarted up as a theory.

It was, therefore, with some astonishment as well as great professional interest that I recently realized how many scholars were working on various aspects of the topic, in a number of different fields, and from a range of theoretical perspectives. The publication of this collection of essays signifies that the study of friendship has gained its long-deserved legitimacy and centrality in the social sciences. In a sense, this volume marks the culmination of a first phase in the solidification of an academic specialty, bringing together the scattered strands of research and theory that have gradually developed over the past two decades. In so doing, we are able to see what has been accomplished in the several disciplines and how differing approaches can be mutually enlightening. At the same time, we become aware of the gaps in research, anomalies in findings, and limitations of theory. And that is what a book such as this should do: bring coherence to the past and point to the future.

In terms of where we are today compared to 20 years ago, the most obvious accomplishment of this collection is to create a dialogue between psychologists and sociologists (and I speak as one who clings tenaciously to Durkheim's dictum that social facts must be explained by social facts). The interplay between "dispositional" and "situational" factors is explicitly recognized by several of the authors. Indeed, friendship may be the perfect test tube for exploring how external factors condition internal processes. That is, aside from its inherent fascination, friendship is a crucial focal point for explicating relationships of more general application. In addition, it is obvious by now that the "meaning of friendship" can be derived only from the point of view of the respondents, that is, that we must reconstruct behavior from the ground up as well as from the societal level down.

Second, one must be impressed by the many directions in which research has spread—across the entire life course, embracing the homeless as well as those more securely embedded in primary groups, and among women and men as well as between them. The variety of theoretical perspectives that yield insight is also impressive—equity and exchange, life span development, the socially structured life course, and various combinations of these factors. There is also the salutary reminder that intimacy has its dangers and that informal relationships can also have negative effects.

Equally clear, I believe, are the directions that future research should take. Most crucially, we need to know whether or not the life course/life span/life cycle models we have constructed have any cross-cultural validity. Many social scientists seriously doubt the existence of any "developmental ground plan" that exists apart from cultural or historical specificity. Before turning to other societies, we should perhaps know more about subgroups within our own—what about the poor who are not homeless, or Mexican-Americans, or inner-city minority populations? Do American Jews have different friendship patterns than born-again Christians? If so, why?

At the other end of the research spectrum, we could use more studies based on social-psychological models, as in the symbolic interaction and ethnomethodological traditions. True, this agenda will add to the confusion of theories and methods that already beset us. But better to thicken the pot than to risk too thin a gruel.

In any event, this collection provides a splendid introduction to the systematic study of friendship and is a necessary launching pad for further exploration of this most existentially fragile but deeply enduring phenomenon.

—Beth B. Hess

Preface

Scholars have neglected the study of older adult friendship until recently. This is unfortunate, because the voluntary nature of friendship conceptually distinguishes it from nonvoluntary relationships with relatives, neighbors, and coworkers. Of course, though not formalized in modern Western society, structural and normative constraints lead individuals to have friends of the same sex, age, race, religion, geographic area, and socioeconomic status. The context in which friendship takes place also affects its content and dynamics. It is the element of choice, however, that makes friendship different from other types of social relationships. Furthermore, friendships vary tremendously because there are fewer constraints on them than on other social relationships. Studying friendship thus enables researchers to examine the interplay between structure and process in a way that is not possible when studying relationships that exhibit less variation.

There are important reasons for studying friendship and aging together. First, friendships usually involve age peers, whereas neighbor and kin relationships are often intergenerational. Age peers are likely to share similar problems, to experience similar losses, and to possess similar resources; they are comparable in status to one another. Friendship thus provides aged individuals with an opportunity to socialize among equals. Second, in addition to sharing similar current realities, older people have had similar past experiences. Because elderly adults have lived long lives, studying their friendships provides a unique opportunity to examine the interplay between the effects of aging and cohort membership. Third, gerontologists have often characterized progression from the middle to the later years of life as a series of losses of roles and choices. Friendship, as a voluntary relationship and enduring role, is thus important to the maintenance of older adults' psychological well-being. Finally, friendships may be relatively more important to old people in the future than they are now. As families scatter over larger areas, future generations of elderly persons may be less likely than current cohorts to be entrenched in extended kinship networks.

Theoretical and methodological advances in older adult friendship research have occurred recently, especially in the fields of sociology and psychology. Researchers whose work does not focus specifically on friendship, however, seem virtually unaware of this progress. They continue to treat friendship as a residual category of social relationships or to use superficial conceptualizations and measurements of it. One reason for this is that the friendship literature is scattered throughout the journals of many disciplines. We hope that this multidisciplinary volume will encourage the incorporation of these recent advancements into research, whether friendship is of central or of peripheral importance to these future studies.

This volume consists of chapters that each review, summarize, integrate, and elaborate on a specific aspect of the friendship literature. The focus is on older adult friendship, but the theoretical and methodological issues should be of interest to those who study social relationships at all stages of the life course. In many cases, a lack of literature on aging and friendship led authors to rely on research about younger persons' friendships to develop theoretical ideas for the study of older persons' friendships. Additionally, some contributors introduce new data to begin to fill gaps in the literature. The purpose of all of the chapters, however, is to review and critique previous work and to articulate theoretical frameworks and associated research strategies for new efforts rather than to report on individual studies.

We invited the authors to write chapters for this book because they have already made contributions to our understanding of friendship. They represent a variety of disciplines: Adams, Allan, and Litwak are sociologists; Crohan, Rook, and Wright are social psychologists; Antonucci, Blieszner, Roberto, and Tesch received training in human development; and Cohen is a psychiatrist.

Our editorial goal was to do more than produce a collection of disparate chapters on aging and friendship. We endeavored, through frequent communication and a workshop with the authors, to construct a volume that says something that the individual chapters do not say by themselves—namely, that to understand friendship, one must study the interplay between structure and process.

We organized the volume around this theme. In Part I, Adams provides the reader with an overview of the conceptual and methodological issues in the field and introduces many of the studies referenced throughout the rest of the volume.

Part II includes theoretical discussions from two perspectives. The first is a structural approach taken by Allan and Adams in their examination of how context promotes or inhibits the friendships of aged adults. Litwak also uses a structural framework to analyze distinctive forms of friendship and the importance of each type of friend to older adults. The second perspective in Part II is developmental. Tesch explores the influence of early personality development and interpersonal relations on late-life friendship. Blieszner discusses the processes by which older adults initiate, maintain, and end friendships.

The authors in Part III elaborate upon the social processes involved in friendship. First, Crohan and Antonucci analyze myriad ways that friends provide social support to older adults. Next, Roberto grounds friend interaction in the theoretical perspectives of social exchange and equity. Then, Rook discusses an aspect of friendship that has received little attention, the causes and consequences of problems in older adults' friendships.

In Part IV, the contributors examine the interplay between structure and process by providing in-depth looks at how social statuses affect friendship. Using a developmental approach, incorporating dispositional and structural explanations, Wright examines the effect of gender on the potential for same-sex and cross-sex friendships. Using a structural approach and network analysis, Cohen demonstrates that homeless old men are not bereft of friendships. Finally, in Part V, Blieszner suggests directions for future research on friendship and aging.

Colleagues warned us that doing an edited volume would be very difficult, but enthusiastic contributors and the terrific help we got from others made it a pleasant though time-consuming experience. We got off to a good start, thanks to some very thorough anonymous reviews and thoughtful, helpful advice from our Sage Editor, Terry Hendrix. Along the way, Suzanne B. Kurth read the entire manuscript and made useful comments, as did students in Blieszner's seminar on adult friendship. Beth B. Hess not only wrote the Foreword to this book, she gave us some constructive advice about the first drafts of the chapters. How fortunate for us that the founding mother of our field is a skilled editor and critic. Near the end, B. Jan McCulloch, Jeanette K. Adams, and Paul Ahlers, graduate students at the University of North Carolina at Greensboro, stepped in to help.

Our universities were also supportive. The Research Council of the University of North Carolina at Greensboro granted Adams funds to cover some of the costs incurred in developing this volume. Laura M. Land, Assistant Director of Housing and Residence Life, Virginia Polytechnic Institute and State University, helped with the arrangements for the contributors' workshop that was held on the campus in Blacksburg. Our colleagues in the Sociology Department at UNCG and the Department of Family and Child Development at VPI and SU encouraged us. Last but not least, Janice Maness, Joan Roach, and Cathy Barnes, secretaries at UNCG, provided us with clerical support.

We agreed early on to list our names in alphabetical order but to divide the editorial work evenly. This book is the product of a joint effort that has strengthened our professional relationship and deepened our friendship. We dedicate it to our Steves.

—Rebecca G. Adams
Greensboro, NC

—Rosemary Blieszner
Blacksburg, VA

PART I

Overview

1

Conceptual and Methodological Issues in Studying Friendships of Older Adults

REBECCA G. ADAMS

Many authors, including myself, have lamented the relative lack of studies on friendship (Adams, 1983; Hess, 1972; Cohen, 1961). If one searches through *Psychological Abstracts* and *Sociological Abstracts*, however, one finds myriad references under the heading. This contradiction is only apparent. Many of the articles classified as studies of friendship discuss it only in passing, combine a measure of friendship behavior with other measures of social behavior to create general indices of various kinds, do not distinguish between neighbors and friends, or discuss friendship abstractly rather than report on studies of actual friendship behavior. After eliminating these references from consideration, one is left with a hodgepodge of studies, designed with different intentions, using different measures and methods, and with different strengths and weaknesses. Depending upon one's disciplinary perspective, personal view of social reality, methodological biases, and larger agenda, one indeed might not consider many of these remaining articles as studies of friendship.

My major purpose in this chapter is to impose some conceptual and methodological order on the unwieldy mass of research on friendship. This effort is clumsy, because researchers often have made independent decisions regarding measurement, questionnaire design, and study design. It is thus impossible to create a typology of studies of friendship with a reasonably limited number of categories. Instead, one must discuss each decision separately.

Most of the research that focuses on friendship as a distinct category of social relationships has been conducted in the last 20 or 25 years. The friendship literature is scattered throughout the journals of many disciplines. Among others, gerontologists have focused a great deal of attention on friendship. This is probably due to the centrality of the study of friendship to activity and disengagement theories, the debate around which has preoccupied gerontologists for almost three decades. More recently, gerontologists have begun studying informal support, some of which is naturally provided by friends. Gerontology is a multidisciplinary field, so friendship scholars who are gerontologists review literature from numerous fields of study. A high level of interdisciplinary communication among gerontologists enhances the quality and creativity of their friendship research. For this reason, this chapter and, indeed, this entire volume focus primarily on studies of older adult friendships. The methodological and conceptual decisions that gerontologists have made in studying friendship reflect those that other friendship researchers have made. Limiting the substantive focus of this chapter to older adult friendships thus does not mean that the conceptual and methodological issues discussed are irrelevant to those who research friendships occurring during other stages of life.

Depending on how one defines, measures, and studies friendship, one reaches different conclusions and gains different knowledge. A second purpose of this chapter, then, is to describe how methodological and conceptual decisions have shaped our impressions of older adult friendship and to speculate about how our view of it might change if studies were conducted differently in the future.

Almost all of the studies of the friendships of older people have been based on data collected using some form of survey research methods. Although researchers using observational or documentary methods have conducted excellent ethnographies on the social lives of older people (e.g., Arth, 1961; Eckert, 1980; Gubrium, 1975; Hochschild, 1973; Hoyt, 1954; Retsinas & Garrity, 1985), they have focused more broadly on social interaction, old age subculture, sociability, or social ties rather than specifically on friendship. Ethnographers have observed many relationships that were undoubtedly friendships. They have not, however, systematically explored what friendship meant to those studied. Often they have assumed that observable social interaction indicated a friendship. This chapter thus focuses mainly on the decisions made by survey researchers studying older adult friendships.

By examining the literature on older adult friendships in this chapter, I attempt to accomplish two purposes—to bring some conceptual and methodological order to the friendship literature and to illustrate the connection between the decisions survey researchers have made about how to study friendship and what we know about it. I also intend this chapter to alert potential friendship researchers to pertinent conceptual and methodological issues, make readers better informed and more critical consumers of friendship research, and serve as an introduction to many of the studies referenced throughout the rest of the volume. Four sections follow. The first three describe and critique the decisions older adult friendship researchers have made about how to define and measure friendship, questionnaire design, and other design issues, respectively. The last section discusses the connection between how researchers have studied older adult friendships and our knowledge of them.

DEFINITION AND
MEASUREMENT OF FRIENDSHIP

Members of our culture use the word *friend* in a variety of ways. Although we typically describe an individual as a friend with confidence that listeners understand our meaning, some might use the term to refer to either a mere acquaintance or an intimate (Allan, 1977; Kurth, 1970; Paine, 1969). As Matthews (1986, p. 155) observed, "there is a great deal of evidence to indicate that the 'culture of friendship' is too diverse to capture with a clearly specified set of norms and expectations." Not only does friendship lack cultural definition, it lacks structural definition. An individual's friends are neither determined by blood ties, as relatives are, nor by residence, as neighbors are (Cohen, 1961; Keller, 1968; Toennies, 1961). Although people tend to choose friends of the same sex, age, race, religion, geographic area, and status level (Adams, 1985a; Blau, 1973; Booth & Hess, 1974; Laumann, 1973), our culture does not require friends to be in structurally similar positions and thus many are not.

The lack of cultural and structural definitions of friendship makes studying it exciting, but difficult. Researchers have coped with the lack of consensus regarding the definition of the word *friend* in three ways:

(a) leaving the responsibility for the interpretation of the word to the people under study, (b) limiting the definition of friendship in some way, or (c) employing inductive methods to determine what the term means to those being studied. I have included examples of each of these approaches in Table 1.1.

The authors of 10 of the articles listed in Table 1.1 left the entire responsibility for the interpretation of the word *friend* to the people under study. These studies typically included global questions about some aspect of friendship behavior (see discussion below). For example, Wood and Robertson (1978, p. 369) asked questions about the "number and frequency of activities engaged in with . . . friends." Incidentally, this is the measurement strategy employed by researchers whose articles, not discussed in this chapter or included in Table 1.1, mention friendship only in passing.

The major problem with allowing respondents to interpret the meaning of the word *friend* entirely by themselves is the difficulty in interpreting study findings. Do they reflect real behavior or definitions of friendship? Attempts to compare findings across studies illustrate the problem best. Although Johnson (1983), Pihlblad and McNamara (1965), and Wood and Robertson (1978) all asked questions about frequency of visiting with friends, one cannot confidently compare their results. One cannot assume that people living in the cultural contexts of a working-class neighborhood in Madison, Wisconsin (Wood & Robertson, 1978), three small towns in central Missouri (Pihlblad & McNamara, 1965), and the San Francisco Bay Area (Johnson, 1983) defined friendships similarly. One can therefore not assume that the measure of visiting was reliable.

To attempt to cope with this problem, the authors of 3 of the 10 studies referred to above divided relationships into types before asking about them. Mancini and Simon (1984) asked their respondents about close and casual friends, and Tesch, Whitbourne, and Nehrke (1981) asked theirs about friends inside and outside of a domiciliary home. Using a data collection methodology developed by Kahn and Antonucci (1980), Shea, Thompson, and Blieszner (1988) had their respondents name their closest friends, not quite so close friends, and acquaintances with whom they wished to become friends. A priori typologies of friendship make comparisons across respondents easier.

A more common method of attempting to cope with this problem is to limit the interpretation of the word *friend* in some way (see Table 1.1). Some studies have thus been limited: to close, intimate, good, or best friends; to between 1 and 5 friends; to proximate friends; by frequency or recency of contact; to nonrelatives; or to nonwork relationships. In other studies, researchers have used friendship as a residual category. That is, they have treated relationships other than kin, work, and neighbor relationships as friendships.

As one can see in Table 1.1, some researchers have limited their respondents use of the word *friend* in more than one way. For example, Roberto and Scott (1986, p. 104) reported that

> respondents were asked about their relationship with both their *best* and *least best* friend. The best and least best, or other friend, was selected by asking the respondents to first give the number of people they considered to be their close friends, *not* including relatives. Close friends were defined as "those special people whose friendship means the most to you." Out of these close friends, the respondents were asked to think of their very best friend who lived in the area and with whom they had had contact within the past 6 months. The respondents were then asked to name one other person who lived in the area and with whom they had had contact within the past 6 months, but whom they considered to be their least best friend in their close-friend network.

Limiting the definition of friendship has both advantages and disadvantages. On one hand, there are practical and theoretical reasons for using this approach. Left without any limitations, respondents name many friendships—perhaps more than are possible to study given the use of certain measurement strategies and the lack of time and other resources. As discussed above, if researchers do not limit its definition, respondents might include many different types of relationships as friendships and thus render comparisons and summaries confusing. Furthermore, sometimes the theoretical question requires the investigator to specify the definition of friendship in some way. For example, Rosow (1967) was interested in the relationship between age density of residential context and social interaction among neighbors, so he studied only local friendships.

On the other hand, limiting the definition of friendship does not solve all problems. It is impractical and unproductive to specify definitional criteria on all of the dimensions of friendship, so most researchers specify criteria on only one or two dimensions. This means that they do not completely solve the comparability problem. For example, if a researcher limits the definition of friendship to those with whom the respondent frequently interacts, the friends included still vary in

TABLE 1.1
Definition and Measurement of Friendship

Study	Leaving it to Respondent	Closeness	Number	Proximate	Contact	Nonkin	Nonwork	Resid.	Other	Inductive
				Approach to Definition of Friendship						
				Limiting it in Some Way						
Adams, 1985a, 1986a, 1986b, 1986c, 1987										X
Babchuk, 1978	X									
Bankoff, 1981									X	
Blau, 1961, 1973		X								
Booth & Hess, 1974		X				X				
Candy, Troll, & Levy, 1981		X	X							
Cantor, 1979		X				X				
Chappell, 1983		X				X				
Cohen & Rajkowski, 1982; Sokolovsky & Cohen, 1981			X		X	X				
Eckert, 1980				X						
Essex & Nam, 1987		X	X							
Ferraro, Mutran, & Barresi, 1984								X		
Fischer, 1982; Fischer & Oliker, 1982										X
Johnson, 1983; Johnson & Catalano, 1983	X									

Reference	1	2	3	4	5	6	7	8	9
Keith, Hill, Goudy, & Powers, 1984		X	X						
Litwak, 1985		X	X						
Lopata, 1977, 1979			X						
Lowenthal & Haven, 1968		X						X	
Mancini, 1980	X								X
Mancini & Simon, 1984	X								
Matthews, 1983, 1986	X								
Pihlblad & Adams, 1972	X								
Pihlblad & McNamara, 1965	X								
Powers & Bultena, 1976	X		X						
Roberto & Scott, 1984		X	X	X	X	X			
Roberto & Scott, 1986		X	X	X	X	X	X		
Rose, 1965							X		
Rosenberg, 1970		X	X		X				
Rosow, 1965, 1967		X		X	X				
Shea, Thompson, & Blieszner, 1988	X	X							
Shulman, 1975		X	X					X	
Simons, 1984	X								
Spakes, 1979	X								
Tesch, Whitbourne, & Nehrke, 1981	X								
Tomeh, 1964									
Usui, 1984		X	X					X	
Weiss & Lowenthal, 1975		X	X						
Wood & Robertson, 1978	X	X						X	

emotional closeness, in physical distance separating them, and in other ways. Furthermore, by limiting the respondents' definitions of the word *friend*, the researcher studies a subtype of friendship rather than friendship in general. As mentioned above, this is sometimes by theoretical intention. Often, however, after limiting the definition of friendship, the researcher discusses findings as though he or she had imposed no limitation. Only careful readers remember the definitional decisions and assess their impact on findings.

The use of a priori structural and social-psychological definitions pose slightly different problems for the researcher. Most persons in our society define friendship social psychologically rather than structurally. For example, we are more likely to mention emotional closeness than physical proximity as an important factor in friendship. Using an a priori structural definition thus imposes artificial limitations on the use of the word *friend*. A useful a priori social-psychological definition would be difficult to develop, however, because people divide friends from nonfriends in different places along, for example, the continuum of perceived loyalty. Given the variation and range of definitions of friendship, it may be more plausible to develop a measure of *degrees of friendship* rather than an a priori definition designed to separate friends from nonfriends. This would not, however, help the researcher who wants to ask questions about specific friendships.

Studies using a priori definitions of friendship have, in some regards, been premature. Researchers still must do more studies of how people define friendship. Very recently, two other researchers (Fischer, 1982; Matthews, 1983) and I (Adams, 1985b) each used inductive approaches to the study of friendship. This body of literature furthers our understanding of how people use the word *friend* in our society.

The other two researchers induced definitions of friendship by studying the characteristics of relationships described as friendships. Matthews (1983) conducted guided conversations with men and women aged 60 or over using friendship as a constant referent. Two definitions of friendship emerged—one emphasizing the special qualifications that particular individuals had, such as a shared past, and one emphasizing the importance of the presence of people in daily life. Fischer (1982) studied the differences between associates who were labeled as friends and those who were not. A cross-section of adults living in northern California applied the label friend broadly to almost all associates who were not kin, coworkers, or neighbors. Friends were likely to be the same age, to have known one another for a long time, and to be involved socially, rather than intimately or economically.

In studying 70 elderly, white, nonmarried, female residents of a Chicago suburb, I distinguished between *characteristics* and *definitions* of friendship (Adams, 1985b). I began interviews by asking the women to define friendship. They tended to define it in social-psychological terms, referring to affect or predisposition to help one another, rather than in structural terms. After defining friendship, the women listed their friends and answered a series of questions about each of them. Their definitions were not closely related to the characteristics of their friends. Women who defined friendships in social-psychological terms and who had friendships conforming to their expectations did, however, tend to have higher friendship satisfaction than others. This suggests their definitions of friendship had meaning for them.

What one learns from reading these three studies in combination is that people use the word friend indiscriminately and have different types of friends, but do know what a real friend means to them. Together, these findings suggest that future investigators should direct efforts toward further understanding of types of friendship and the social and psychological factors that affect how people define and use the word *friend*. More inductive studies, particularly replications, are essential to progress further in this area. These studies are likely to be slow in appearing in the literature. Although the three studies described here used strikingly different empirical methods, all were very time consuming. Unfortunately, the structure of the academy discourages people from doing time-consuming studies and from replicating studies originally conducted by other researchers.

Summary

It would be satisfying to end this section with a discussion of a valid and reliable typology of friendship. Instead, this paragraph summarizes the warnings contained in the previous pages. First, leaving the responsibility for the interpretation of the word *friend* entirely to the people being studied leads to problems of comparability and interpretation of findings. Second, limiting the definition of friendship does not completely solve these problems and results in the study of a subtype of friendship rather than of friendship in general. Scholars must exercise caution in reading the resulting studies, because authors often discuss their findings as though they are about friendship in general when they are about a subtype of it. Third, inductive studies of friendship, including ethnographies, though very informative and necessary if we are to develop and refine a friendship typology, are also very time consuming. At this stage, friendship researchers must decide which of these three problems they are willing to endure.

QUESTIONNAIRE DESIGN

In addition to deciding how to handle the definition and measurement of friendship, researchers must decide how to ask questions about it. Among other things, they must decide whether to refer to friendship in general or specific relationships, on the unit or units of analysis, and whether to use close-ended or open-ended questions or both.

Question Referent
and Unit of Analysis

Friendship researchers have asked questions about friends in general, one specific friend (e.g., a confidant), each of a subset of members of some social network (e.g., three hotel friends, five best friends), or each member of an entire network (e.g., very close friends, recent contacts, all friends). This decision about which alternative referent to use is intricately related to whether the dyad, the respondent, or the respondent's network is the unit of analysis. For the purposes of this discussion, and in Table 1.2, I combined studies that used the respondent as the unit of analysis and those that used the respondent's network as the unit of analysis, because most studies that used one, used both. If the questions are about one specific friend or are global questions about friends in general, the respondent is the unit of analysis by default. If, however, questions are about each of two or more friends, the researcher can opt to use the respondent, the dyad, or both as units of analysis.

Although the evidence is limited, it seems quite clear that researchers obtain the most accurate data by asking questions about each member of an entire network and calculating summary scores for each respondent. Global questions require respondents to describe friendships as if they were all similar (e.g., Do you expect your friends to help you?), to calculate averages across friendships (e.g., On the average, how often do you see each of your friends?), or to sum over friendships (e.g., How many times did you visit a friend last week?). Even asking someone how many friends they have leads them to guess rather than to calculate an answer carefully. Focusing questions on specific relationships increases the possibility of receiving accurate, carefully considered answers. Asking about any fewer than all members of a specified network can also cause inaccuracy. Are three close friends really representative of all close friends? Probably not.

A problem arises, however, when researchers gather information on each network member and want to report findings using the dyad as the unit of analysis. Respondents vary in how many relationships they report. This means people who name many friendship dyads contribute more to generalizations about friendship than people who name few. Investigators can solve this problem in two ways. The researcher can either (a) ask the respondent to list a certain size subset of all friends named (e.g., Of the friends you have just named, which three are your closest friends?) and report on only those friends at the dyadic level or (b) control for size of network when using the dyad as the unit of analysis. The latter solution is the most satisfactory. It is, however, time consuming and requires a larger sample size, because size of network enters each analysis.

Question Structure

Most of the friendship surveys of older adults have relied exclusively on close-ended or structured questions. Matthews's (1983, 1986) study was a notable exception, because her interviews were guided conversations solely composed of open-ended questions. Other studies have included both close-ended and open-ended questions (e.g., Adams, 1985a, 1986b, 1987; Eckert, 1980; Johnson, 1983; Johnson & Catalano, 1983; Shea et al., 1988; Weiss & Lowenthal, 1975).

There are several reasons for including open-ended questions in a survey. First, sometimes a researcher does not know enough about a topic to create a comprehensive list of possible responses. Eckert (1980), for example, used an open-ended question to ask his respondents what they liked most about a friend.

Second, quoting respondents brings data to life for the reader. Weiss and Lowenthal (1975) effectively used this technique when describing the dimensions of friendship. Reporting that 36% mentioned similarity as a friendship quality means more when one reads what a respondent said: "We went through a lot of things together in high school; you

TABLE 1.2
Questionnaire Design

Study	Global	One Relationship	Each of Subset	Each of Network	Combination	Other	Respondent	Dyad
Adams, 1985a, 1986a, 1986b, 1986c, 1987				X			X	X
Babchuk, 1978				X			X	X
Bankoff, 1981	X						X	
Blau, 1961, 1973	X						X	
Booth & Hess, 1974				X			X	
Candy, Troll, & Levy, 1981			X					X
Cantor, 1979				X			X	X
Chappell, 1983					X		X	
Cohen & Rajkowski, 1982; Sokolovsky & Cohen, 1981				X				X
Eckert, 1980			X					X
Essex & Nam, 1987		X					X	
Ferraro, Mutran, & Barresi, 1984	X						X	
Fischer, 1982; Fischer & Oliker, 1982				X			X	X
Johnson, 1983; Johnson & Catalano, 1983	X						X	

The header spans: "Question Referent" covers Global, One Relationship, Each of Subset, Each of Network, Combination, Other; "Unit of Analysis" covers Respondent, Dyad.

Study	1	2	3	4	5	6	7	8
Keith, Hill, Goudy, & Powers, 1984		X					X	
Litwak, 1985	X	X						
Lopata, 1977, 1979		X				X	X	
Lowenthal & Haven, 1968		X						
Mancini, 1980		X						X
Mancini & Simon, 1984		X						X
Matthews, 1983, 1986	X	X	X					
Pihlblad & Adams, 1972		X						X
Pihlblad & McNamara, 1965		X						X
Powers & Bultena, 1976		X						X
Roberto & Scott, 1984		X						X
Roberto & Scott, 1986		X	X					
Rose, 1965		X						X
Rosenberg, 1970		X			X			
Rosow, 1965, 1967	X	X						X
Shea, Thompson, & Blieszner, 1988	X	X	X					
Shulman, 1975		X				X		
Simons, 1984				X				
Spakes, 1979								X
Tesch, Whitbourne, & Nehrke, 1981		X		X				
Tomeh, 1964		X				X		
Usui, 1984		X		X				
Weiss & Lowenthal, 1975		X						
Wood & Robertson, 1978		X						X

29

know, parties, drinking, all that. You have all these experiences and it just sort of binds you" (pp. 52-53).

Third, open-ended questions are useful in interpreting quantitative relationships between variables. For example, in the survey of elderly women referred to above, I asked my respondents whether they preferred their friends to know one another (Adams, 1983). These findings were useful in interpreting a negative relationship between network density and having a friend to ask for advice on money matters. A respondent observed: "You run the risk of gossip" (p. 208). Quoting another was useful in interpreting a positive relationship between network density and receiving help in an emergency: "I think they should know one another. You can transmit information quickly" (p. 208).

Finally, Gibson and Aitkenhead (1983), who did a large-scale survey of an elderly population, found that using an instrument including both open-ended and close-ended questions helped stimulate respondent interest and avoid respondent fatigue. Friendship surveys, particularly those including questions about each network member, can be quite lengthy. This is a compelling reason for including a few open-ended questions.

Like many other good ideas, including open-ended questions on a survey can be expensive because of the greater costs entailed during the interviewing and coding process (Converse, 1984). One can minimize the cost of including open-ended questions by asking them of only a subset of the entire sample. In order to use open-ended questions economically, survey researchers must have clear ideas of what findings they want to illustrate and what relationships they plan to analyze before fielding a study.

Summary

Although there are good theoretical and practical reasons for designing friendship questionnaires in many different ways, asking questions about each friend in a network and calculating summary scores for analyses with the respondent as the unit of analysis seems to be the best way to obtain accurate information. No research, however, confirms this conclusion. Dyadic analyses should always control for the total number of persons in the network. Open-ended questions about friendship are quite useful to the researcher, but not a necessity unless one desires in-depth information.

STUDY DESIGN ISSUES

Researchers must also decide what population to study, how to sample it, how to collect the data, and what study design to use. Similarly, to the decisions mentioned previously, they can make these decisions on theoretical or practical grounds.

Population and Sample

Apparently all of the studies including more than a passing reference to older adult friendship have been of local or special populations (see Table 1.3). In most cases, the investigator studied the population because it was convenient and available or for theoretical reasons unrelated to the study of friendship. There were, of course, some exceptions in which researchers chose populations for theoretical reasons related to the study of friendship (e.g., Bankoff, 1981; Cohen & Rajkowski, 1982; Rosenberg, 1970; Rosow, 1967; Shea et al., 1988; Weiss & Lowenthal, 1975). For whatever reasons researchers have chosen to study special or local populations, however, the existence of only this type of study makes it impossible to generalize about the friendships of older adults. This is not to say that studies of special populations are inherently useless in this regard. The existing studies, however, were not replications and very few reported on the responses to the same questions, so they make a limited contribution to a general knowledge of friendship among older people.

Not only have the studies of older people's friendships tended to be of local or special populations, they have tended to be of healthy, middle-class respondents. Researchers have investigated very few working-class or low-income populations. Some exceptions are the studies by Cantor (1979), Cohen and Rajkowski (1982), Sokolovsky and Cohen (1981), Eckert (1980), Ferraro, Mutran, and Barresi (1984), Rose (1965), and Rosenberg (1970). Even fewer frail populations have been studied. See Ferraro et al. (1984), Johnson (1983), Johnson and Catalano (1983), and Tesch et al. (1981) for exceptions.

Most of the samples were probability ones of some kind (see Table 1.3). Unfortunately, many of the studies that focused specifically on friendship used nonprobability samples, had very small sample sizes, or both (e.g., Adams, 1985a, 1986a, 1986b, 1986c, 1987; Bankoff, 1981; Cohen & Rajkowski, 1982; Eckert, 1980; Fischer, 1982; Fischer & Oliker, 1983; Matthews, 1983, 1986; Roberto & Scott, 1984; Rosow,

TABLE 1.3
Population and Sample

Study	Population	Sample Type	N
Adams, 1985a, 1986a, 1986b, 1986c, 1987	Unmarried elderly women in Chicago suburb	Purposive	70
Babchuk, 1978	45+ in Lincoln and Omaha, NE	Probability	800
Bankoff, 1981	2 widow support groups	Saturation	447
Blau, 1961, 1973	2 NY state health districts	Unknown	500
Booth & Hess, 1974	Midwest urban middle-aged and aged	Probability	800
Candy, Troll, & Levy, 1981	Retired and employed teachers, female high school students	Purposive	172
Cantor, 1979	NY inner city elderly	Probability	1,552
Chappell, 1983	65+, receiving no home care, in Winnipeg, Manitoba, Canada	Probability	400
Cohen & Rajkowski, 1982; Sokolovsky & Cohen, 1981	SRO hotel occupants in NYC	Probability	161
Eckert, 1980	SRO hotel occupants in California	Availability	43
Essex & Nam, 1987	50+ women in Madison, WI	Probability	356
Ferraro, Mutran, & Barresi, 1984	Census Survey of low income, aged, and disabled	Probability	3,683
Fischer, 1982; Fischer & Oliker, 1982	Urban northern California adults	Purposive	1,050
Johnson, 1983; Johnson & Catalano, 1983	Acute care hospital admissions in San Francisco Bay Area	Saturation	167
Keith, Hill, Goudy, & Powers, 1984	Married men in towns and cities in midwestern state	Probability	1,200
Litwak, 1985	65+ in NY metropolitan area and in 2 Florida counties	Availability/Probability	1,818

Lopata, 1977, 1979	Social Security benefactors in Chicago	Probability	1,169
Lowenthal & Haven, 1968	San Francisco community resident aged	Probability	280
Mancini, 1980	65+ in urbanized area of southeastern city	Probability	104
Mancini & Simon, 1984	Residents of high rise in Roanoke, VA	Saturation	91
Matthews, 1983, 1986	Senior students, agency referrals, others	Availability	63
Pihlblad & Adams, 1972	65+ in 64 small towns in Missouri	Probability	1,551
Pihlblad & McNamara, 1965	65+ in 3 small towns in central Missouri	Saturation	151
Powers & Bultena, 1976	60+, noninstitutionalized, in 5 Iowa counties	Unknown	269
Roberto & Scott, 1984	White, urban, middle-class women, 65+	Probability	71
Roberto & Scott, 1986	64+ in southwestern city	Probability	116
Rose, 1965	Adults in 2 lower-income communities in Rome	Probability	251
Rosenberg, 1970	45+, members in working class, Philadelphia, PA	Probability	1,596
Rosow, 1965, 1967	Apartment residents, 62+, in Cleveland, OH	Purposive	1,200
Shea, Thompson, & Blieszner, 1988	Residents of rural retirement community	Saturation	27
Shulman, 1975	Residents of inner-city suburb	Unknown	198
Simons, 1984	Elderly in midwestern county	Purposive	308
Spakes, 1979	National survey of 55+ in 3 community types	Purposive	873
Tesch, Whitbourne, & Nehrke, 1981	Male residents of VA center in Bath, NY	Saturation	54
Tomeh, 1964	Adults in Detroit area	Purposive	801
Usui, 1984	60+ in Jefferson County, KY	Probability	704
Weiss & Lowenthal, 1975	Families of high school students (including pre-retired)	Purposive	216
Wood & Robertson, 1978	Grandparents in working-class neighborhood in Madison, WI	Probability	257

1965, 1967; Shea et al., 1988; Tesch et al., 1981; Weiss & Lowenthal, 1975). Although one cannot be sure without more complete information, it seems that the more in-depth and focused the study of friendship, the more problematic the sample.

Method of Data Collection

Perhaps due to the complexity of the topic, very few researchers have used mail, telephone, or self-administered questionnaires to do surveys of friendship. I used a combination of mail questionnaires and telephone interviews to do a follow-up survey of the friendships of the older women mentioned above (Adams, 1987). I already had extensive background information on them from the in-depth interviews conducted a year earlier, so the mail questionnaire could be short. Simons (1984) mailed questionnaires to older adults in a Midwestern county. Candy, Troll, and Levy (1981) used self-administered questionnaires to study the friendships of high school females, teachers, and retired teachers. Because almost all of the surveys on the topic of friendship have relied on face-to-face interviews, one cannot comment on the relative validity, reliability, or response rates obtained by using different data collection methods.

Study Design

Friendships are more vulnerable to change than other social relationships, because participation in them is voluntary. Although many researchers have found a relationship between aging and friendship patterns (see Brown, 1981, for a review of articles on this topic), very few of them have reported longitudinal data. Furthermore, because most studies of friendship have been recent, the observations are primarily of one cohort. It is thus possible that some of the observations about the relationship between aging and friendship patterns are really about differences between middle-aged and elderly cohorts. For example, it is possible the relatively lower level of friendship interaction among the elderly (Brown, 1981) was always characteristic of their cohort. If so, the current middle-aged cohort will not necessarily exhibit the same pattern when it ages.

In order to study friendship change, some researchers have asked their respondents retrospective questions about how their friendships had changed over time (e.g., Lopata, 1979). Matthews (1986) focused her entire interview on friendships through the life course. She introduced the concept of *populated bibliography*—the idea that people pass through a chain of interpersonal relationships. She argued that one can understand friendship style only in a biographical context.

Although retrospective data are better than cross-sectional data, they have their limitations. As Matthews (1986) observed, retrospective data often distort what really happened. This problem is magnified by the topic of friendship, because remembering an ex-friend requires recalling feelings rather than a structurally determined relationship.

The few existing longitudinal studies support the view of older people's friendships as highly dependent on circumstances. Johnson and Catalano (1983) reported on a decline in support from friends among highly impaired elderly people between their release from a hospital and nine months later. Ferraro et al. (1984, p. 252) reported that "the length of time widowed is associated with changes in health and friendship support reported by older widows." Shea et al. (1988) documented changes in resource exchange by friends following relocation to a retirement community. My study (Adams, 1987) showed that, over a three-year period, patterns of friendship change varied by middle-class status group, but that the members of each group tended to have reversed their middle-aged friendship patterns. The "members of high society" who had had casual cosmopolitan networks saw old age an opportunity to cherish a few close relationships, the "pillars of the community" began exploring relationships outside of their neighborhood, and the "marginal women" had time to explore casual relationships for the first time in their lives.

Summary

If we are to improve our general knowledge of friendship among older people, researchers must replicate studies of local or special populations so they can compare findings and must do studies of national populations so they can note patterns across groups. They also must do in-depth studies of older adult friendship using probability samples; determine the relative validity and reliability of collecting data on friendship with face-to-face interviews, telephone interviews, mail questionnaires, and self-administered questionnaires; and conduct longitudinal studies of friendship.

CONCLUSIONS

It should now be clear why the lengthy listing of references in collections of social science abstracts under the heading of friendship is not inconsistent with the lamentations of researchers about the lack of studies in the area. The articles and books discussed in this chapter are among those most focused on older adult friendships. After reviewing these studies, one concludes that we would know more if researchers had made different methodological and conceptual decisions. This is not to say that this literature is without merit. In addition to providing important foundation knowledge, it suggests directions for future research on friendship.

These suggestions are easy to summarize. Friendship researchers must be more self-conscious about the methodological and conceptual decisions they make and should study friendship in ways that have not been commonly used in the past. Below, I discuss some specific limitations of the current literature, their possible implications for our understanding of older people's friendships, and suggestions for ways to expand our knowledge of friendship through future research endeavors.

Researchers have typically left the interpretation of the word *friend* to respondents without studying their definitions or have set a priori limitations on the meaning of the word, so we know very little about what friendship means to older people. Researchers have often imposed middle-aged criteria on the friendships of older adults (e.g., measuring friendship involvement by frequency of interaction or limiting the study of friendship to those one sees frequently). This approach leaves the impression that older adults have limited involvement in friendship. Recent studies using inductive methods have begun to correct this impression (e.g., Adams, 1986b; Matthews, 1986). Ethnographic studies would also be useful in this regard.

Researchers have often asked questions about friendship in general or asked about only a subset of some group of friends. As Cohen and Rajkowski (1982) observed, this approach probably underestimates the variability of people's friendships. They suggested, as I do here, asking questions about each member of a respondent's entire network. While several researchers have done this, no one has conducted methodological experiments using the various measurement tactics. Asking questions about each member of the network is very time consuming, so it is important to know what one gains in accuracy by doing it. Of course, using network methodology has other advantages, not discussed here, such as being able to construct contextual measures such as density, multiplexity, and so forth.

Because most researchers have used only structured questions, they have missed the opportunity to capture the range of possible responses to questions and to understand the relationship between variables from the older person's point of view. Once again, it is possible that researchers have interpreted data with inappropriate frameworks for lack of appropriate ones.

Because friendship researchers have studied only local or special populations, we have very little general knowledge of friendship and a limited sense of the sources of its variation. At the very least, researchers must begin to replicate studies to expand this knowledge and to develop reliable methods for studying friendship. Studies of general populations, such as national ones, large enough to control for key subcultural and contextual variables, would also help develop a general knowledge of friendship. The subsequent step would be to replicate national studies in more than one cultural context.

The tendency for the studies most focused on friendship to use nonprobability samples further limits generalization. It probably also truncates the range of relationships studied. It is very possible that very busy people and very frail ones, for example, elude all but the most persistent researchers. When researchers do not choose a sample according to the rules of probability theory, no estimate of this type of bias is possible. This, once again, leads to a lack of understanding of the variability of older people's friendships.

Although it is doubtful that telephone, mail, or self-administered surveys are better than face-to-face ones, researchers need to compare the results obtained using different data collection methods. Perhaps investigators could eliminate some of the other shortcomings of friendship research from specific projects if they could collect data accurately and completely using one of the less expensive techniques. For example, a researcher might be able to afford a probability sample when doing a telephone survey but not when doing face-to-face interviews.

Very few researchers have done longitudinal studies of friendship, so older people's networks probably seem less dynamic than they are. When comparing friendships across categories of a cross-sectional variable rather than across time, researchers tend to infer uni-dimensional change. For example, Brown (1981), who reviewed the findings of cross-sectional studies, could conclude only that age-related declines had a negative effect on friendship activity rather than being able to discuss the variety of ways in which friendships change as people age.

In reading the remaining pages of this volume, I am impressed with how much research remains to be done, but also with the creativity of those who have already made contributions. Friendship researchers are an adventurous bunch. They have to be in order to study a type of relationship as elusive as friendship. Now that the preliminary work has been done, it is time for friendship researchers to try new methods, develop a better conceptual understanding of friendship, and to monitor their progress carefully.

REFERENCES

Adams, R. G. (1983). *Friendship and its role in the lives of elderly women.* Unpublished doctoral dissertation, University of Chicago.

Adams, R. G. (1985a). People would talk: Normative barriers to cross-sex friendships for elderly women. *The Gerontologist, 25,* 605-611.

Adams, R. G. (1985b, November). *The permeable boundaries of friendship: A longitudinal study of elderly women.* Paper presented at the 38th Annual Meetings of the Gerontological Society of America, New Orleans.

Adams, R. G. (1986a). A look at friendship and aging. *Generations, 10,* 40-43.

Adams, R. G. (1986b). Emotional closeness and physical distance between friends. *International Journal of Aging and Human Development, 22,* 55-76.

Adams, R. G. (1986c). Secondary friendship and psychological well-being. *Activities, Adaptation and Aging, 8,* 59-72.

Adams, R. G. (1987). Patterns of network change: A longitudinal study of friendships of elderly women. *The Gerontologist, 27,* 222-227.

Allan, G. (1977). Class variations in friendships patterns. *British Journal of Sociology, 28,* 389-393.

Arth, M. J. (1961). American culture and the phenomenon of friendship in the aged. *The Gerontologist, 1,* 168-170.

Babchuk, N. (1978). Aging and primary relations. *International Journal of Aging and Human Development, 9,* 137-151.

Bankoff, E. A. (1981). Effects of friendship support on the psychological well-being of widows. In H. Z. Lopata & D. Maines (Eds.), *Research in the interweave of social roles: Friendship* (pp. 109-139). Greenwich, CT: JAI.

Blau, Z. S. (1961). Structural constraints on friendships in old age. *American Sociological Review, 26,* 429-439.

Blau, Z. S. (1973). *Old age in a changing society.* New York: New Viewpoints.

Booth, A., & Hess, E. (1974). Cross-sex friendship. *Journal of Marriage and the Family, 36,* 38-47.

Brown, B. B. (1981). A life-span approach to friendship: Age-related dimensions of an ageless relationship. In H. Z. Lopata & D. Maines (Eds.), *Research in the interweave of social roles: Friendship* (pp. 23-50). Greenwich, CT: JAI.

Candy, S. G., Troll, L. E., & Levy, S. G. (1981). A developmental exploration of friendship functions in women. *Psychology of Women Quarterly, 5,* 456-487.

Cantor, M. H. (1979). Neighbors and friends. *Research on Aging, 1,* 434-463.

Chappell, N. L. (1983). Informal support networks among the elderly. *Research on Aging, 5,* 77-99.

Cohen, C. I., & Rajkowski, H. (1982). What's in a friend? Substantive and theoretical issues. *The Gerontologist, 22,* 261-266.

Cohen, Y. A. (1961). *Social structure and personality.* New York: Holt, Rinehart & Winston.

Converse, J. M. (1984). Strong arguments and weak evidence: The open/closed questioning controversy of the 1940's. *Public Opinion Quarterly, 48,* 267-282.

Eckert, J. K. (1980). *The unseen elderly: A study of marginally subsistent hotel dwellers.* San Diego: Companile.

Essex, M. J., & Nam, S. (1987). Marital status and loneliness among older women: The differential importance of close family and friends. *Journal of Marriage and the Family, 49,* 93-106.

Ferraro, K. F., Mutran, E., & Barresi, C. M. (1984). Widowhood, health and friendship support in later life. *Journal of Health and Social Behavior, 25,* 245-259.

Fischer, C. S. (1982). *To dwell among friends.* Chicago: University of Chicago Press.

Fischer, C. S., & Oliker, S. J. (1983). A research note on friendship, gender, and the life cycle. *Social Forces, 62,* 124-133.

Gibson, D. M., & Aitkenhead, W. (1983). The elderly respondent: Experiences from a large-scale survey of the aged. *Research on Aging, 5,* 283-296.

Gubrium, J. F. (1975). *Living and dying at Murray Manor.* New York: St. Martin's.

Hess, B. (1972). Friendship. In M. W. Riley, M. Johnson, & A. Foner (Eds.), *Aging and society: Vol. 3. A sociology of age stratification* (pp. 357-393). New York: Russell Sage.

Hochschild, A. R. (1973). *The unexpected community.* Englewood Cliffs, NJ: PrenticeHall.

Hoyt, G. C. (1954). The life of the retired in a trailer park. *American Journal of Sociology, 59,* 361-370.

Johnson, C. L. (1983). Fairweather friends and rainy day kin: An anthropological analysis of old age friendships in the United states. *Urban Anthropology, 12,* 103-123.

Johnson, C. L., & Catalano, D. J. (1983). A longitudinal study of family supports to impaired elderly. *The Gerontologist, 23,* 612-618.

Kahn, R., & Antonucci, T. (1980). Convoys over the life course: Attachment, roles and social support. In P. B. Bates & O. G. Brim (Eds.), *Life span development and behavior* (Vol. 3, pp. 253-286). New York: Academic Press.

Keith, P. M., Hill, K., Goudy, W. J., & Powers, E. A. (1984). Confidants and well-being: A note on male friendship in old age. *The Gerontologist, 24,* 318-320.

Keller, S. (1968). *The urban neighborhood: A sociological perspective.* New York: Random House.

Kurth, S. B. (1970). Friendships and friendly relations. In G. McCall, M. M. McCall, N. K. Denzin, G. D. Suttles, & S. B. Kurth (Eds.), *Social relationships* (pp. 136-170). Chicago: Aldine.

Laumann, E. O. (1973). *Bonds of pluralism.* New York: John Wiley.

Litwak, E. (1985). *Helping the elderly.* New York: Guilford.

Lopata, H. Z. (1977). The meaning of friendship in widowhood. In L. Troll, J. Israel, & K. Israel (Eds.), *Looking ahead: A woman's guide to the problems and joys of growing older* (pp. 93-105). New York: Prentice-Hall.

Lopata, H. Z. (1979). *Women as widows.* New York: Elsevier.

Lowenthal, M. F., & Haven, C. (1968). Interaction and adaptation: Intimacy as a critical variable. *American Sociological Review, 33,* 20-30.

Mancini, J. A. (1980). Friend interaction, competence, and morale in old age. *Research on Aging, 2,* 416-431.

Mancini, J. A., & Simon, J. (1984). Older adults' expectations of support from family and friends. *Journal of Applied Gerontology, 3,* 150-160.

Matthews, S. H. (1983). Definitions of friendship and their consequences in old age. *Ageing and Society, 3,* 144-155.

Matthews, S. H. (1986). *Friendships through the life course.* Beverly Hills, CA: Sage.

Paine, R. (1969). In search of friendship: An exploratory analysis in "middle-class" culture. *Man, 4,* 505-524.

Pihlblad, C. T., & Adams, D. L. (1972). Widowhood, social participation and life satisfaction. *International Journal of Aging and Human Development, 3,* 323-330.

Pihlblad, C. T., & McNamara, R. L. (1965). Social adjustment of elderly people in three small towns. In A. Rose & W. A. Peterson (Eds.), *Older people and their social world* (pp. 49-73). Philadelphia: F. A. Davis.

Powers, E. A., & Bultena, G. L. (1976). Sex differences in intimate friendships of old age. *Journal of Marriage and the Family, 38,* 739-747.

Retsinas, J., & Garrity, P. (1985). Nursing home friendships. *The Gerontologist, 25,* 376-381.

Roberto, K. A., & Scott, J. P. (1984). Friendship patterns among older women. *International Journal of Aging and Human Development, 19,* 1-10.

Roberto, K. A., & Scott, J. P. (1986). Friendships of older men and women: Exchange patterns and satisfaction. *Psychology and Aging, 1,* 103-109.

Rose, A. M. (1965). Aging and social interaction among the lower classes of Rome. *Journal of Gerontology, 20,* 250-253.

Rosenberg, G. S. (1970). *The worker grows old.* San Francisco: Jossey-Bass.

Rosow, I. (1965). The aged, family, and friends. *Social Security Bulletin, 28,* 18-20.

Rosow, I. (1967). *Social integration of the aged.* New York: Free Press.

Shea, L., Thompson, L., & Blieszner, R. (1988). Resources in older adults' old and new friendships. *Journal of Social and Personal Relationships, 5,* 83-96.

Shulman, N. (1975). Life-cycle variations in patterns of close relationships. *Journal of Marriage and the Family, 37,* 813-821.

Simons, R. L. (1984). Specificity and substitution in the social networks of the elderly. *International Journal of Aging and Human Development, 18,* 121-139.

Sokolovsky, J., & Cohen, C. I. (1981). Measuring social interaction of the urban elderly. *International Journal of Aging and Human Development, 13,* 233-244.

Spakes, P. R. (1979). Family, friendship, and community interaction as related to life satisfaction of the elderly. *Journal of Gerontological Social Work, 1,* 279-293.

Tesch, S., Whitbourne, S. K., & Nehrke, M. F. (1981). Friendship, social interaction, and subjective well-being of older men in an institutional setting. *International Journal of Aging and Human Development, 13,* 317-327.

Toennies, F. (1961). Gemeinschaft and gesellschaft. In T. Parsons, E. Shils, K. D. Naegele, & J. R. Pitts (Eds.), *Theories of society* (pp. 191-201). New York: Free Press. (original work published in 1897)

Tomeh, A. K. (1984). Parents, friends, and familial sex role attitudes. *Sociological Inquiry, 54*, 72-88.

Usui, W. M. (1984). Homogeneity of friendship networks of elderly blacks and whites. *Journal of Gerontology, 39*, 350-356.

Weiss, L., & Lowenthal, M. F. (1975). Life-course perspectives on friendship. In M. F. Lowenthal, M. Thurnher, D. Chiriboga, & Associates (Eds.), *Four stages of life* (pp. 48-61). San Francisco: Jossey-Bass.

Wood, V., & Robertson, J. F. (1978). Friendship and kinship interaction: Differential effect on the morale of the elderly. *Journal of Marriage and the Family, 40*, 367-375.

PART II

Structural and Developmental Perspectives

2

Aging and the
Structure of Friendship

GRAHAM A. ALLAN
REBECCA G. ADAMS

Discussions of friendship nearly always observe that, in comparison to other kinds of relationships, choice plays a very large part in friendship. Of all our relationships, friendship is the most voluntary and the least institutionalized. It is not imposed by circumstance but developed by those involved for reasons of their own. Similarly, its content and organization are essentially private rather than a matter for social prescription. As Jerrome (1984) and other social anthropologists have pointed out, such an open form of relationship is not tolerated in all societies. In many, appropriate patterns of friendship behavior are quite highly institutionalized, so a far greater level of social control is exercised over friendship matters than in most industrial societies. In this light, the freedom permitted friendships in industrial societies stems from the very different social and economic dependencies existing within them compared with friendships occurring in societies dominated by other forms of production. In societies where social and economic cooperation within a locality are crucial, the development of friendship ties is likely to come under more scrutiny, both because these ties may affect the material interests of others and, of course, because the local network is more dense and thus gossip flows readily.

Yet this very comparison leads to the question of whether the freedom regarding friendship in societies such as ours is as great as it initially appears. Although friendship behavior is not socially prescribed in quite the way it is in some other societies, there are nonetheless quite evident regularities in the way friends treat each other and, indeed, in the expectations people have about friendships in general. There may be no rituals or ceremonies that celebrate and legitimize friendship, or any codified sanctions that can be imposed, but the transactional basis of friendship is still clearly norm-governed and people breaking these norms leave themselves open to criticism, albeit informal. Similarly, although in theory there are no real limits on who can become friends, in practice the position is very different with friends nearly always having broadly similar social characteristics (Lazarsfeld & Merton, 1954; Verbrugge, 1977). Furthermore, if the social formation of different societies generates different patterns of friendship within them, then it also follows that individuals located differently within a society have their friendship options structured differently. If nothing else, the opportunities open to them for servicing and developing friendships are in part shaped by their position within the social structure.

What we are suggesting here, then, is that though people may have more choice over their friendships than they do over many of their other relationships, they are still nonetheless bound by social conventions that circumscribe their freedom of choice. Friendship, in other words, is structured and patterned in ways that, to a large degree, lie outside individual control. The purpose of this chapter is to analyze how friendship is externally structured, concentrating particularly on patterns of friendship among the elderly, and to show that approaches emphasizing choice alone are too simple. If we are to understand the nature and social significance of friendship properly, then researchers need to focus attention on structural aspects of the relationship as well as on its more voluntary properties. Where appropriate, we draw on the research literature to illustrate our arguments, but some of the discussion is more tentative because research on the social structure of friendship patterns is not as fully developed as it might be.

CHARACTERISTICS OF FRIENDSHIP

The principal focus of this chapter is on how the social and economic conditions under which people live pattern their opportunities to interact with friends and to develop sociable ties. In essence, we argue that friendship, in generic terms, involves systems of exchange that are more available to some people than to others, depending on their particular social position. In order to understand this statement, consider the exchange that friendship, in its various guises, involves. We recognize, of course, that friendship can take various forms and, in normal use, the term can refer to quite a wide variety of relationships. In this respect, the problems social scientists have experienced in conceptualizing and operationalizing friendship (Adams, this volume) closely reflect the ambiguities and tensions in our everyday ideas about it.

One of the more important ambiguities within our cultural conception of friendship arises from the distinction between a friend as a more or less regular sociable contact on the one hand, and as someone with whom one has developed a high level of intimacy, trust, and loyalty on the other (Kurth, 1970; Matthews, 1986). In practice, most friendships involve elements of both, though to differing degrees. Nonetheless, the distinction—between Naegale's (1958) "just a friend" and what most people recognize as real friends—is important to the way people think about and make sense of their relationships. Writers such as Matthews (1986), Adams (1986), and Shea, Thompson, and Blieszner (1988) have recently emphasized this theme in their analysis of the elderly's friendships, pointing out the significance of time as it relates to biography and personal history in the elderly's perception of closeness. A related issue stems from the ambiguity between choice and contextual determination within some sociable relationships. People may not fully recognize some ties that have many similar properties to pure friendship as such because they see them as being consequent upon common participation within a particular setting rather than upon purposeful selection of the others as individuals. The more they see a specific context as defining a relationship and setting its parameters, the less likely they are to recognize it as friendship per se. Important too, as Allan (1979) suggested, the extent to which people routinely frame sociable relationships in this way may vary systematically between different social groups rather than simply being a matter of individual choice.

Because of the ambiguities over what counts as friendship, many researchers limit their investigation to a small number of best or close friends, a strategy that also simplifies survey data collection (see Adams, this volume). This approach results in a somewhat narrow appreciation of the role of informal sociability in people's lives. For this reason, and because of its greater congruence with a structural perspective, the approach adopted here is broader. Our concern is with examining the range of sociable relationships that entail elements of friendship. Thus rather than being limited to a narrow cultural conception of real friendship, our perspective focuses on informal social participation more generally, recognizing that relationships are not all defined or organized in the same fashion.

Yet given the variations in the organization of sociable relationships, most forms of friendship in this generic sense nonetheless share some common structural characteristics. The most significant of these is that all forms of friendship are premised on a rough equality (Hess, 1972; Paine, 1969). Unlike many other kinds of relationships, friendship does not entail authority, patronage, or any other sort of structural hierarchy. Those who are friends—or mates, or buddies, or pals, or whatever—see and treat one another as being equal within the relationship. Although this does not necessarily mean that at any time exchanges are equitable between those who are friends, an effective or putative balance of exchange—achieved through what Naegale (1958) terms "infrequent reciprocity"—is normally sustained. How broad the exchanges are, in terms of intimacy, value, or nature, varies, as does the time dimension of the friends' exchange. Because of the trust generated in them, continuing imbalance is less significant in close friendships than in others (Roberto & Scott, 1986). With these other friendships, however, people usually spend a good deal of effort to ensure balanced exchanges with neither side wishing to be seen as abusing the friendship by failure to reciprocate in appropriate ways. This can, incidentally, limit the social involvement of older adults as declining health or financial circumstances inhibit their abilities to reciprocate.

The structural equality at the heart of friendship is also reflected by the marked tendency for those involved in the relationships to occupy more or less equivalent positions within the social structure. Friendship rules do not necessitate this, but their conventional organization certainly encourages it. Although there are numerous exceptions, not the least among the elderly, friends are normally of the same age cohort, class position, marital status, gender, and so on. One obvious reason for this is that those we meet sociably, and find interesting and compatible, are likely to be people who have broadly similar interests and experiences to us. We simply have more in common and more opportunity to meet with people whose life circumstances are similar to our own. As important though, this common structural position also means that equivalence of exchange within the relationship is easier to manage. Where resources and commitments are similar and where no external indicator of hierarchy exists, the relationship can be quite readily seen as premised upon equality. As investigators of unemployment and divorce, for example, have noted, when an individual's social location alters in any significant way, his or her friendship circles also begin to change accordingly (Binns & Mars, 1984; Hart, 1976; McKee & Bell, 1986; Spanier & Casto, 1979).

Importantly, this structural equivalence is a contingent rather than an intrinsic characteristic of friendship. It is, for example, possible to sustain an equal relationship by limiting the boundaries of interaction to specific settings that help render external social inequalities less significant. Oxley (1974) found that this was how mateship—distinct in form as well as terminology from friendship—was organized in the Australian mining town he studied. Similarly, it is possible for people with different social characteristics and in different structural positions to sustain friendships more narrowly defined. They are likely to experience some tension, however, over the equivalence of exchange within the relationship. What, for example, counts as a fair or reciprocal exchange when one side has significantly more resources than the other? How under these circumstances can the friends construct the relationship so friendship does not slide into patronage and inequality?

FRIENDSHIP AND EXTERNAL STRUCTURE

So far we have discussed how people pattern and structure friendship as a generic form of relationship. Having done this, we can now consider how factors over which elderly people have relatively little control can pattern their involvement in such relationships. The focus here is on the *external structure*—on how present and, to some extent, past material and social circumstances shape the elderly's patterns of friendship. The central issue is the extent to which older individuals have the "personal space" (Deem, 1982) and opportunity within the patterning of their daily lives to engage sociably with others, to form new friendships, and to service existing ties. To some degree, of course, the extent to which people—old or young—avail themselves of opportunities for meeting with others and developing friendship networks is a matter of personality and individual resolve. Yet clearly too, individuals do not have complete freedom in these matters; the parameters of the choices they are able to make are set by broader structural aspects of their life-styles. From this perspective, friendship is just one element within the totality of people's experience, and, like other elements within it, needs to be viewed in its relationship to the whole.

In the main, structural studies of friendship have been dominated by two distinct approaches, neither of which, for different reasons, is entirely satisfactory. The first, and the one that ties in most closely with the perspective informing this chapter, focuses on how different aspects of social structure affect patterns of friendship. The difficulty with many of these studies is that they concentrate on one specific structural characteristic, such as class, gender, urbanism, or family stage, and simply correlate this with friendship behavior. As a result, they isolate rather than integrate the consequences of different structural factors. Although some forms of this kind of analysis are more sophisticated and consider the impact of many social structural variables simultaneously, they do not always highlight their cumulative patterning adequately. In other words, though such approaches certainly yield interesting and important findings, they often make it difficult to specify how the full range of different factors that determine structural location impinge on one another and collectively shape the opportunities for developing and servicing friendships.

The second structural approach common in friendship research is the network perspective (see Cohen, this volume, for a discussion of this approach). Developing from anthropological research in the 1950s and 1960s (Barnes, 1954; Bott, 1957; Mitchell, 1969), the purpose of this perspective is to examine how the patterning of social networks exerts an independent influence on social behavior. An attraction of this approach is that it allows the use of quite sophisticated mathematical analysis techniques, though this may sometimes lead to a greater concern for mathematical structure than for sociological substance. This raises a more fundamental problem with the approach: the tendency to treat the concept of structure in a quite narrow fashion. Rather than being concerned with those features of social structure that have traditionally dominated much sociology—class, gender, ethnicity, and so forth—network analysts have, with some exceptions (Fischer, 1982; Wellman, 1985), focused predominantly on the configurational structure of networks in their accounts of behavior. In this chapter, we do not elucidate further this distinct idea of structure, as our concern is much more with how broader features of social and economic organization pattern friendship opportunities.

Thus the remainder of this chapter draws more on the first structural approach mentioned above. Rather than discussing the impact on friendship of the full range of structural factors, however, our strategy is to examine four of the major structural changes that are commonly experienced in the course of aging: retirement, widowhood, declining health, and relocation. For analytical purposes, we discuss separately the consequences of each of these processes for friendship patterns, but we recognize that this somewhat mechanistic approach is not fully appropriate as often people experience two or more of these shifts in their circumstances concurrently. Nonetheless, our intention is to illustrate how different aspects of aging can affect friendship and demonstrate the importance of considering structural as well as more personal characteristics for understanding the patterning of friendship in old age.

OLDER ADULTS' FRIENDSHIPS

The traditional image of the elderly is one of a dependent group whose horizons become narrowed as their opportunities for social and economic involvement gradually diminish. Such imagery is, of course, quite misleading. Although the social and physical conditions of aging foster some similarity, the divisions among the elderly are of greater importance, especially given the wide age span subsumed under the term (Neugarten, 1974). But even if we separate the elderly into more discriminating age cohorts, the differences and divisions between their experiences, past and present, remain. Aside from the pervasive influence of gender, the elderly's different material resources—in particular their pension rights and their housing conditions—are bound to influence the pattern of their activities. So too, though linked to economic position, the relative health or infirmity of the elderly creates divisions between them that are not just a correlation of chronological age.

But as well as divisions within the elderly population, we also realize that reaching retirement age and being, as it were, officially recognized as old does not of itself mean people's patterns of sociability become more limited. Although some avenues, such as employment, may be restricted, others continue to provide mechanisms for servicing sociable relationships. People can accrue as well as lose friendships at this phase of their lives (Adams, 1987; Jerrome, 1981; Shea et al., 1988). For example, Jerrome's (1981) respondents used a number of strategies for maintaining and developing their friendship circles. Joining clubs and recreational associations was a major device, but equally many built on relationships with neighbors or ex-colleagues, turning these into more fully fledged friendships in a way that circumstances or predisposition had not previously allowed. From these analyses, it is evident friendships do not just passively dissipate in old age, as many models of the aging process imply, but, as in other life cycle phases, alter and change in line with the overall social circumstances of those concerned.

Work and Retirement

Retirement obviously has different repercussions for people depending on how completely they have been retired and removed from their previous work. The two genders systematically differ in how they experience this and, consequently, in the impact it has on their friendship behavior. The members of the current cohort of older women were much less likely to have worked for pay than their male counterparts. Employment tends to be quite central to men's identity (especially though not only for the generations currently of retirement age), but less so to women's. Indeed, for the majority of women, retirement from paid work represents in some senses a less radical break with their personal traditions than it does for men. This difference is reflected in how retirement affects friendship circles, though not in entirely straightforward ways.

How much men's friendships are altered by their retirement depends on the extent to which these were based on work contacts and embedded in the work setting. Some work-based friendships continue for a while after retirement, though unless there is some other basis to the solidarity—locality or common association membership, for example—they are prone to erosion over time as they lose the reinforcement the work setting provided. This is particularly so for working-class males; research has suggested they activate work-based relationships outside the work context less often (see Allan, 1979, for a review).

Work organizations, however, are not the only kind in which men generate and service ties of friendship and sociability. Friendships also arise through common membership in formal or semiformal organizations such as sports clubs, churches, recreational societies, and political parties. Material circumstances, physical condition, personality, and previous patterns affect how involved men are in such leisure associations during retirement. For those without adequate pensions, the loss of income upon retirement may result in a withdrawal from some of these activities. So too, in later old age, some men have relatively few surviving male peers with whom to sustain friendships. On the other hand, for some of those not so impoverished or gender isolated, the greater time available in retirement allows them to become more active in different leisure organizations and thus to extend their friendship networks. Interestingly, work experience may itself play a subtle role in this, for different forms of work can result in people having different levels of skill at, and interest in, generating sociable relationships. For instance, those professionals whose income has depended on their ability to service and retain individual clients are likely to be more adept at developing sociable networks in retirement than workers whose material interests and work practices have not been so dependent upon sustaining personal patronage in this way.

For women, retirement from waged labor has rather different consequences. In general, they base their identity less on their employment and more on their other work, that is, on their homemaking responsibilities, which for many continue to make demands on their time. As with men, retirement from employment results in a loss of sociable contact for women and the demise of friendships principally serviced in the work context. How adequately other friendships can compensate for this deficit varies. For some women, the burden of domestic labor becomes heavier because of their own or their husband's ill health and, in some cases, through the need to provide care for now very elderly parents; this leaves them with relatively little opportunity for servicing friendships (Allan, 1986; Nissel & Bonnerjea, 1982). Others find they can now organize domestic work to create more space within their schedules for socializing than was possible when they were also in employment.

Other factors also affect the space for friendship in older women's lives. One important issue is the availability of leisure organizations of different forms to facilitate older women meeting their peers and servicing friendships. In the United States, women of all ages belong to a wide range of social, charitable, recreational, and cultural organizations and, in addition, older women belong to social centers and clubs catering specifically to the elderly. Women dominate these latter organizations. In Britain, on the other hand, leisure associations for females are rare, both in old age and in earlier life phases (Deem, 1982; Dixey & Talbot, 1982). In general, members of the middle class are more likely to belong to associations, a factor that helps account for older working-class women's relatively greater involvement with kin (Allan, 1979, 1985).

Older women's material circumstances also influence their sociable activities in other ways. For example, many of those on minimum pensions may not have sufficient resources to engage in much sociability. Similarly, married women who are financially dependent on their husbands' occupational pensions may also feel somewhat constrained in their leisure relationships. Although studies have not specifically examined the distribution of household resources among the elderly, other research has shown that wives without independent incomes rarely feel they have the same right as their husbands to spend money on themselves (Hunt, 1978; Pahl, 1983). One further important factor affecting the scheduling of episodes of sociability is the availability of private transportation. Fear of going out alone, especially at night in urban areas, can discourage some elderly women without access to cars from greater involvement with their friends.

Whatever the opportunities for sociability older women have struc-tured into their routines, in some respects they appear better equipped to generate and sustain ties of friendship than men. In particular, women involved extensively in privatized domestic labor—the dominant pattern for the now elderly generations of married women for whom employ-ment was not the norm—have often become skilled at servicing and sustaining friendships without much organizational support. In this sense their lifetime experience has involved them in "relationship work" that may hold them in good stead in retirement (Mason, 1987). Such structural gender differences as these are consonant with reports in the research literature that men tend to have a wider range of sociable contacts than women but that women are better at creating more intimate friendships (Bell, 1981; Hess, 1979; Pleck, 1976; Seiden & Bart, 1976).

Widowhood

Marital status influences the friendship circles that people maintain. In particular, with respect to the elderly, the popular view is that widowhood limits people's involvement with their friends. Some research lends support to this view (e.g., Booth, 1972), though most emphasizes the need to consider other factors apart from widowhood alone. Certainly, the processes involved seem to be more subtle than the basic loss-of-friendship model implies. In general, researchers agree that widowhood leads to changes in the personnel of friendships, but that it does not necessarily entail a reduction in the overall level of contact individuals have with their friends. What matters, as Blau's (1961) influential analysis first illustrated, is the social context of widowhood. Because of the tendency for structural balance within friendship, over time the widowed become less involved with their still married friends and find their friendship circles biased more to other widows. Consequently, Blau argued, those who are widowed early often find themselves relatively isolated because most of their peers are still married. In contrast, those who are widowed nearer the average age of widowhood have less difficulty generating friendships as there is a larger pool of other widows available. Indeed, as Blau pointed out, for the same reasons of structural balance, those still married are more isolated in later old age than those widowed as there are few other married couples surviving. In a somewhat similar vein, Petrowsky (1976) argued that the concentration of widows in a locality affects friendship, with friendships being easier to generate where there are more widows living locally than where there are few.

Following from this, widowhood probably affects males and females in quite different ways. In general, widowers experience structural discrepancy more often, simply because women tend to live longer and, of course, marry men older than they. Given that gender is also a relevant aspect of structural equivalence within friendship, widowers are likely to find that their friendship circles decrease both because a number of their male friends die and because those still living tend to be married. To some extent, some widowers may be able to compensate for this by maintaining sociable relationships that are effectively bound into, and defined by, specific contexts—clubs, bars, and so forth—so that discrepancies in marital status are rendered largely irrelevant (Oxley, 1974).

In the main, women are less isolated in their widowhood than men simply because theirs is a more common experience. More of their friends are likely to be widowed at around the same time and, even when this is not so, there is typically a larger pool of others in a similar position with whom they can develop friendships. Of course, we should not underestimate the difficulties of doing this if few institutionalized contexts for initiating relationships exist. In this light, the social centers and clubs specifically catering to the elderly in the United States provide an important forum for integrating widows socially.

The processes by which friendship circles alter in widowhood are worth discussing more fully. Clearly, clean breaks with previous friends are unlikely. Indeed, in Lopata's (1979) studies, many widows continued to nominate couple friends, while nonetheless recognizing the relationships had altered and interaction was less frequent. Sometimes contact is lost through geographical mobility, when, for example, the widow moves to be nearer to a child. In other cases, previous friendships may cease because the primary tie was with the late spouse rather than with the surviving widow. More often though, the decline of the friendship results from the difficulties both sides experience in carrying on as before under changed circumstances. Maintaining the balance of exchange and reciprocating equally when the units within the tie are different presents minor problems and tensions for which friend partners cannot readily find solutions. Whether it is a matter of no longer having a common set of everyday experiences, of feeling uncomfortable in social settings dominated by couples, of having difficulty in sustaining the cross-gender tie, of not being sure of the rules that govern reciprocity of exchange, or whatever, the consequence is that these relationships become less comfortable and easy than they were previously.

Treating the widowed as an homogenous group is, of course, risky. Although widowhood does structure some aspects of experience in similar ways, it is important to emphasize again that its impact on friendship patterns varies depending on the specific material and social circumstances of those involved. Widowhood is just one, albeit important, aspect of their overall social situation. A range of other factors, including the adequacy of their financial provision, influences aspects of friendship behavior. Equally, as Bankoff (1981) argued, widowhood, like divorce, involves a process through time rather than just being a steady state. What widowed persons want from friends, as well as who those friends are, changes as the initial pain of bereavement becomes muted and they embrace new roles.

Declining Health

The elderly's level of health also has repercussions for their patterns of sociability and friendship. While the majority of the elderly are sufficiently fit to lead fully independent lives, a good number suffer from various infirmities or disabilities that have some impact on their opportunities for involvement with friends. A substantial amount of literature discusses the restrictions on social interaction that result from declines in the physical conditions of elderly people in a wide variety of contexts. From Townsend's (1957) classic study of the elderly in Bethnal Green, London, onwards, researchers have shown how ill health and physical disability limit opportunities for servicing friendships and developing new ties (Arling, 1976; Retsinas & Garrity, 1985; Rose, 1965). In line with the general argument of this chapter, however, declines in health do not affect elderly people's friendship patterns uniformly. Social circumstances and context affect how much poor health inhibits ability to service friendships.

For example, at least two studies have shown that illness or physical handicap can act as friendship resources in some contexts. Rosow (1967) reported that older people in poor health who lived in residential retirement hotels had more contact with local friends than their healthy neighbors. He suggested that this resulted from the greater local dependence of the unhealthy elderly. Adams (1986) found that in age-segregated buildings, compared to women with no physical limitations, those with physically limiting conditions had more local friends, more emotionally close local friends, denser friendship networks, and had more frequent contact with friends. She argued, as did Hochschild (1973) before her, that older persons often feel better when they have a relationship with someone who is worse off. In age-segregated housing, helping behavior was visible and people who helped others gained status and respect. Having a physically limiting condition in such a setting thus attracted the helpful friend. In age-integrated settings, the reverse situation existed—having a physically limiting condition restricted opportunities for friendship activities. Not only were opportunities for local friendship less numerous, but the visibility of people with physically limiting conditions was less, thereby making it less likely a good Samaritan would find them or be amply rewarded for their efforts.

Of course, not all the elderly's friends live locally. Adams (1986), for example, found that, on the average, over half the friendships her respondents reported were long-distance. As in Matthews's (1986) research, these friendships were often both long lasting and considered to be particularly close. The impact of infirmity and ill health on such long-distance friendships varies. On the one hand, contact can often be maintained as previously, through letters and telephone calls. On the other hand, opportunities for face-to-face interaction may become curtailed when poor health makes traveling and, indeed, extensive entertaining difficult.

Although researchers have not studied the intervening effects of gender on the relationship between declines in health and friendship patterns, one can speculate what they might be. Women experience fewer restrictions on activity than men, despite suffering from chronic conditions more often (Hess & Markson, 1980). This is because the chronic conditions women tend to have, such as arthritis, are less disabling than those that men tend to have, such as heart conditions. Furthermore, women are given more latitude to show signs of physical weakness and thus probably do not find illness as much of an embarrassment. One would thus expect declining health to have less of an impact on the friendships of women than on those of men.

Relocation

Older people do not move as often as others do, but there are age-related incentives for relocation: loss of neighborhood roles to youth, having too large a home and high equity, increased or prohibitively high maintenance costs, loss of mobility due to infirmity, no longer being able to drive, and lessened income (Regnier, 1975). Important too, often in combination with these reasons, older people may move to live nearer to their children or siblings or to live in a more agreeable climate.

Relocation involves separation from friends and the generation of new contacts. Whether people maintain old friendships, alter their everyday friendship behavior, and develop new friendships varies depending on the characteristics of the new residential situation and on those of the mover. Different contexts offer different opportunities for organizational involvement, place different normative constraints on friendship, have populations at different levels of functional impairment, and have different degrees of age density. Older persons' adjustment to these circumstances depends not only on the actual characteristics of the setting, but on the similarity of it and their previous environments (Prager, 1986).

The characteristics of the environment and of older persons sometimes interact to affect their friendship opportunities. For example, the physical characteristics of the environment can be of crucial importance to the formation of friendships by frail elderly persons (Moos, David, Lemke, & Postel, 1984). So too social factors play their part. Interestingly, given the general significance of equality within friendship, some settings serve to deemphasize the relevance of status differences.

For instance, Retsinas and Garrity (1985) showed that social and economic characteristics did not affect friendship interaction in a nursing home situation because these characteristics were not visible. The degree of handicap and the level of care required were the important criteria. Similarly, Adams (1986) showed that previous marital status was not related to friendship patterns in age-segregated housing, but was significant elsewhere in the community. A move to age-segregated housing was a break with the past and equalized the situations of women with various marital histories.

Most of the scant research in this area is on older women rather than on older men or both sexes. Men and women, however, move to different kinds of environments and for different reasons, mainly because of the gender differential in longevity. More women than men, for example, live in age-segregated housing and in nursing homes. They are also much more likely to be living alone. Women are thus more likely to live in environments with good opportunities for friendship with people in similar life circumstances and, because they live alone, probably are more likely to be motivated to pursue relationships.

In order to answer the question of how relocation affects friendship behavior adequately, a longitudinal research design is necessary. Unfortunately, most longitudinal studies have focused on the effects on morbidity of moves to institutions (Borup, 1983; Horowitz & Schulz, 1983). Although some researchers have discussed the social and emotional impact of relocation in general terms, there appears to be only one longitudinal study that specifically examines the effects of relocation on friendship patterns (Shea et al., 1988). Unfortunately, this study started shortly after older adults moved to a retirement community rather than before. The results, however, are informative. Over a four-month period, old friendships remained stable in resource exchange and affection, while newly developed friendships increased on both dimensions. It would be interesting to know whether this situation continued in the longer run.

In the absence of longitudinal studies, we can glean some information relevant to understanding how relocation affects friendship patterns from cross-sectional studies comparing people in various types of settings or from case studies of friendship behavior in settings to which older people often move. There have been case studies of friendship activity in nursing homes (Gubrium, 1975; Tesch, Whitbourne, & Nehrke, 1981), public housing (Hochschild, 1973), planned retirement communities (Osgood, 1982), single-room occupancy hotels (Cohen & Rajkowski, 1982; Eckert, 1980), and trailer parks (Hoyt, 1954).

Clearly though, there are methodological problems in jumping too readily to conclusions about the effects of relocation from studies such as these, especially as all of them focus on age-dense or age-segregated environments. Longitudinal studies that examine friendship patterns before and after relocation are undoubtedly needed. Ideally, such studies should not just focus on mobility to locations catering specifically or mainly to the elderly, or to the infirm or handicapped elderly. Long-term studies comparing the changes in friendship patterns of older people moving to a wide variety of environments would be most informative, particularly if they focused on the independent elderly as well as on those in need of greater support.

CONCLUSIONS

In this chapter, we have deliberately adopted a perspective emphasizing how structural circumstances over which the individual has relatively little control pattern friendships. Rather than focusing on friendship choice or on the personal and voluntary character of friendship, we have sought to demonstrate how an individual's structural location influences his or her opportunities for developing and servicing friendships. More specifically, our concentration on some of the major changes that regularly accompany old age has highlighted the importance of examining the interplay among different structural elements. These distinct elements do not operate in isolation, but interact with one another so as to encourage or discourage, facilitate, or hinder different patterns of friendship from emerging. Consequently, it is not sufficient just to assess the correlation between friendship behavior and individual structural factors such as material circumstances, gender, domestic situation, or what have you. Instead, to understand them properly, researchers need to analyze patterns of friendship within the context of the overall constellation of structural characteristics that constitute an individual's social location.

Because of our general approach, we have paid little heed to variations in people's friendships. Clearly, there are important qualitative differences in people's friendships (Jerrome, 1981; Matthews, 1983). Matthews, for example, identified two different patterns of friendship in later life, one marked by gregariousness and the other by greater reserve. Persons with the former pattern take advantage of the various opportunities for sociability with others and form new friendships quite readily. Those with the latter tend to regard only people they have known for a relatively long period as true friends.

These differences clearly entail different notions of what being a friend means; they also involve different histories and experiences of friendship. In other words, older people do not conjure up their definitions of friendship and their ways of organizing sociability out of nothing, but instead build upon patterns established over their life courses. Consequently, in explaining how these discrete patterns emerge, the structural characteristics pertaining to people's earlier friendship behavior need exploring. In general, one would expect those who had most access to sociable settings and most practice in forming friendships in earlier phases to be most adept and skilled in forming friendships in later life, and consequently to have broader rather than narrower conceptions of friendship.

Although the process is clearly not so straightforward as this, what matters is the continuing interaction between structure and personality. The argument of this chapter has been that structure—the patterning of circumstances and relationships in ways that are not solely of the individual's own choosing—is important within this dialectic and should not be forgotten or ignored in friendship studies. To be appreciated properly, however, it is important to undertake longitudinal studies of friendship so that investigators can map changes in friendship patterns against changes in people's structural location. Ideally such studies of the elderly would start with people before they reached retirement age and follow them through as they aged, examining changes in the composition and process of their friendship networks. It goes without saying that, as yet, such studies do not exist for the elderly, or indeed for other social groups.

REFERENCES

Adams, R. G. (1986). Emotional closeness and physical distance between friends: Implications for elderly women living in age-segregated and age-integrated settings. *International Journal of Aging and Human Development, 22*, 55-76.

Adams, R. G. (1987). Patterns of network change: A longitudinal study of friendships of elderly women. *The Gerontologist, 27*, 222-227.

Allan, G. A. (1979). *A sociology of friendship and kinship*. London: Allen & Unwin.

Allan, G. A. (1985). *Family life: Domestic roles and social organization*. Oxford: Basil Blackwell.

Allan, G. A. (1986). Friendship and care for elderly people. *Ageing and Society, 6*, 1-12.

Arling, G. (1976). The elderly widow and her family, neighbors and friends. *Journal of Marriage and the Family, 38*, 757-768.

Bankoff, E. A. (1981). Effects of friendship support on the psychological well-being of widows. In H. Z. Lopata & D. Maines (Eds.), *Research in the interweave of social roles: Friendship* (pp. 109-139). Greenwich, CT: JAI.

Barnes, J. A. (1954). Class and community in a Norwegian island parish. *Human Relations, 7*, 39-58.

Bell, R. (1981). *Worlds of friendship*. Beverly Hills, CA: Sage.

Binns, D., & Mars, G. (1984). Family, community and unemployment: A study in change. *Sociological Review, 32*, 662-695.

Blau, Z. (1961). Structural constraints on friendships in old age. *American Sociological Review, 26*, 429-439.

Booth, A. (1972). Sex and social participation. *American Sociological Review, 37*, 183-192.

Borup, J. H. (1983). Relocation mortality research: Assessment, reply, and the need to refocus on the issues. *The Gerontologist, 23*, 235-242.

Bott, E. (1957). *Family and social network*. London: Tavistock.

Cohen, C. I., & Rajkowski, H. (1982). What's in a friend? Substantive and theoretical issues. *The Gerontologist, 22*, 261-266.

Deem, R. (1982). Women, leisure and inequality. *Leisure Studies, 1*, 29-46.

Dixey, R., & Talbot, M. (1982). *Women, leisure and bingo*. Leeds: Trinity & All Saints College.

Eckert, J. K. (1980). *The unseen elderly: A study of marginally subsistent hotel dwellers*. San Diego: Campanile.

Fischer, C. S. (1982). *To dwell among friends: Personal networks in town and city*. Chicago: University of Chicago.

Gubrium, J. F. (1975). *Living and dying at Murray Manor*. New York: St. Martin's.

Hart, N. (1976). *When marriage ends*. London: Tavistock.

Hess, B. B. (1972). Friendship. In M. W. Riley, M. Johnson, & A. Foner (Eds.), *Aging and society: A sociology of age stratification* (pp. 357-393). New York: Russell Sage.

Hess, B. B. (1979). Sex roles, friendship and the life course. *Research on Aging, 1*, 494-515.

Hess, B. B., & Markson, E. W. (1980). *Aging and old age*. New York: Macmillan.

Hochschild, A. R. (1973). *The unexpected community*. Englewood Cliffs, NJ: Prentice-Hall.

Horowitz, M. J., & Schulz, R. (1983). The relocation controversy: Criticism and commentary on five recent studies. *The Gerontologist, 23*, 229-234.

Hoyt, G. C. (1954). The life of the retired in a trailer park. *American Journal of Sociology, 59*, 361-370.

Hunt, P. (1978). Cash transactions and household tasks. *Sociological Review, 26*, 555-571.

Jerrome, D. (1981). The significance of friendship for women in later life. *Ageing and Society, 1*, 175-197.

Jerrome, D. (1984). Good company: The sociological implications of friendship. *Sociological Review, 32*, 696-718.

Kurth, S. B. (1970). Friendships and friendly relations. In G. McCall, M. M. McCall, N. K. Denzin, G. D. Suttles, & S. B. Kurth (Eds.), *Social relationships* (pp. 136-170). Chicago: Aldine.

Lazarsfeld, P., & Merton, R. (1954). Friendship as social process. In M. Berger, T. Abel, & C. H. Page (Eds.), *Freedom and control in modern society* (pp. 18-66). Princeton, NJ: Van Nostrand.

Lopata, H. Z. (1979). *Women as widows*. New York: Elsevier.

Mason, J. (1987). *Marriage, ageing and inequality: A study of continuity and change in long term marriage*. Unpublished doctoral dissertation, University of Kent.

Matthews, S. H. (1983). Definitions of friendship and their consequences in old age. *Ageing and Society, 3,* 144-155.

Matthews, S. H. (1986). *Friendships through the life course*. Beverly Hills, CA: Sage.

McKee, L., & Bell, C. (1986). His unemployment, her problem: The domestic and marital consequences of male unemployment. In S. Allen, A. Waton, K. Purcell, & S. Wood (Eds.), *The experience of unemployment* (pp. 134-149). Basingstoke: Macmillan.

Mitchell, J. C. (1969). The concept and use of social networks. In J. C. Mitchell (Ed.), *Social networks in urban situations* (pp. 1-50). Manchester: Manchester University Press.

Moos, R. H., David, T. G., Lemke, S., & Postel, E. (1984). Coping with intra-institutional relocation: Changes in resident and staff behavior. *The Gerontologist, 24,* 495-502.

Naegale, K. (1958). Friendship and acquaintances: An exploration of some social distinctions. *Harvard Educational Review, 28,* 232-252.

Neugarten, B. L. (1974). Age groups in American society and the rise of the young-old. *Annals of the American Academy of Political Sciences, 415,* 187-198.

Nissel, M., & Bonnerjea, L. (1982). *Family care for the handicapped elderly: Who pays?* London: Policy Studies Institute.

Osgood, N. J. (1982). *Senior settlers: Social integration in retirement communities*. New York: Praeger.

Oxley, H. G. (1974). *Mateship and local organization*. Brisbane: University of Queensland.

Pahl, J. (1983). The allocation of money and the structuring of inequality within marriage. *Sociological Review, 31,* 237-262.

Paine, R. (1969). In search of friendship. *Man, 4,* 505-524.

Petrowsky, M. (1976). Marital status, sex and the social networks of the elderly. *Journal of Marriage and the Family, 38,* 749-756.

Pleck, J. (1976). Man to man: Is brotherhood possible? In N. Glazer-Malbin (Ed.), *Old family/new family* (pp. 229-244). New York: Van Nostrand.

Prager, E. (1986). Components of personal adjustment of long distance movers. *The Gerontologist, 26,* 676-680.

Regnier, V. (1975). Neighborhood planning for the urban elderly. In D. Woodruff & J. Birren (Eds.), *Aging: Scientific perspectives and social issues* (pp. 295-312). New York: Van Nostrand.

Retsinas, J., & Garitty, P. (1985). Nursing home friendships. *The Gerontologist, 25,* 376-381.

Roberto, K. A., & Scott, J. P. (1986). Friendships of older men and women: Exchange patterns and satisfaction. *Psychology of Aging, 1,* 103-109.

Rose, A. M. (1965). Aging and social interaction among the lower classes of Rome. *Journal of Gerontology, 20,* 250-253.

Rosow, I. (1967). *Social integration of the aged*. New York: Free Press.

Seiden, A. M., & Bart, P. B. (1976). Woman to woman: Is sisterhood powerful? In N. Glazer-Malbin (Ed.), *Old family/new family* (pp. 189-228). New York: Van Nostrand.

Shea, L., Thompson, L., & Blieszner, R. (1988). Resources in older adults' old and new friendships. *Journal of Social and Personal Relationships, 5,* 83-96.

Spanier, G. B., & Casto, R. F. (1979). Adjustment to separation and divorce: An analysis of 50 case studies. *Journal of Divorce, 2,* 241-253.

Tesch, S., Whitbourne, S. K., & Nehrke, M. F. (1981). Friendship, social interaction, and subjective well-being of older men in an institutional setting. *International Journal of Aging and Human Development, 13,* 317-327.

Townsend, P. (1957). *The family life of old people.* London: Routledge & Kegan Paul.

Verbrugge, L. M. (1977). The structure of the adult friendship choices. *Social Forces, 56,* 576-597.

Wellman, B. (1985). Domestic work, paid work and net work. In S. Duck & D. Perlman (Eds.), *Understanding personal relationships* (pp. 159-185). Beverly Hills, CA: Sage.

3

Forms of Friendships
Among Older People
in an Industrial Society

EUGENE LITWAK

Many sociologists have suggested that the movement of human society from an agricultural to an industrial order weakened, if not destroyed, primary group ties such as friends, kin, and neighbors. They have argued that an industrial society requires rapid change that leads to populations with cultural diversity. In addition, a modern society requires appointments by merit and rational distribution of labor that cause friends and relatives to be scattered geographically and socially. It also requires impersonal, instrumental, and economic incentives that destroy altruistic motivations of love and trust as well as long-term commitments. For all of these reasons, many social scientists felt that the modern industrial order led to the demise of primary groups such as friends and family (Nisbet, 1969; Stein, 1960; Toennies, 1940).

In this chapter, I argue that primary groups are viable in industrialized societies, highlight the distinctive structure of friendship ties, show the types of tasks friends optimally manage, and apply this formulation to the pattern of friendships among older people. A key point of this

AUTHOR'S NOTE: Data for this chapter were gathered under a grant from the National Institute on Aging, grant number RO1 AG04577-01A1. The Institute is in no way responsible for the interpretations presented in this chapter.

65

presentation is that older people in a modern society typically need three types of friends to manage friendship activities. They need long-term friends to oversee those activities associated with roles that tend to be stable over a lifetime, such as ethnic and religious ones, as well as those activities based on their early years that they seek to preserve. They need intermediate-term friends to manage activities associated with slowly changing roles, such as occupational changes, marital shifts, residential moves, and alterations in parental roles. Finally, they need short-term friends to deal with immediate and rapid changes in roles, such as those associated with being a newcomer in a retirement community, activities during a vacation trip, or peer interactions in a nursing home.

CHARACTERISTICS OF FRIENDSHIP
DEFINED BY PRIOR RESEARCHERS

One of the chief characteristics of friendships that past writers have stressed is noninstrumental emotional bonding (Allan, 1979; Suttles, 1970). That is not sufficient, however, to differentiate friendship relations from other types of primary groups, such as marital or kinship ties. Two additional characteristics are often added to this definition. First, friendships are more elective (Allan, 1979; Suttles, 1970); friends have far greater freedom to drop a tie or to create one. By contrast, marital ties require legal mandates for either initiation or termination, and other kinship ties, such as parent and child, are defined by legal-biological bonds making it virtually impossible to end them except by death. One ends neighborhood ties only by moving a household to a new location. A second differentiating characteristic of friendship ties is the emphasis on common values or statuses (Blau, 1961; Jackson, 1977; Lazarsfeld & Merton, 1954; Rosow, 1967; Suttles, 1970). For some (Blau, Blum, & Schwartz, 1982), similarity of statuses and roles applies to all primary group affiliations, not just friendships.

Suttles (1970) touched on yet another way of differentiating friendship, by the type of tasks it can uniquely manage. He pointed out that larger social norms govern society. These norms cannot clearly cover all of the idiosyncratic elements of interpersonal relations. As a result, individuals often engage in activities that seem to depart from definitions of reality because they are only partially covered by the larger social norms. Friendships provide alternative definitions of reality by bringing together individuals who share the same idiosyncratic interpersonal definitions. The idea that friends provide definitions of reality in idiosyncratic situations is similar to a proposal made by Katz and Lazarsfeld (1955) that primary groups provide definitions of reality in uncertain situations. Suttles argued that because larger social norms do not legitimate these idiosyncratic definitions, people view them as deviant. Friendships thus involve a very important element of trust because a betrayal could lead to serious punishment. Suttles provided a rationale as to why the emotional bonds that characterize friendships are uniquely suited to manage a major life task, that is, providing definitions of reality for those aspects of life not covered by social norms.

Some argue that friendship bonds in modern society may be qualitatively different from those of the past. Silver (1987) pointed out that, with the development of a market economy, work and nonwork activities become increasingly differentiated. For the first time, individuals are able to consider emotional ties very separately from their immediate economic-instrumental needs. As a result, friendship ties take on a far more personal emotional character. Parsons (1949) made a similar argument for marital ties and Zelizer (1985) did so for parent-child relations. Silver suggested it is indeed a paradox that those who rail most against the inhumane materialism of modern market economies and long for the more humane bonds of friendship that typify the past do not understand that the evolvement of pure emotional ties is possible only when work and family can be separated through the market economy and the consequent spread of formal organizations.

VIABILITY OF PRIMARY
GROUPS IN MODERN SOCIETY

To understand the special nature of friendships in a modern society, it is necessary to understand more generally how the primary groups, of which they are a major subunit, can exist alongside formal organizations that have such discrepant requirements. In this section, I argue that friendship ties take on their special character because of the need to deal with the conflicting demands of the large-scale formal organization.

The logic of the argument becomes clear if first one examines the rationale for the destruction of primary groups in a modern society. For instance, Weber (1947) asserted that large-scale formal organizations optimize technical knowledge or task simplification (i.e., dividing complex tasks into components that make them simpler and, therefore, faster and easier to handle). These organizations optimize technical knowledge because they appoint people on the basis of their technical knowledge and get rid of them if they do not perform up to par. They further protect technical knowledge through use of impersonal economic incentives that prevent nepotism. By contrast, primary groups recruit people on the basis of birth, love, or common interests based on everyday socialization. Members make lifelong commitments to each other and encourage nepotism by relying on internalized commitments of affection or duty for motivation. Weber further asserted that people with technical knowledge or the capacity for task simplification generally manage most tasks better than those without technical knowledge. As such, they antiquate primary groups. Even where the primary groups can manage some tasks better than the formal organizations (e.g., preservation of the family), the formal organizations and the primary groups cannot simultaneously exist in a strong form because they have contradictory structures. Either the primary groups introduce nepotism into the formal organizations or the formal organizations introduce contractualism into the primary groups. Weber's argument was implicit in the formulations of many of the sociologists in the late 1880s and first half of the 1900s (Ogburn, 1953; Toennies, 1940) and even some in the 1960s (Nisbet, 1969; Stein, 1960).

Parsons (1949) was one of the first of the modern sociologists to argue that both formal organizations and primary groups can and must exist in strong form in the modern society. His claim was based on the notions that only the primary group can provide early socialization and adult tension management and that these are essential to any society's survival. He recognized the contradictory structures of formal organizations and primary groups, but argued that they could exist in a strong form in a society if they were kept isolated from each other. The mechanism he saw for isolating the two groups was to alter the primary group structure so that only one person linked the primary group with the formal organization. Because the two groups handle very different tasks this guarantees maximum isolation. Such considerations led Parsons to conclude that there should be only one type of primary group, that is, the husband and wife and young children, and only one person in that primary group should have a major occupational career. This, in turn, means that relationships with adult children and other traditional kinship ties are attenuated. Such links mean that the adult child who is a major breadwinner is linked to a parent or adult sibling who is also a major breadwinner. By logical extension, it would also eliminate adult friendship and neighbor ties because these also connect two adults in the labor force, either directly if they are in the labor force or indirectly through their spouses.[1] In short, if Parson's views were correct, friendship ties would be very weak in a modern industrial society.

Parsons' postulates were rejected (Litwak & Figueira, 1968) on several grounds. First, formal organizations seem to work best when they have close working relationships with primary groups (Katz & Lazarsfeld, 1955; Litwak, 1985). Second, primary groups other than the marital dyad play a key role in most areas of life (Litwak, 1985). Third, formal organizations, along with primary groups, play critical roles in those areas exclusively assigned by Parsons to the primary groups. For instance, the therapeutic professions have a central role in adult tension management, and pediatricians and professionals in child development have important roles in early socialization of the child. Finally, primary groups are pivotal to most areas of life, not only to the two suggested by Parsons (Litwak, 1985).

Mayhew (1970), a student of Parsons, sought to rectify these errors by contending that primary groups actually help in all areas of life. He suggested that this is because they are cheaper than formal organizations. He was not able, however, (a) to indicate for which tasks they were cheaper or when being cheaper was important or (b) to offer a good solution as to how primary groups could live in close contact with large-scale organizations if he dispensed with Parsons' suggestion that their activities could be isolated. Leaving such questions unanswered makes Mayhew's formulation suspect. For instance, it would be cheaper to have one's spouse perform major surgery rather than to hire a surgeon, but few people would choose that alternative. Clearly, Mayhew had in mind that primary groups would be cheaper for some types of activities, but he never specified the criteria for demarcating them. He was also aware of the need to explain how formal organizations and primary groups exist in a strong form without destroying each other, but he had, at most, some ad hoc speculations.

Fischer (1982) presented the most interesting and systematic data on friendships in a modern society. He, however, was not interested in many questions that are of basic concern to this inquiry. For instance, he did not ask what are the unique contributions of friends or other primary groups as contrasted to formal organizations. Rather he started out with the assumption that interpersonal ties, typical of primary groups, were vital to social existence (Fischer, 1982). Therefore, he did not address the assertions made by people such as Weber— that formal organization would antiquate primary groups because they could handle most tasks more effectively. Rather, he addressed another question raised by Weber: How could primary groups exist in a seemingly inconsistent social milieu? Weber was referring to the milieu of large formal organizations, and Fischer was referring to the atmosphere of large urban communities. Nevertheless, Fischer was concerned with many of the same kinds of inconsistency that Weber noted; for example: How could a primary group exist if its members came from heterogenous cultures?

Unlike Weber, Fischer often solved the problem of inconsistencies by suggesting that inconsistencies were more apparent than real. For instance, he argued there is no inconsistency between heterogenous populations in cities and the development of strong community ties, because in an urban area there is a large enough population so that even the smallest minority groups have enough members to form a homogenous subcommunity. Fischer never addressed the question of how these homogenous subgroups can exist alongside large-scale formal organizations that have the opposite structure. For instance, how does one prevent the nepotism of the subcommunities from corroding the technical expertise of the formal organizations? As a consequence, he did not see a need to explain theoretically the differences in structure between primary groups in the present society and those of the past. Rather he adopted the role of an empirical explorer: What are the primary group relations that exist in an urban society as contrasted with nonurban society? He and his colleagues uncovered all kinds of nuances of groups and structure that were not readily apparent to the average observer. They pointed out that informal ties can exist across social distance, which is contrary to the expectations of the traditional urban theorist (Jackson, Fischer, & Jones, 1977) that there are at least two different types of friendships, whereas most writers thought of friendship as single phenomenon (Jackson, 1977), and that friends, neighbors, and kin seem to do different things (Fischer, 1982). These nuggets of information are strewn throughout his works and are a major contribution to our knowledge of modern society. In this chapter, I take their work the next step, by showing that their findings can be systematically related to each other through a task-specific theory of group structure. This process leads to a theoretical definition of friendships that shows why they are viable in a modern society as well as to a statement of the kinds of tasks they can best manage.

A TASK-SPECIFIC
THEORY OF FRIENDSHIP

To understand the unique structure and role of friendship groups in a modern society, it is necessary to provide a better answer than prior writers gave to Weber's assertions of the technical superiority of the monocratic bureaucracy and its conflicting structure with primary groups. To deal properly with Weber's first assertion, one must address two specific questions: (a) For what tasks is technical knowledge unnecessary, and (b) why are primary groups superior to formal organizations for managing these nontechnical tasks?

Tasks for Which
Primary Groups Are Optimal

Technical knowledge is not necessary under at least two circumstances. First, an activity may be so simple that no amount of technical knowledge can improve upon it. For instance, to save a person who has fallen asleep with a cigarette in his or her hand, all one needs to do is to remove the cigarette. Doctors or fire fighters, with all of their specialized training, would do no better than the ordinary individual.

Technical knowledge also is not useful where the activity is so unexpected that the expert cannot get to the scene in time to make a difference whereas the primary group member can. This is true even when the expert's knowledge is more useful. For instance, if during the course of a tornado, a man is knocked unconscious and his leg broken in his burning house, it would take too long for a doctor to get there to pull him out before he is consumed by the flames. A family member or a neighbor is more likely to be available to pull him out before he is killed. It would be better to have a doctor pull him out so as not to aggravate the leg or any other injuries. It is still better, however, to have a less well-trained individual who can help in time than a professional who cannot.

Given that there are at least two situations where technical knowledge provides no advantages, the question arises: Why is the primary group more efficient in such instances? Why cannot the formal one be equally efficient or even more so? The answer lies in a consideration of the same dimensions of structure that gave the formal organization its superiority in the management of technical knowledge. First, recruitment of people on the basis of technical training, when technical training is not necessary, is unnecessarily costly (Litwak, 1985). Where technical knowledge is not necessary, motivating individuals through impersonal economic incentives so as to guard against favoritism does not guarantee superior performance. Economic motivation requires close supervision because individuals so motivated move to satisfy personal rather than group goals if their work or their work outcomes cannot be observed. By contrast, those motivated by typical primary group mechanism of internalized commitments of duty or affection require virtually no supervision. As a result, where technical tasks are not necessary, primary groups can usually guarantee a more motivated individual (Litwak, 1985). Finally, the large size and detailed division of labor of monocratic bureaucracies lead to unnecessary long lines of communication where tasks cannot benefit from technical knowledge or task simplification. The small numbers and diffuse relations of primary groups give them shorter and therefore faster lines of communication where technical tasks are not required (Litwak, 1985). In short, where technical tasks are not required, the primary group is cheaper, faster, and motivates people better.

Assuming that individuals seek to optimize their goals, the above is the theoretical basis for asserting that friendship groups, as a form of primary group, are likely to exist in robust forms in the modern industrial society.[2] It is a theoretical answer to Weber, which also incorporates the Suttles statement that friendship groups provide definitions of reality when people are confronted by idiosyncratic situations not covered by social norms and the Katz and Lazarsfeld (1955) view that primary groups provide definitions of reality in uncertain situations. It also points out the limitations of these prior formulations. It is not just friendships that deal with idiosyncratic aspects of norms but all primary groups, kin, spouse, and neighbors. For instance, there may be some generalized norms on sexual behavior for married couples but the husband and wife generally fix the precise rules that govern this activity (e.g., which days of the week). Furthermore, it is not just definitions of reality that these groups provide but any nontechnical task, be it a social-emotional or an instrumental one. For instance, studies have shown (Kendig, 1986; Shanas, 1979) that close to 90% of the services provided to older people who are in need of help comes from kin rather than from the formal organizations that are set up to provide such help. The logic of this formulation also suggests that a market economy that forces primary groups to divest themselves of technical activities leads to primary groups with the distinctive emotional bonding indicated by Silver (1987).

Furthermore, to understand why primary groups work and what differentiates friendships from other primary groups, it is necessary to consider all elements of the primary group structure, not just trust. For instance, we must take into account the fact that the primary group members need not have specialized training and have varying degrees of diffused ties, long-term commitment, common life-style, and group size. In this presentation, I have not attempted to consider all of the dimensions of groups or the full range of supportive arguments and data because I have developed this elsewhere (Litwak, 1985).

The Coexistence of Conflicting Groups

To understand the unique character of friendship as contrasted to other primary groups, it is necessary to address the next issue raised by Weber's formulation, that is: How can primary groups and formal organizations simultaneously exist in a strong form in a given society? One important point that many of the prior theorists overlooked is that formal organizations and primary groups not only have contradictory structures, they also have overlap in goals. This overlap provides strong incentives for coordination despite conflicts produced by their structures. The complementariness of their goals is very obvious once one understands the strengths of each, because most tasks have both predictable and unpredictable elements to them as well as both technical and nontechnical ones. As a consequence, most tasks require both formal organizations and primary groups.

It is necessary to understand that conflict by itself does not prevent two groups from working alongside each other (Litwak, 1985). Russia and United States have done so for many years. The critical issue is how to prevent potential conflict from exploding into destructive warfare. I have suggested three solutions to this dilemma (Litwak, 1985). First, mechanisms exist that regulate the contact between formal organizations and primary groups so they are sufficiently close to coordinate but not so close as to destroy each other (Litwak, 1985; Litwak, Meyer, & Hollister, 1977). This positioning of the two groups does not eliminate the conflict but reduces it to a level that permits coordination. A second procedure for managing conflict is to alter the structure of the formal organization so that it moderates the conflict with the primary group. The third procedure is the one central to this chapter—to alter the structure of the primary group in order to reduce the friction to a workable level, while retaining its key features so it can manage nontechnical tasks. The analysis of this mechanism permits the specification of the unique structure of friendship groups as well as the kinds of tasks they can optimally control.

To illustrate the forms of modifications, consider four of the typical dimensions of primary groups (Cooley, 1909; Litwak, 1985): (a) long-term commitments, (b) common life-styles, (c) continuous face-to-face contact or proximity, and (d) small size. The demands of the formal organization for a rational distribution of labor often means that members of a primary group might be subject to pressures for differential geographic mobility as well as differential social mobility. The question arises, how can the kinship system be modified to deal with the fact that members might be scattered in different cities, have different occupations, and have differential economic success?

I start from the premise that the one thing kinship systems cannot give up is that of long-term commitment, such as the tie between parent and child. Given that premise, the kinship system must give up continuous face-to-face proximity and a homogenous life-style if it is to exist in a modern industrial society. In an industrial society such modifications are possible since (a) frequent exchanges can be managed over geographic distance with modern means of communication and transportation and (b) many exchanges do not require a common life-style, for example, household services to older people (Litwak, 1985). The lack of close proximity or a common style of life means, however, that the new kinship type (i.e., the modified extended family) cannot manage tasks that require close continuous proximity or tasks that require homogenous life-styles. For instance, kin who are not next door neighbors may be unavailable to provide transportation in a medical emergency. They can provide emotional support to a widow through weekly telephone calls, however.

By contrast, the neighborhood group faced with the same problem of differential mobility cannot give up the primary group dimension of continuous proximity and retain the essence of a neighborhood. To meet the formal organizational demand for differential mobility, it must give up long-term commitment and, to a lesser extent, homogenous life-styles. Again, the modern industrial system makes the former possible by encouraging the development of mechanisms that speed up the integration of newcomers and ease the departure of old-time residents (Fellin & Litwak, 1963; Litwak, 1985). Typical of mechanisms that speed up integration of newcomers are (a) organizations designed to incorporate newcomers into the community (e.g., churches that have social events for newcomers, welcome wagons, newcomer clubs) and (b) national media and organizations that cut across class, race, ethnic, and regional differences and provide a common basis for newcomers' quick integration. These are sufficient to sustain the modern neighborhood, but they clearly are structurally different from traditional primary groups. Modern neighborhoods cannot manage tasks that require long-term commitments. For example, neighbors usually cannot provide the continuous care required by chronically ill older people. These long-term commitments are typically managed by kin (Litwak, 1985). As suggested above, however, neighbors manage other tasks that kin cannot handle, such as providing emergency first aid.

How does the modern marital household typically meet the demand for differential mobility? It cannot give up continuous proximity or long-term commitment. It deals with the problem of differential mobility by keeping its membership restricted to a two-adult family. This minimizes the likelihood of differential mobility because at most only two people can be in the labor force (Gerstel & Gross, 1984; Marwell, Rosenfeld, & Spilerman, 1979).[3] Even though it survives, the modern marital household is not the same as in the past. It cannot manage tasks that require more than two adults. For instance, if one person dies or is seriously injured and the other needs emotional succor, no one is left in the household to give it. The kinship system can manage this even if its members do not live in the same household.

As a consequence of primary groups having to live alongside formal organizations, primary groups have become structurally differentiated so that each type manages some of the tasks of the traditional primary group and relies on other primary groups to manage other tasks.

UNIQUE DIMENSIONS
OF FRIENDSHIP GROUPS

With all of this in mind: What are the special structural features of friendship groups? As others have noted, friendship groups give individuals the maximum discretion to enter or depart. This structural feature provides individuals with the ability precisely to match values, personalities, roles, or statuses with their friends. This raises a question: Which tasks benefit most from matching statuses, roles, or values? It is clear when considering the range of services provided to older people that some tasks require matching of values and statuses and other tasks are best managed by people with different statuses and values. For instance, younger rather than same-age people can best assist extremely old persons (i.e., 85+) who are chronically ill and need everyday household services. At an advanced age, friends who are age peers generally are too frail to provide such services. By contrast, if one is a recently widowed older woman who seeks to learn how to manage the everyday nitty-gritty of living, such as eating by oneself, going to social affairs without a spouse, or discussing TV programs or books of mutual interest, then the person most likely to supply all of this is another widow of the same age with matching socioeconomic status.

More generally, all individuals have a range of roles and values. Prior investigators who spoke about the communality of values and roles tended to select those that were both pertinent and matched. They ignored those that required heterogeneity or those that were different and not pertinent. For instance, Fischer (1982) argued that homogeneity of statuses is characteristic of social ties and then presented evidence that contradicted this assertion by showing that kin who are part of an individual's network are systematically less likely than friends to be of the same age, same marital status, and same occupation. If Fischer had chosen to concentrate on kinship ties and on the variables of age, gender, and occupation, he would have concluded that differences in statuses were the chief characteristic of primary group ties. Blau et al. (1982), when predicting who would get married, matched people on ethnicity and income but ignored that people must be of opposite genders. Their conclusion ignored the thesis of complementary needs (Ktsanes & Ktsanes, 1962), which suggests that individuals with different personality needs and values are most likely to marry. If they had concentrated on the gender differences and the associated inter-personal skills and values indexed by these differences, they could have made the case that differences were central. The empirical fact is that for some tasks having different values is important and for others having similar values is important.

What differentiates the friendship group from other groups is that it can concentrate uniquely on those tasks that require very precise matching of values and roles. The question arises as to how this structure has been affected by modern industrial demands. Modern society has enormously increased the complexity of occupations and the range of roles that individuals can choose. Thus two friends entering the occupational world after graduating from college are unlikely to go into precisely the same occupation. One may become a chemist and the other an engineer. If they enter the same occupation, such as engineering, they may move into different branches, that is, one into aeronautical and the other into mechanical. If they enter into the same precise sub-specialization, one may move into a managerial slot, while the other remains in the field. In short, the likelihood that two individuals who start out as friends in their teens will end up in the same precise occupation is much lower than would be the case in an agricultural community. The number of options for marital roles has also increased enormously. It is possible to be married or to remain single. If married, it is possible to get a divorce or to remain married. It is also possible to have children or not to have children. It is possible to go to work when the child is young or to stay out of the labor force. It is possible to retire or to remain in the labor force. Finally, it is possible to have any combination of these factors at different times in one's life span. All of these changes lead to major changes in one's life-style. In addition, science and technology produce so many innovations that statuses change so quickly that a slightly older person can no longer act as a role model for one younger.

Achieving precise matching given this kind of complexity requires not one friendship group, but several types. My hypothesis is that the older person in a modern industrial society is optimally served by at least three different types of friendship groups based on time. The first is long-term friends who reflect roles that generally do not change (such as ethnicity and religion). They also reflect temporally defined activities. For instance, memories of one's teen-age years, which are valuable to an older individual, can be shared only by long-term friends. The second type of friends are the intermediate-term friends who reflect slowly changing major roles (e.g., occupation or marital status). These friends change several times over a life span, but not very frequently. And, finally, there are short-term friends, who deal with immediate and frequent changes in roles and statuses (e.g., newcomer in a retirement community or a nursing home).

Each of these friendship types faces somewhat different structural problems. The long-term friends have the same problem as kinship groups: How do they maintain their contact over distance, when in a modern society long-term friends are subject to differential mobility? Unlike kinship groups, which are defined bio-legally, friendship ties are held together only by common interests and affection. Such bonds require far more frequent reinforcement to survive. Short-term friends suffer from the same problems as neighbors, that is, short tenure. They need mechanisms of quick integration but, unlike the neighbors, they do not have the reinforcing quality of continuous proximity that ensures a certain amount of contact. It requires far more energy to maintain short-term friends than short-term neighbors. The intermediate-term friends may have the best of both worlds. They have lesser need for communicating over distance and for mechanisms of quick integration.

EMPIRICAL EVIDENCE FOR DIFFERENT TYPES OF FRIENDS

If the above analysis is correct, those who have all three types of friends are most advantaged. What evidence is there for different types of friends? The most compelling evidence comes from the work of Jackson (1977). He pointed out that people tend to form friends based on work, ethnicity, and age and that these friendships differ. Ethnic friends tend to be long term and involve childhood friendships and kin-based friendships. By contrast, work ties are shorter in duration and not based on kinship or childhood friends. Furthermore, he pointed out that ethnic-based childhood friends are neither seen as frequently nor live as close as occupationally based friends. Despite this, people often see childhood friends as being emotionally closer than occupationally based ones. All of this is very consistent with the notion that people have long-term and intermediate-term friends. The ethnic are the former and the occupational are the latter. Jackson's evidence suggests that long-term friends are much more subject to problems of communicating over distance. He referred to the shorter-term friends as friends of "convenience" and to the longer-term friends as friends of "commitment." These labels are somewhat judgmental and detract from my finding that these different types of friends do different things that are equally vital. Individuals benefit from having both types of friends.

I also provided some data consistent with the thesis of three types of friends. My study (Litwak, 1985) consisted of respondents who were 65 years old or older and lived in New York City and its surrounding suburbs or in Dade or Broward County in Florida. I asked them how long they had known most of their friends and gave them three choices: 3 years or less, 4 to 10 years, or more than 10 years. I called the first short-term, the second intermediate-term, and the last long-term friends. This was not the ideal question, because theoretically I should have identified those who had all three types of friends rather than forcing the respondents to choose only one type. Also, among older people, the category of 10 years or more classifies some intermediate-term friends with long-term ones. Despite these problems, the findings were similar to Jackson's. First, I found, like Jackson, that those who had long-term friends tended to live farther away from their friends than those who had short-term ones. Also, like Jackson reported, long-term friends were more likely to say that they had friends of the same age than short-term or intermediate ones. Similar to Jackson, I found that those with long-term friends were more likely to feel emotionally closer to them.

Cohen (1980, pp. 236-239), using a national sample, also provided supportive evidence. He reported that those individuals whose friendships were based on ethnicity were not as likely to see their friends as often as those who had nonethnic friends and that this was partly the case because their ethnic friends lived farther away. In other words, three different studies, done at different times, with very different populations, came up with very similar findings consistent with a task-specific framework of friendship. This suggests a very robust formulation.

In addition, I sought to show that each type of friend provided a different type of service. Ideally, long-term friends are uniquely suited to deal with tasks that do not require immediate proximity but do demand common life-style; these friendships are formed around slowly changing roles or roles referring to early periods of their lives. Illustrative of such tasks would be spending yearly vacations together, reminiscing about earlier times, and giving advice on how to deal with basic retirement issues, such as how to deal with spouses who do not know what to do with themselves because of retirement. None of these activities requires continuous proximity and all can be managed by telephone or by ad hoc visits. This type of service also requires someone in the same age group and sharing the same style of life. These services refer to typical problems that are likely to be experienced by long-term friends despite their distance. The question I used that came closest to this formulation asked respondents who they would seek out as a companion for their favorite free-time activity. This type of service would definitely require someone with a common life-style and age homogeneity. The question is less than ideal insofar as free-time activities could imply either the need for close proximity (e.g., playing cards) or living apart (e.g., going on a yearly vacation together). It was, however, the only item available (Litwak, 1985). A question that is more suited to a short-term friend, because it stressed close proximity and not age homogeneity, asked who older people would seek out if they needed an emergency loan of a small household item (e.g., salt during the middle of a meal).

When the extremes of short- and long-term friends are considered, the patterns are fairly clear. Long-term friends were more likely to serve as companions for free-time activities than short-term friends. By contrast, the short-term friends were more likely than the long-term ones to provide emergency loans of small household items. In summary, long-term friends and short-term friends tended to provide different services.[4] The data also highlight the central role of the intermediate-type friends. People with intermediate-type friends reported the same percentage who provide free-time companions (a long-term service) as those with long-term friends. They also reported the same percentage providing short-term services as those with short-term friends.

To get some estimate of the importance of having all three types of friends and to demonstrate the relationship between distance and services, I classified all respondents in terms of whether most of their friends lived within a 10-block area, most lived outside of a 10-block area, or their friends were equally mixed between those living within and out of a 10-block area. Since short-term friends tend to live in close proximity and long-term friends tend to be separated by distance, I made the assumption that those who had equal numbers of friends who lived near and far were also most likely to have both types of friends. If that assumption is made, the data show that those who have both types of friends are more likely to receive long-term services (e.g., companion-ship for free-time activities) than those having either short- or long-term friends, are almost as likely as those with short-term friends to receive services requiring proximity (providing emergency loans of small household items), and are more likely than those with only long-term friends to receive such services.

The data also demonstrate the extent to which some services require physical proximity. Those with friends who lived within a 10-block area were far more likely to have friends who would provide emergency loans of small household items than those whose friends all lived outside the 10-block area. By contrast, they had no advantage at all for services that do not require proximity, such as providing a companion for free-time activities.

The data further show that some services depend on life-styles associated with common age. I asked respondents if most of their friends were the same age, mostly older, or mostly younger. If they said they were mixed, I classified them as being in the same age group. Those having same-age friends were more likely to choose their friends as companions for free-time activities than those who had younger or older ones. By contrast, having same-age friends provided no advantage for receiving an emergency loan of small household items.

The central point of this discussion is that in a modern society one kind of friend generally cannot match on all key statuses and therefore different types of friends are necessary for different tasks.

The Dynamics of Friendship Change

Friendship patterns and the types of services delivered may radically alter with shifts in the stages of the life span. For instance, those who are in their teens would not easily differentiate between long-term and intermediate-term friends. Paradoxically, people who enter the very advanced period of aging may be in the same position with most of their long-term friends having died. This is especially likely if they are residents of a nursing home where turnover through mortality may be as high as 30% per year. My study (Litwak, 1985) showed that approximately 60% of the community members said they had known most of their friends for 10 or more years. Among the institutionalized aged, 41% said they had such long-term friends. My study also showed that sicker older people selected friends who were younger. This, in part, is because those who are sicker are also older and their age peers are more likely to have died. It also reflects the fact that sicker people require services that demand physical vigor typical of younger people who also live nearby. For instance, my data showed that people who were sick and single were almost twice as likely as those who were married and healthy to have friends that were younger than they were. People in intermediate states (e.g., married and sick or single and healthy) were slightly less likely to have friends who were younger than themselves than those who were sick and single. If an investigator were examining a middle-aged or even younger population, the problem of health would be a minor one. The investigator would assume that all individuals have sufficient resources to communicate with friends throughout the city. As a result, age homogeneity might be far more significant in these younger age groups.

Matching on gender may also play a different role for older people than for younger ones. With retirement and physical frailties produced by advanced aging, the gender differences may become much less important than they were at a younger age. Household tasks may be increasingly shared and physical frailties may reduce both husband and wife to common leisure-time activities (e.g., playing cards). The kind of services that must be delivered to the advanced aged are often household services or social-emotional ones that females are more typically socialized to do than males. Insofar as these changes take place, gender may play a decreasing role in choosing friends as people reach advanced ages.

To highlight this phenomenon, all respondents in my study were asked if their friends were mostly men, mostly women, or equally mixed between men and women. As previous writers noted, the highest percentage, 51%, said most of their friends were the same gender. Only 3% said they were the opposite gender. What was surprising was that 46% said they had equal numbers of friends of both genders. Examining the gender groups separately showed that the female respondents were most likely to say their friends were exclusively of the same gender. Of the 765 females, 69% said that most of their friends were females. Among the 374 men, only 20% said their friends were mainly males. The men overwhelmingly (72%) said their friends came from both gender groups. This could be, in part, a statistical artifact because women outnumber men in this age group, but the findings suggested that the male response went beyond the chance probabilities. A second explanation is that men are more likely to be married than women and married people are more likely to have mixed gender friends (Lopata, 1979). In Western society, mixed gender friendship ties are easily confused with courtship behavior. As a result, people see them as competitive to marriage unless they are held jointly with one's spouse. They also are discouraged among single people unless they are viewed as preliminary to courtship behavior. At the same time, if the very advanced aged require more and more services associated with the traditional female role, and if there is also increasing gender homogenization among the advance elderly, there may be more and more incentives for men to choose female friends.

My data (Litwak, 1985) show that married people, be they male or female, were more likely to say that their friends come from a mixed gender group than single respondents were. At the same time, these figures show that males are more likely to make this statement than females. Of the married females, only 58% made this statement, but 79% of the married men did so; 21% of the single females made this statement, but 54% of the single men did so. Men also were more likely to say their friends were predominantly women than women were to say that their friends were predominantly men. This holds true for both married and single respondents. Again, these differences go beyond the chance probabilities based on there being more women than men in the sample. In short, the evidence suggests that insofar as advancing age leads to homogeneity of gender roles and puts a greater weight on services identified with traditional female roles, there may be incentives for men to cross gender boundaries.

I am not arguing that it is the differences in gender roles that are crucial to formation of friendships but that it is the growing similarity in roles and changing needs that cause advanced elderly males to choose females as friends.

Some Apparent Exceptions and Some Expansions

Allan (1979), in his objections to an earlier statement of this theory, suggested that primary groups (such as friends, kin, spouse, and neighbors) are not necessarily associated with the structural features I have said typically characterize them. For example, neighbors may in some instances be long term, and kin and friends may be neighbors. In my recent work (Litwak, 1985), I tried to clarify this point. The task-specific theory suggests that groups can manage only those tasks that have matching dimensions. From this theoretical point of view, when kin live next door as neighbors they should perform the same functions as neighbors. Similarly, where neighbors have long-term contacts, they may perform some of the functions of kin. Where kin share the same occupation and marital status, they may perform the same function as friends. I provided some empirical documentation at this point in my book (Litwak, 1985). These are not exceptions to the task-specific theory, but exceptions to the idea that, under the impact of modern industrialization, primary groups will differentiate.

The question then arises: To what extent are these examples even exceptions to the latter hypothesis? My claim is that primary groups must typically differentiate in a modern industrial society (Litwak,

1985) and that modern society could not function if the majority of primary groups did not follow the lines suggested by a task-specific theory. The majority of primary groups in my data did follow this predicted direction. Moreover, in my book, I also utilized the task-specific framework to predict which primary group structure will not follow the typical pattern. As such, these atypical cases are not violations of the larger theoretical framework. The hypothesis that in a modern society primary groups will develop a differential structure is to a large extent based on the idea that they are subject to differential mobility. In a modern society, there are some groups not subject to such differential mobility; it is those groups that have a more traditional primary group structure. These seeming exceptions consist of people who either are not in the labor force, are in a segment of the labor force that is not subject to differential mobility, or who implicitly or explicitly reject the values of a modern society. In a modern industrial society, they can exist only as a minority. For example, unskilled laborers are less subject to differential mobility than many others. Unskilled laborers are not pressured toward differential mobility, but only toward joint family or primary groups mobility. Any unskilled labor is easily substituted for any other. Therefore, if a job is open to one member of the primary group, it is also open to others. Also, because unskilled laborers are poor, there is an incentive for primary group members to remain in geographical proximity (Gans, 1962; Litwak, 1985; Young & Willmott, 1957). The reason is that they have to use primary group members as substitutes for formal organizational services they cannot afford. For instance, the poor person who, because of ailments, cannot use public transportation to go to the store has to call on a primary group member to help with the shopping. By contrast, rich persons can pay the store to deliver or pay for a taxi to take them to the store and back.

A second group not subject to differential mobility are the very old who are single and sick (Litwak & Longino, 1987). They are out of the labor force and so do not experience any pressure for differential mobility. Like poor people, they need services that only their children or younger kin can provide (Litwak, 1985). A third group that rejects differential mobility are those (such as the Amish) who have, as a matter of cultural norms, given up on the modern industrial society (Huntington, 1981). They reject automotive travel and electricity. Modern society can tolerate them as long as they are a small minority. By definition, however, society would not be modern if they were a substantial group in the population. In short, Allan was correct in pointing out that not all people follow the typical pattern of primary group differentiation, but he was wrong in assuming this is inconsistent with the task-specific theory or even the theory that primary groups typically differentiate in a modern society.

Some might argue that science and technology will in the future reduce uncertainty and make technical knowledge necessary for all tasks. Consequently, formal organizations will take over in the future. It is important to understand that modern science and technology are as likely to create uncertainty through the profusion of innovations (Bennis, 1966; Terryberry, 1968) as to reduce it by eliminating areas of ignorance (Litwak & Figueira, 1968). Science and technology also have the same probability of simplifying tasks so that the ordinary individual can manage them (e.g., the developments in personal computers) as they have of complicating them so that only experts can manage, for example, super computers (Litwak & Figueira, 1968). As a consequence, nontechnical tasks and primary groups will be with us for the foreseeable future.

SUMMARY AND CONCLUSION

The thesis of this chapter is that friendship groups share with all primary groups internalized noninstrumental commitments, a lack of technical expertise, and an absence of a detailed division of labor. Primary groups manage vital nontechnical tasks associated with uncertainty that are endemic to a modern society better than formal organizations do. Under the impact of modern industrialization, friendship groups have increasingly differentiated from other primary groups in their emphasis on a common life-style and extreme flexibility in initiating and terminating social ties. Because of these structural features, friends are better able than other primary groups to provide services that require very precise matching of social statuses and values. In a modern society, however, there are so many role options, changing at different speeds, that the only way individuals can match roles with others is to have at least three types of friends: short-term, intermediate-term, and long-term. The importance of each varies with the stage in the life span. The very young find that long-term and intermediate-term friends may not be distinguishable; for the extremely old there are not as many long-term friends and the concentration may be on intermediate-term and short-term friends. For those between these age extremes, all three types may prove vital. Each type of friend provides a different type of service.

This formulation includes many of the views of past writers. For instance, it incorporates the idea that friendships are based on strong emotional ties, that friends have matching statuses and values, that affiliation is on an elective basis, and that friendship provides a definition of reality when dealing with idiosyncratic elements of norms. It adds to these formulations by incorporating all elements of the primary groups, not simply emotional bonding and communality of life-styles, and by showing how the total configurations differ among friendship, marital, kinship, and neighbor relationships, and formal organizations. It indicates systematically what types of tasks friends can optimally manage in addition to providing definitions of reality, and it shows how these tasks differ from those managed by other primary group structures. Finally, it agrees with the view, expressed by Silver (1987), that friendship groups in a market economy are more likely to be defined by pure emotional bonds than were friendships in the premarket economies of Western society. I would add only that this is true of all primary group ties, as Parsons (1949) argued for marital ones, and Zelizer (1985) documented for parent-child relations. The paradox is that these pure emotional relations occur with the rise of large-scale formal organizations, which cause many observers to see primary group ties as diminishing rather than changing. All of this is encompassed in a theory that can be expanded to include all types of group structures (Litwak, 1985) not simply those discussed in this chapter.

NOTES

1. It might be possible to consider friendships between women if, as Parsons argued, men tend to be the chief breadwinners. It is important to recognize, however, that there would still be an indirect tie to each woman's husband, which could constitute a threat under Parson's formulation. Insofar as the women were single, one could not assume that they were not the major breadwinners.

2. This formulation holds for social-emotional tasks as well as instrumental tasks. For instance, we assume that psychiatrists and other therapeutic professionals are better able to manage those aspects of emotional stress that can be reduced by technical knowledge, and the primary group members are better able to manage those that do not require technical knowledge.

3. Gerstel and Gross (1984) pointed out that some can make use of commuter marriages to deal with this problem but they view this as an atypical or temporary solution.

4. The percentage differences, though in the right direction, are not large. This reflects the poor definition of long-term friends as well as the ambiguity of questions used to measure services.

REFERENCES

Allan, G. A. (1979). *A sociology of friendship and kinship*. London: Allen & Unwin.

Bennis, W. G. (1966). *Changing organizations*. New York: McGraw-Hill.

Blau, P., Blum, T., & Schwartz, J. E. (1982). Heterogeneity and intermarriage. *American Sociological Review, 45*, 45-61.

Blau, Z. (1961). Structural constraints of friendships in old age. *American Sociological Review, 26*, 428-438.

Cohen, S. M. (1980). *Interethnic marriage and friendship*. New York: Arno.

Cooley, C. H. (1909). *Social organization*. New York: Scribner's.

Fellin, P., & Litwak, E. (1963). Neighborhood cohesion under conditions of mobility. *American Sociological Review, 28*, 364-376.

Fischer, C. S. (1982). *To dwell among friends: Personal networks in town and city*. Chicago: University of Chicago Press.

Fisher, C. S., Jackson, R. M., Stueve, C. A., Gerson, K., & Jones, L. M., with Baldassare, M. (Eds.). (1977). *Networks and places: Social relations in the urban setting*. New York: Free Press.

Gans, H. J. (1962). *The urban villager*. New York: Free Press.

Gerstel, N., & Gross, H. (1984). *Commuter marriage: A study of work and family*. New York: Guilford.

Gordon, M. M. (1964). *Assimilation in American life*. New York: Oxford University Press.

Huntington, G. E. (1981). The Amish family. In C. H. Mindel & R. W. Habenstein (Eds.), *Ethnic families in America: Patterns and variations* (pp. 295-325). New York: Elsevier.

Jackson, R. M. (1977). Social structure and friendship choice. In C. S. Fischer, R. M. Jackson, C. A. Stueve, K. Gerson, & L. M. Jones, with M. Baldassare (Eds.), *Networks and places: Social relations in the urban setting* (pp. 39-58). New York: Free Press.

Jackson, R. M., Fischer, C. S., & Jones, L. M. (1977). The dimensions of social networks. In C. S. Fischer, R. M. Jackson, C. A. Stueve, K. Gerson, & L. M. Jones, with M. Baldassare (Eds.), *Networks and places: Social relations in the urban setting* (pp. 39-58). New York: Free Press.

Katz, E., & Lazarsfeld, P. F. (1955). *Personal influence*. Glencoe, IL: Free Press.

Kendig, H. L. (1986). Intergenerational exchange. In H. Kendig (Ed.), *Ageing and families: A social networks perspective* (pp. 85-109). Sydney: Allen & Unwin.

Ktsanes, T., & Ktsanes, V. (1962). The theory of complementary needs in mate selection. In R. F. Winch, R. McGinnis, & H. R. Barringer (Eds.), *Selected studies in marriage and the family* (rev. ed., pp. 517-531). New York: Holt, Rinehart & Winston.

Lazarsfeld, P. F., & Merton, R. K. (1954). Friendship as social process: A substantive and methodological analysis. In M. Berger, T. Abel, & C. H. Page (Eds.), *Freedom and control in modern society* (pp. 18-66). New York: Van Nostrand.

Litwak, E. (1985). *Helping the elderly: The complementary roles of informal networks and formal systems.* New York: Guilford.

Litwak, E., & Figueira, J. (1968). Technological innovation and theoretical functions of primary groups and bureaucratic structures. *American Journal of Sociology, 73,* 468-481.

Litwak, E., & Longino, C. F. (1987). Migration patterns among the elderly: A developmental perspective. *The Gerontologist, 27,* 266-272.

Litwak, E., Meyer, H., & Hollister, C. D. (1977). The role of linkage mechanisms between bureaucracies and families: Education and health as empirical cases in point. In R. J. Liebert & A. W. Imershine (Eds.), *Power paradigms and community research* (pp. 121-152). Beverly Hills, CA: Sage.

Lopata, H. Z. (1979). *Women as widows.* New York: Elsevier.

Marwell, G., Rosenfeld, R., & Spilerman, S. (1979). Geographic constraints on women's careers in academia. *Science, 205,* 1225-1231.

Mayhew, L. (1970) Ascription in modern societies. In E. O. Laumann, P. M. Siegel, & R. W. Hodge (Eds.), *Logic of social hierarchies* (pp. 308-323). Chicago: Markham.

Nisbet, R. (1969). *Community and power* (2nd ed.). New York: Oxford University Press.

Ogburn, W. F. (1953). The changing family. In R. Winch & R. McGinnis (Eds.), *Selected readings in marriage and the family* (pp. 75-77). New York: Henry Holt. (Original work published in 1938)

Parsons, T. (1949). The social structure of the family. In R. Anshen (Ed.), *The family: Its function and destiny* (pp. 173-201). New York: Harper & Row.

Rosow, I. (1967). *The social integration of the aged.* New York: Free Press.

Shanas, E. (1979). The family as a support system in old age. *The Gerontologist, 19,* 169-174.

Silver, A. (1987). *Friendship in social theory: Personal relations in classic liberalism.* Unpublished manuscript.

Stein, M. (1960). *Eclipse of community.* New York: Harper & Row.

Suttles, G. D. (1970). Friendship as a social institution. In G. J. McCall (Ed.), *Social relationships* (pp. 95-135). Chicago: Aldine.

Terryberry, S. (1968). The evolution of organizational environments. *Administrative Science Quarterly, 12,* 590-613.

Toennies, F. (1940). *Fundamental concepts of sociology* (C. P. Loomis, Trans.). New York: American Book Company. (Original work published in 1887)

Weber, M. (1947). *The theory of social economic organization.* (A. M. Henderson & T. Parsons, Eds. & Trans.). New York: Oxford University Press. (Original work published 1921)

Young, M., & Willmott, P. (1957). *Family and kinship in East London.* London: Routledge & Kegan Paul.

Zelizer, V. A. (1985). *Pricing the priceless child: The changing social value of children.* New York: Basic Books.

4

Early-Life Development and Adult Friendship

STEPHANIE A. TESCH

Investigators of late-life friendship have observed that older adults vary widely in the quality, function, and meaning they attach to friendship, if they have friends at all. Describing a relatively small sample of 75- to 95-year-olds, Erikson, Erikson, and Kivnick (1986, pp. 126-127) wrote:

> Our subjects report widely divergent patterns of new friendship in their current lives. Some speak with a kind of social disdain, demanding to choose their friends in old age as they did in younger years, on the basis of quality and not simply of proximity and imposed living conditions. Some . . . long for the kind of friend they seem unable to find. . . . Some philosophically eschew "getting too chummy with your neighbor," preferring to "do things with friends but keep intimate conversations inside the family."

Sarah Matthews (1986) found that individual differences in the nature and number of late-life friendships were continuous with patterns of friendship established early in life. Using guided, autobiographical interviews with elderly informants, Matthews identified "independents" who were involved in friendly relations throughout life but were unable to name any particular person as a friend; "discerning" individuals who named a small number of very important, very close friendships that were quite distinct from their relationships with friendly acquaintances; and persons using the "acquisitive" style of friendship who had adapted to changing circumstances by making new friends throughout life, with the expectation that potential friends would always be available.

Although life changes such as marriage or relocation led to the fading of friendships for many of Matthews's (1986) informants, others were able to maintain friendships over great distances for many years, indicating that variations in late-life friendship style may partially reflect individual differences in personality and social orientation, factors with a lifelong developmental history. Thus a life span developmental approach may contribute greatly to our understanding of the significance of friends or lack of them in late adulthood.

OVERVIEW OF THE DEVELOPMENTAL PERSPECTIVE

The antecedents of late-life friendship may be sought in various aspects of personality development and in the interpersonal relationships of earlier life. Whereas researchers have addressed the relationship between early personality development and later social orientation primarily in theoretical terms, they have investigated age trends in the nature of friendship empirically, often without relying on a specific theory. In addition, researchers have studied individual differences in interpersonal orientation in young adults without discussion of their possible influence on later-life relationships.

In this chapter, I discuss three theories of social and emotional development with implications for adult social relationships: the interpersonal theory of Sullivan (1953), attachment theory based on the work of Bowlby (1982), and the psychosocial theory of Erikson (1963). In addition to reviewing representative research relevant to each theoretical approach, I discuss intimacy motivation (McAdams, 1985) as a potentially useful construct for investigating individual differences in adult friendship. Finally, I argue that existing empirical data and certain theoretical concepts support a dialectical model of continuous, mutual influence between personality development and friendship.

THEORIES OF SOCIAL AND EMOTIONAL DEVELOPMENT

Sullivan's Interpersonal Theory

Psychiatrist Harry Stack Sullivan (1953) argued that personality does not exist apart from its interpersonal context: personality development is equivalent to the development of interpersonal relationships, and vice versa. Peers become important in the juvenile era (age 6 or so), and each succeeding developmental level is defined by a shift in the nature of peer relations.

Upon entering the social world of school, the juvenile is affected by the experiences of social subordination to extrafamilial authority figures, including peer bullies, and of social accommodation to persons with different habits and values. Although the widening interpersonal experiences of a new era can remedy deficits in personality due to limitations of earlier social environments, arrests in development can also occur in the juvenile era, with lasting consequences for interpersonal relations. Specifically, the school environment promotes the development of competition and compromise, adaptive qualities that in unfavorable circumstances can evolve into "outstandingly troublesome traits" in adulthood (Sullivan, 1953, p. 232). Furthermore, the juvenile may acquire many durable stereotypes, including sex stereotypes, that may create obstacles to later relationships. Finally, juveniles may learn to disparage others, a habit that interferes with the development of self-worth as well as regard for the worth of others.

Around the age of 9 or 10, the era of preadolescence begins when the child develops "a specific new type of interest in a particular member of the same sex who becomes a chum or a close friend" (Sullivan, 1953, p. 245). Sullivan used the terms *love* and *intimacy* to describe this chumship, characterized by collaboration in the pursuit of mutual goals and validation of personal worth. The intimate communication that permits the preadolescent to see the self through the eyes of the chum may correct various personality warps from the juvenile era, such as the egocentric craving for special attention and the expectation of universal popularity. According to Sullivan, the failure to establish a close, same-sex friendship before puberty interferes with the development of a positive but realistic self-system and the ability to relate well to individuals and groups. The preadolescent need for the intimate companionship of a same-sex friend is so strong that failure to satisfy this need results in loneliness, a condition that may motivate even a previously isolated child to seek a chum.

In early adolescence, the emergence of the lust dynamism presents the challenge of coordinating the needs for security, intimacy, and sex, which often oppose or interfere with each other. The power of the need for intimacy plus the desire for sexual contact may push the socially backward adolescent into relationships that have the potential to correct some personality deficits and facilitate the acquisition in interpersonal skills. Adolescence ends with the appearance of a "mature repertory of interpersonal relations" (Sullivan, 1953, p. 297), a level of functioning that many people never attain. To avoid anxiety, the self-system may create internal restrictions on interpersonal contact and in areas of interest. In other words, close friendships in childhood and adolescence lead to adult self-esteem, interpersonal effectiveness, and openness to experience. At the same time, these personal qualities are necessary for mature adult relationships.

Validation of the chum concept. Several researchers have examined chumships. A study by McGuire and Weisz (1982) supported the theoretical importance of chumship for enhancing interpersonal sensitivity. They found that compared to fifth and sixth graders without a chum, those with a chum (a stable, reciprocated friendship with high behavioral involvement) were significantly higher in altruism and affective perspective-taking ability, skills unrelated to peer popularity. Similarly, both sixth grade boys and fifth to sixth grade girls with chums were more altruistic than control groups matched on level of peer status and intelligence (Mannarino, 1976, 1979). Of course, investigators cannot establish direction of effects by correlational research; they must gather longitudinal evidence to determine whether children with greater social concern are more likely than others to form chumships or whether the chumship promotes greater social sensitivity and concern for others. A third possibility is that certain types of parent-child relationships may foster social sensitivity and capacity for intimate friendship (Mannarino, 1979).

Childhood peer relations and adult outcomes. Henry Maas (1968) conducted a valuable longitudinal analysis of preadolescent chumship and adult personality using data from the Berkeley Guidance Study. On the basis of a personality assessment done around age 30, Maas identified 24 "warm" adults, rated above average on warmth and capacity for intimacy and below average on avoiding interpersonal closeness. Conversely, the 20 aloof adults scored below the mean on capacity for intimacy and warmth and above the mean on "keeps people at a distance"; "avoids close interpersonal relationships." Maas had access to data on preadolescent friendships from yearly interviews conducted with each child from the ages of 8 to 12. Contrary to prediction, having a preadolescent chum did not appear to be a prerequisite for intimacy capacity in adulthood: about half the children in both the warm and the aloof subsamples had mutual friendships lasting a year or more. Aloof males were likely to have reported spoiled friendships requiring a new chum, whereas most warm males had had the same chum from ages 8 to 12. In addition, warm adults appeared to have had higher peer status as children, because they were much more likely than the aloof adults to have had friendships with children three or more years older than they were. Moreover, aloof females usually had only one or two friends after the age of 10 or so whereas warm females were still involved in play groups of four friends or more. Finally, the warm subsample had been more accepting of opposite-sex playmates than had the aloof group, supporting Sullivan's concerns about juvenile stereotyping and disparagement. In other words, the aloof subsample appeared to have experienced more rejection and to have been more rejecting of peers, consequently expressing feelings of loneliness and boredom during the preadolescent period.

Whereas Mannarino (1976, 1979) and McGuire and Weisz (1982) observed chumship to be uniquely associated with interpersonal concern and sensitivity, Maas (1968) concluded that the experience of chumship was neither necessary nor sufficient for development of the capacity for adult intimacy. Maas's definition of chumship, however, did not include the specific behavioral criteria used in the more recent investigations in which only about 30% of children surveyed met the criteria for chumship (see Mannarino, 1980). In any case, the experience of truly close friendship in childhood or early adulthood is evidently no guarantee of interpersonal satisfaction in old age. Paradoxically, Matthews (1986) found that adults whose accounts of friendship were most similar to Sullivan's chumship, the discerning, were also the most vulnerable to loneliness in later life. Of those with a discerning style of friendship, many had lost their few friends by old age and had no hope of establishing new relationships that would satisfy their need for intimate companionship. Adams (1986) observed a related phenomenon in elderly women whose closest, long-time friends tended to be geographically distant. Thus capacity for intimacy does not necessarily go hand in hand with active, intimate friendships, particularly in old age when poor health, lack of transportation, or other factors may interfere with social contact (see Allan & Adams, this volume).

Maas's (1968) work did support Sullivan's view that the quality of childhood peer relations in general is related to interpersonal functioning in adults. This finding was consistent with a more recent analysis of all the Berkeley Guidance subjects with complete data up to age 40. Ratings of childhood peer relations were strongly correlated with adolescent peer relations, which correlated positively with midlife marital satisfaction and sociability in males and overall adult outcomes (mental health, marital satisfaction, sociability) in both sexes (Skolnick, 1986).

The Attachment Approach

A second theory of early-life development with potential implications for life span social development is the study of the child's emotional attachment to the primary caretaker. In the ethological tradition, Bowlby (1969) described infant behaviors such as crying, smiling, proximity seeking, and so on as functions of a biologically based attachment behavior system. Ainsworth's "strange situation" procedure classifies infant attachment patterns on the basis of overt responses to separation and reunion with the mother or primary caretaker. Securely attached infants strong positive emotion when reunited with mother and are easily comforted by her presence; insecure-avoidant infants show no separation distress and actively avoid the mother when reunited; and insecure-ambivalent infants appear anxious during separation and reunion, seeking proximity but also showing anger and resistance (see Ainsworth, 1982). These patterns of attachment usually remain consistent during infancy and have been found to predict later social behavior, with secure attachment at age 1 associated both with greater peer sociability around age 2 (Pastor, 1981) and age 3½ (Sroufe, 1979) and with greater peer popularity at ages 4 and 5 (LaFreniere & Sroufe, 1985).

Adult outcomes of early attachment experience. Although the emotions associated with infant attachment are probably most likely to be reactivated by the experience of falling in love, attachment can be an element of any adult relationship that is of central emotional importance, including some friendships (Weiss, 1982, 1986). For friendship to qualify as attachment, the individual must display

> need for ready access to the attachment figure, desire for proximity to the attachment figure in situations of stress, heightened comfort and diminished anxiety when in the company of the attachment figure, and a marked increase in discomfort and anxiety on discovering the attachment figure to be inexplicably inaccessible. (Weiss, 1982, p. 173)

In later life, these characteristics might occur in friendships between unmarried women who have lived together for years, or between pairs of friends who have no other close relationships.

Theoretically, the early attachment relationship leads to the formation of mental models of the self and of relationships. These models
are based on experience, guide interpersonal behavior, and are partly
unconscious and therefore resistant to change (Bowlby, 1973). Research
linking adults' attachment orientation (their internal working models of
relationships) with the security of their own child's attachment (Main,
Caplan, & Cassidy, 1985; Ricks, 1985) and with the experience of adult
romantic love (Hazan & Shaver, 1987) has indirectly supported
Bowlby's assertion that security of attachment in infancy affects later
social relationships. In addition, adults who experienced disruption of
their childhood attachments via parental divorce have described
themselves as more lonely than adults from intact families (Shaver &
Rubenstein, 1980).

Despite these interesting parallels between childhood and adult
experiences, there is evidence that the influence of early attachment on
later relationships may be fairly weak in some cases. In the research on
adult attachment orientation, all the investigators described notable
exceptions to their basic findings—individuals with very negative early
experiences or insecure working models of attachment who nevertheless
had emotionally secure relationships as adults (Hazan & Shaver, 1987;
Main et al., 1985; Ricks, 1985). Furthermore, Skolnick and her
colleagues found that although the mother-child relationship predicted
mental health and marital satisfaction at age 40 in the Berkeley
Guidance sample, child and adolescent peer relationships were better
predictors of adult functioning than were the maternal variables
(Skolnick, Tschann, & Leino, 1985). Moreover, Skolnick's (1986) stage-
state analysis of infant attachment, childhood peer relations, adolescent
peer relations, and adult outcomes showed that the two most common
developmental pathways were the consistently negative path (insecure
attachment, below-average child, adolescent, and adult outcomes) and a
discontinuous pattern of insecure attachment followed by above-
average peer relations in childhood and adolescence and positive adult
outcomes. Similarly, Vaillant (1977) found that childhood relations
with the mother (assessed retrospectively in interviews with parents of
college sophomores) were unrelated to social adjustment at age 45 to 50
in his subsample from the Grant Study of Harvard men. Men whose
childhood environments were favorable overall, however, were nearly
twice as likely as men with unfavorable childhoods to have friends at
middle age (Vaillant, 1977). In addition, social adjustment in adolescence was strongly related to midlife social adjustment.

The weak correlation between mother-child relations and adult social relations in the Berkeley and Harvard longitudinal studies may be due in part to lack of precise or in-depth data on infant attachment or quality of adult friendship. Until investigators obtain further evidence, however, it appears that internal working models of close relationships formed in infancy are indeed subject to modification during maturation, and that experience with peers may be as important as child-parent bonds for later social relationships. These conclusions are compatible with Sullivan's (1953) hypothesis that the friendships of childhood and adolescence can be therapeutic for self-worth and capacity for intimacy. The attachment approach has provided evidence in support of other aspects of Sullivan's theory, too, such as the transmission of anxiety from the mother to the infant. Moreover, interpreting Sullivan's (1953) argument that one cannot experience true loneliness until around puberty can be restated in attachment terms. For Weiss (1982), loneliness reflects the lack (not merely the absence) of an attachment figure, a state that commonly occurs in adolescence when one relinquishes parents as attachment figures but has not yet formed new, enduring attachments. Whereas Bowlby focused almost exclusively on the role of the mother, Sullivan emphasized the importance of peers in social development.

Alternative views of early experience. When continuity does occur in attachment orientation, it is possible that mother-infant attachment indirectly affects later friendships in at least two ways. For one, the social competence observed in securely attached children may evolve from higher levels of exploration in early childhood (Ainsworth, 1982), activity that promotes interaction with peers. Second, warm and sensitive parents may serve as role models for interpersonal behavior. For example, Gold and Yanof (1985) observed that teenage girls who wanted to become like their mothers were more intimate and identified more with their closest girlfriends. A democratic relationship with a respected mother also correlated with the degree of mutual influence between girlfriends.

Erikson's Psychosocial Theory

In revising Freudian psychosexual stages into a psychosocial theory, Erikson (1959, 1963) focused on the development of ego strength throughout life. In each of eight age-related stages the individual faces a decisive encounter with the social environment in which opposing tendencies create a critical turning point in personality development. A balance of these opposing tendencies represents a favorable resolution of the crisis (Erikson et al., 1986), promoting favorable development in later stages. Conversely, a preponderance of the negative disposition at a given stage interferes with favorable resolutions of later crises. Thus development at each stage is partly a reflection and partly a reintegration of the important experiences of all earlier stages.

The intimacy versus isolation crisis. The first of the adult psychosocial crises is that of intimacy versus isolation, in which the healthy personality develops "the capacity for eventual commitment to lasting friendships and companionship in general and, in particular, for the genital mutuality suggested in Freud's theory of psychosexuality" (Erikson et al., 1986, p. 37). Orlofsky, Marcia, and Lesser (1973) operationalized the intimacy versus isolation construct by using interview data on quality of friendships and heterosexual relationships to locate college males in one of five intimacy statuses representing various modes or phases in the resolution of the intimacy crisis. Men in the "isolate" status had no current friendships. Those in the statuses of "stereotyped relationships" and "pseudointimate" had many friends of both sexes but their relationships lacked depth or closeness. Men located in the "intimate" and "preintimate" statuses had lasting friendships characterized by openness, responsibility, mutuality, and affection. Researchers later expanded the intimacy status measure by adding the "merger" status, representing a tendency to form dependent relationships (Levitz-Jones & Orlofsky, 1985) lacking in codetermination (Tesch & Whitbourne, 1982).

In an elegant reconceptualization of Erikson's theory, Logan (1986) argued that the eight stages represent a repeated cycle of development that occurs first in childhood and again in adulthood, with the identity crisis of adolescence serving as a pivotal link between the two cycles. In this scheme, the intimacy versus isolation crisis of adulthood is a recapitulation of both the trust versus mistrust and the autonomy versus shame and doubt crises of early childhood. This hypothesis is consistent with Orlofsky's (1978) finding that college males located in the intimate and preintimate statuses scored higher on autonomy than those in the pseudointimate plus stereotyped statuses, who in turn scored higher than isolate-status males. Similarly, college women located in the intimate and preintimate statuses showed greater individuation (self-reliance) and less defensiveness on a projective measure of separation anxiety than did women in the merger status or a low-intimacy group consisting of the pseudointimate, stereotyped relationships, and isolate statuses. Women in the latter two categories also showed more signs of anxious attachment than did the high-intimacy women. This approach links adult intimacy with early childhood experiences of attachment and separation-individuation.

Age differences in friendship. According to Erikson's theory, the quality of friendship should deepen during the transition from adolescence to adulthood, due to the increased importance of interpersonal commitment in the intimacy versus isolation stage. When investigators analyzed descriptions of actual friendship, both adolescents and adults tended to emphasize similarity and reciprocity (Candy, Troll, & Levy, 1981; Goldman, Cooper, Ahern, & Corsini, 1981; Weiss & Lowenthal, 1975). Compared to adolescents, however, adult women at all ages were less likely to mention "humorous and entertaining" as an important quality in a friend. In addition, when the researchers asked teenagers and adults of various ages to rate the importance of several functions in their closest friendships, women but not men showed decreases in the self-centered functions of status and power from adolescence to middle adulthood (Candy, 1978; Candy et al., 1981). In further support of Erikson's theory, university alumni in their mid-20s were more likely than university students to be located in intimacy statuses characterized by long-term commitment (intimate and merger), whereas students were more likely to be located in a combined stereotyped-isolate category (Whitbourne & Tesch, 1985). Prager (1983) observed that men in committed intimacy statuses (intimate and pseudointimate) were older than those in uncommitted statuses (preintimate and stereotyped), but among women, older age was more related to depth of relationships than to commitment.

Development of friendship concepts. Both age changes and age differences have appeared in definitions of friendship. For example, LaGaipa (in press) reinterviewed at the age of 22 to 26 years people who had written essays on the nature of friendship when they were preadolescents. Although an early focus on intimacy predicted an expressive focus in adulthood, there was more change than continuity in friendship concepts. Most of the participants had progressed to more empathic conceptions of friendship between preadolescence and early adulthood. Weiss and Lowenthal (1975) found that 20-year-olds were less likely than high school students to cite similarity of interests and experiences as an important characteristic of the ideal friend, a trend also among the middle-aged and preretired adults. Homogeneity in descriptions of one's three closest friends decreased from high school to young adulthood and middle age, indicating greater awareness of differences among friends in the older groups. Consistent with these findings, Tesch and Martin (1983) observed that university alumni in their mid-20s were more likely than college students to permit differences between friends when defining this relationship.

Any cross-sectional age comparison may be clouded by cohort differences, and interpersonal relationships are no exception. Rands and Levinger (1979) asked college students to judge the frequency of various behaviors in several types of relationships among today's young adults and asked elderly adults to make similar judgments about relationships between young adults of 50 years ago. They found several generational differences, particularly with regard to good friends and close friends, with the younger generation reporting higher rates of self-disclosure, expression of affection, and expression of both praise and criticism between friends than the older one. These findings contrast with the fact that older adults describe the intimacy of their current relationships in terms similar to younger groups (Candy et al., 1981; Goldman et al., 1981; Weiss & Lowenthal, 1975), indicating that expectations of intimacy in friendship may have increased from early to late adulthood in today's elderly. If this represents a continuing historical trend toward greater openness in friendships, then ties with friends may be an increasingly important aspect of life for future cohorts of older adults.

Whereas mean age differences in friendship and intimacy probably reflect modal or normative developmental trends, Erikson (1963) implied that resolutions of the intimacy versus isolation crisis may range from the extremes of interpersonal avoidance to lifelong partnerships of love and trust. Moreover, the tension between intimacy and isolation persists throughout adulthood: "Like the young adult, the elder must reconcile a sense of closeness with the experience of being alone, consolidating once more the capacity for love" (Erikson et al., 1986, p. 104). Among adults, therefore, one should expect both interindividual variations and intraindividual change in friendship at all ages; empirical investigation of styles of friendship or intimacy capacity in old age, however, has just begun. Furthermore, Erikson and his colleagues theorized that in later life, memories of interpersonal experiences may be as important for the older person's sense of intimacy as are current interactions (Erikson et al., 1986). Thus investigations of intimacy development in late life might profitably include a life review of previous important relationships, plus an examination of earlier phases of existing relationships. Matthews's (1986) friendship biographies provide an illustration of this approach.

Summary of the
Developmental Theories

The three theories of emotional development discussed here pertain to early-life experiences that may have formative effects on the individual and therefore lasting consequences for interpersonal relationships. For Sullivan, early relationships with parents and peers establish a dynamic self-system of motivation and perception that functions to maintain a sense of interpersonal security through the avoidance of anxiety. For Erikson, the childhood development of ego qualities, especially basic trust and autonomy, affects the balance of intimacy and isolation in adulthood. Attachment theory does not directly address the issue of personality formation, but the representational models of self and relationships formed in infancy are thought to influence later close relationships (Bowlby, 1969). Each of these theories has received partial empirical support, but neither longitudinal nor retrospective data have strongly confirmed one of these viewpoints. Researchers may have underestimated the links between childhood and adult social development because of measurement error, particularly with regard to adult capacity for intimacy.

INTIMACY AS A
DIMENSION OF PERSONALITY

Recently, McAdams (1985) defined and operationalized the construct of intimacy motivation as a dimension of adult personality, providing a vehicle for the investigation and explanation of individual differences in interpersonal relationships. He defined the intimacy motive as "a recurrent preference or readiness for experiences of warm, close, and communicative exchange—interactions with others deemed ends rather than means to other ends. Intimacy motivation energizes, directs, and selects behavior in certain situations" (McAdams, 1985, p. 77). One can assess the strength of the intimacy motive with the Thematic Apperception Test (Murray, 1943) in which the investigator scores stories written in response to pictures for the presence of specific themes. Autobiographical and naturalistic research with college students has established the reliability and validity of this measure. Strength of intimacy motivation was correlated with reports of friendship, love, communication, sharing, helping, or touching in descriptions of peak experiences and great learning experiences (McAdams, 1982) and with frequency of interpersonal thoughts, frequency of conversations or letter writing, and greater positive affect in interpersonal situations (McAdams & Constantian, 1983). McAdams and his colleagues also linked the intimacy motive to differences in friendship, with college students high in intimacy motivation reporting more dyadic as opposed to group friendship episodes, more self-disclosure and listening in their friendship encounters, and more trust and concern for the other in their descriptions of their best friends (McAdams, Healy, & Krause, 1984).

Researchers have examined the developmental significance of intimacy motives in at least two age groups to date. In fourth and sixth graders, friendship motivation (a precursor of the intimacy motive) was positively correlated with factual knowledge of best friends, friendship depth, 7-month stability of best friend choice, and teacher ratings of social competence (McAdams & Losoff, 1984). Friendship motivation was not related to peer popularity, intelligence, or teacher ratings of extraversion. In adults, intimacy motivation at age 30 predicted overall psychosocial adjustment, particularly marital enjoyment and enjoyment of job, at age 47 in Vaillant's subsample from the Grant Study (McAdams & Vaillant, 1982). Achievement, affiliation, and power motivation were not significantly related to midlife adjustment in this sample. Thus researchers have linked individual differences in intimacy motivation with differences in quality of friendship at various ages, long-term psychosocial development, memories, thought, and everyday behavior.

In other efforts to identify personality correlates of friendship and intimacy, the trait of femininity/expressiveness (Spence & Helmreich, 1978) has been associated with quality of same-sex (Williams, 1985) and opposite-sex friendships (Tesch, 1985) among young adults, and with marital happiness in middle-aged adults (Antill, 1983). Intimacy motivation might be an impetus for the cultivation of personal expressiveness, leading to the endorsement of feminine traits such as warm, kind, helpful, and so on.

INVESTIGATING INDIVIDUAL
DEVELOPMENT AND FRIENDSHIP

Theories of individual emotional development have stimulated research on childhood and young adult sociability that generally supports the notion of a relationship between early social experience and later psychosocial functioning. The evidence, however, is not consistent with a strongly deterministic point of view, in which early social experience serves as a prototype for all later relationships of primary importance. Instead, both research and theory point to continuing, mutual influence between social experience and individual development. Several components of a life span theory of friendship can be extracted from existing theoretical and empirical evidence:

(a) Attachment research indicates long-term effects of the mother-infant relationship for some people, explained in terms of internal working models of self and relationships. Although these internal representations appear to change dramatically for many people, the mechanisms or circumstances for change have not yet been widely investigated from the attachment perspective.

(b) Sullivan (1953) postulated a major source of change in interpersonal functioning and argued that, by middle childhood, peers were as important as parents in the development of the individual. Current experts in child development share this view (Hartup, 1978; Youniss, 1980).

(c) From the perspective of Erikson's theory, the nature of adult relationships is a function of personality development and thus indirectly a function of early experience. McAdams's work on the intimacy motive supports this conceptual approach. Individual differences in personality were related to cognitive and behavioral differences in childhood and young adult friendship and to psychological adjustment in middle age.

Thus personality and interpersonal relationships appear to be inseparable developmental components, each affecting the other concurrently and over time. A dialectical (Riegel, 1976) or transactional (Sameroff, 1975) model of development best represents this process. In such a model, continuity or change in the person is a function of continuity or change in the social environment, with the social environment subject to the influence of the person. In the words of Robert Hinde (1982, p. 66): "the properties of an interpersonal relationship are influenced by the personalities of the participants, and the personalities of the participants are determined in part by the relationships in which they are and have been involved." In this sense, friendship can be either an independent or a dependent variable in the study of aging (see Tesch, 1983).

By definition, a theory of development must account for both intraindividual change and variations of intraindividual change (Baltes, Reese, & Nesselroade, 1977). Therefore, a developmental approach to adult friendship requires investigation of various patterns of social development, as in Skolnick's (1986) analysis of early-life relationships and adult sociability. This approach emphasizes individual differences rather than average tendencies, an orientation that runs counter to our most common research strategies. For example, Sullivan (1953) and Erikson (1963) disagree on whether the capacity for intimacy first emerges in childhood or adulthood, and both theories have instigated research intended to determine whether friendships at a certain age are particularly important for social and personality development. A transactional approach, however, can accommodate multiple turning points in interpersonal development, with the potential for change continuing through life. Indeed, one representative sample of older adults included 6 persons out of 100 who reported that they did not have close friendships until later life (Roberto, Kimboko, Janonis, & Masters, 1985). In terms of varying developmental pathways, some appropriate questions might be: For whom or under what circumstances do friends have a crucial role in individual development at a particular age? Is childhood friendship especially important for children who have had insecure attachments at home? Is young adult intimacy more poignant for those whose childhood peers neglected or rejected them? In adulthood, are friends invaluable for some and irrelevant for others?

In addition to the investigation of differences in intraindividual development and friendship, a transactional or dialectical model is compatible with the search for enduring individual differences in interpersonal relationships. Styles of friendship could persist for long periods of time if individuals consistently avoid or approach relationships in certain ways, leading to consistent responses from others. For example, the adult "loner" or "independent" may have a history of detachment from peers that extends from childhood to late adulthood (see Gubrium, 1975; Orlofsky, 1978). Conversely, autobiographical research by Matthews and Gill (1982) revealed that elderly adults who recalled at least one close friend in childhood were much more likely to have had several good friends through life (the acquisitive friendship strategy) than those who recalled only nonspecific friendly relations in childhood. In addition, some researchers have found more stability in social development of males than females (Candy, 1978; Skolnick, 1986), an indication that socialization for the male role may restrict opportunities for interpersonal growth (Lewis, 1978; Tognoli, 1980; Wright, this volume).

In summary, theory and research on early-life development suggest several avenues for investigation of adult friendship. These include an emphasis on individual differences in late-life friendship and the role of personality or motivational factors in the initiation, maintenance, or termination of friendship in old age. In turn, a person's history of friendship experiences might help to predict or explain adaptation to varying life circumstances in later years. Processes of change in the meaning and function of friendship across the life span, particularly the factors that contribute to stability or change in friendship, await further investigation. Finally, as recommended by Beth Hess in 1972, researchers should analyze the forms and functions of friendship over time in relation to other important interpersonal ties such as those with parents, siblings, spouses, and children.

REFERENCES

Adams, R. G. (1986). Emotional closeness and physical distance between friends: Implications for elderly women living in age-segregated and age-integrated settings. *International Journal of Aging and Human Development, 22*, 55-76.

Ainsworth, M.D.S. (1982). Attachment: Retrospect and prospect. In C. M. Parkes & J. Stevenson-Hinde (Eds.), *The place of attachment in human behavior* (pp. 3-30). New York: Basic Books.

Antill, J. K. (1983). Sex role complementarity versus similarity in married couples. *Journal of Personality and Social Psychology, 45*, 145-155.

Baltes, P. B., Reese, H. W., & Nesselroade, J.R. (1977). *Life-span developmental psychology: Introduction to research methods.* Monterey, CA: Brooks-Cole.

Bowlby, J. (1969). *Attachment and loss, Vol. 1: Attachment.* New York: Basic Books.

Bowlby, J. (1973). *Attachment and loss, Vol. 2: Separation-anxiety and anger.* New York: Basic Books.

Bowlby, J. (1982). Attachment and loss: Retrospect and prospect. *American Journal of Orthopsychiatry, 52*, 664-678.

Candy, S. G. (1978, August). *A comparative analysis of friendship functions through the adult years.* Paper presented at the 86th Annual Convention of the American Psychological Association, Toronto.

Candy, S. G., Troll, L. E., & Levy, S. G. (1981). A developmental exploration of friendship functions in women. *Psychology of Women Quarterly, 5*, 456-472.

Erikson, E. H. (1959). Identity and the life cycle [Monograph]. *Psychological Issues, 1,* 1-171.

Erikson, E. H. (1963). *Childhood and society* (2nd ed.). New York: Norton.

Erikson, E. H., Erikson, J. M., & Kivnick, H. Q. (1986). *Vital involvement in old age.* New York: Norton.

Gold, M., & Yanof, D. S. (1985). Mothers, daughters, and girlfriends. *Journal of Personality and Social Psychology, 49,* 654-659.

Goldman, J. A., Cooper, P. E., Ahern, K., & Corsini, D. (1981). Continuities and discontinuities in the friendship descriptions of women at six stages in the life cycle. *Genetic Psychology Monographs, 103,* 153-167.

Gubrium, J. F. (1975). Being single in old age. *International Journal of Aging and Human Development, 6,* 29-41.

Hartup, W. W. (1978). Children and their friends. In H. McGurk (Ed.), *Issues in childhood and social development* (pp. 130-170). London: Methuen.

Hazan, C., & Shaver, P. (1987). Romantic love conceptualized as an attachment process. *Journal of Personality and Social Psychology, 52,* 511-524.

Hess, B. (1972). Friendship. In M. W. Riley, I. Johnson, & A. Foner (Eds.), *Aging and society, Vol. 3: A sociology of age stratification* (pp. 359-393). New York: Russell Sage.

Hinde, R. A. (1982). Attachment: Some conceptual and biological issues. In C. M. Parkes & J. Stevenson-Hinde (Eds.), *The place of attachment in human behavior* (pp. 60-76). New York: Basic Books.

LaFreniere, P. J., & Sroufe, L. A. (1985). Profiles of peer competence in the preschool: Interrelations between measures, influence of social ecology, and relation to attachment history. *Developmental Psychology, 21,* 56-69.

LaGaipa, J. J. (in press). Friendship expectations. In R. Burnett (Ed.), *Accounting for relationships.* London: Methuen.

Levitz-Jones, E. M., & Orlofsky, J. L. (1985). Separation-individuation and intimacy capacity in college women. *Journal of Personality and Social Psychology, 49,* 156-169.

Lewis, R. A. (1978). Emotional intimacy among men. *Journal of Social Issues, 34,* 108-121.

Logan, R. D. (1986). A reconceptualization of Erikson's theory: The repetition of existential and instrumental themes. *Human Development, 29,* 125-136.

Maas, H. S. (1968). Preadolescent peer relations and adult intimacy. *Psychiatry, 31,* 161-172.

Main, M., Kaplan, N., & Cassidy, J. (1985). Security in infancy, childhood, and adulthood: A move to the level of representation. *Monographs of the Society for Research in Child Development, 50,* 66-104.

Mannarino, A. P. (1976). Friendship patterns and altruistic behavior in preadolescent males. *Developmental Psychology, 12,* 555-556.

Mannarino, A. P. (1979). The relationship between friendship and altruism in preadolescent girls. *Psychiatry, 42,* 280-284.

Mannarino, A. P. (1980). The development of children's friendships. In H. C. Foot, A. J. Chapman, & J. R. Smith (Eds.), *Friendship and social relations in children* (pp. 45-64). New York: John Wiley.

Matthews, S. H. (1986). *Friendships through the life course: Oral biographies in old age.* Beverly Hills, CA: Sage.

Matthews, S. H., & Gill, K. (1982, November). *Friendship strategies developed through the life course.* Paper presented at the 35th Annual Meeting of the Gerontological Society of America, Boston.

McAdams, D. P. (1982). Experiences of intimacy and power: Relationships between social motives and autobiographical memory. *Journal of Personality and Social Psychology, 42,* 292-302.

McAdams, D. P. (1985). *Power, intimacy and the life story: Personological inquiries into identity.* Homewood, IL: Dorsey.

McAdams, D. P., & Constantian, C. A. (1983). Intimacy and affiliation motives in daily living: An experience sampling analysis. *Journal of Personality and Social Psychology, 45,* 851-861.

McAdams, D. P., Healy, S., & Krause, S. (1984). Social motives and patterns of friendship. *Journal of Personality and Social Psychology, 47,* 828-838.

McAdams, D. P., & Losoff, M. (1984). Friendship motivation in fourth and sixth graders: A thematic analysis. *Journal of Social and Personal Relationships, 1,* 11-27.

McAdams, D. P., & Vaillant, G. E. (1982). Intimacy motivation and psychosocial adjustment. *Journal of Personality Assessment, 46,* 586-593.

McGuire, K. D., & Wesz, J. R. (1982). Social cognition and behavior correlates of preadolescent chumship. *Child Development, 53,* 1478-1484.

Murray, H. A. (1943). *Thematic apperception test.* Cambridge, MA: Harvard University Press.

Orlofsky, J. L. (1978). The relationships between intimacy status and antecedent personality components. *Adolescence, 13,* 419-441.

Orlofsky, J. L., Marcia, J. E., & Lesser, I. M. (1973). Ego identity status and the intimacy versus isolation crisis of young adulthood. *Journal of Personality and Social Psychology, 27,* 211-219.

Pastor, D. L. (1981). The quality of mother-infant attachment and its relationship to toddlers' initial sociability with peers. *Developmental Psychology, 17,* 326-335.

Prager, K. J. (1983). Development of intimacy in young adults, a multidimensional view. *Psychological Reports, 52,* 757-756.

Rands, M., & Levinger, G. (1979). Implicit theories of relationship: An intergenerational study. *Journal of Personality and Social Psychology, 37,* 645-661.

Ricks, M. H. (1985). The social transmission of parental behavior: Attachment across generations. *Monographs of the Society for Research in Child Development, 50,* 211-227.

Riegel, K. F. (1976). The dialectics of human development. *American Psychologist, 31,* 689-700.

Roberto, K. A., Kimboko, P. J., Janonis, C. C., & Masters, J. L. (1985, November). *Friendships over time: A look back.* Paper presented at the 38th Annual Meeting of the Gerontological Society of America, New Orleans.

Sameroff, A. (1975). Transactional models in early social relations. *Human Development, 18,* 65-79.

Shaver, P., & Rubenstein, C. (1980). Childhood attachment experience and adult loneliness. In L. Wheeler (Ed.), *Review of personality and social psychology* (Vol. 1, pp. 42-73). Beverly Hills, CA: Sage.

Skolnick, A. (1986). Early attachment and personal relationships across the life course. In P. B. Baltes, D. L. Featherman, & R. M. Lerner (Eds.), *Life-span development and behavior* (Vol. 7, pp. 174-206). Hillsdale, NJ: Lawrence Erlbaum.

Skolnick, A., Tschann, J., & Leino, V. (1985, August). *Attachment and life span development: A structural equation analysis.* Paper presented at the 93rd Annual Convention of the American Psychological Association, Los Angeles.

Spence, J. T., & Helmreich, R. L. (1978). *Masculinity and femininity: Their psychological dimensions, correlates, and antecedents.* Austin: University of Texas Press.

Sroufe, L. A. (1979). The coherence of individual development. *American Psychologist, 34,* 834-841.

Sullivan, H. S. (1953). *The interpersonal theory of psychiatry* (I. S. Perry & M. L. Gawel, Eds.). New York: Norton.

Tesch, S. A. (1983). Review of friendship development across the life span. *Human Development, 26,* 266-276.

Tesch, S. A. (1985). The psychosocial intimacy questionnaire: Validational studies and an investigation of sex roles. *Journal of Social and Personal Relationships, 2,* 471-488.

Tesch, S. A., & Martin, R. R. (1983). Friendship concepts of young adults in two age groups. *Journal of Psychology, 115,* 7-12.

Tesch, S. A., & Whitbourne, S. K. (1982). Intimacy and identity status in young adults. *Journal of Personality and Social Psychology, 43,* 1041-1051.

Tognoli, J. (1980). Male friendship and intimacy across the life span. *Family Relations, 29,* 273-279.

Vaillant, G. E. (1977). *Adaptation to life.* Boston: Little, Brown.

Weiss, R. S. (1982). Attachment in adult life. In C. M. Parkes & J. Stevenson-Hinde (Eds.), *The place of attachment in human behavior* (pp. 171-184). New York: Basic Books.

Weiss, R. S. (1986). Continuities and transformation in social relationships from childhood to adulthood. In W. W. Hartup & Z. Rubin (Eds.), *Relationships and development* (pp. 95-110). Hillsdale, NJ: Lawrence Erlbaum.

Weiss, L., & Lowenthal. M. F. (1975). Life-course perspectives on friendship. In M. F. Lowenthal, M. Thurnher, D. Chiriboga, & Associates (Eds.), *Four stages of life* (pp. 48-61). San Francisco: Jossey-Bass.

Whitbourne, S. K., & Tesch, S. A. (1985). A comparison of identity and intimacy statuses in college students and alumni. *Developmental Psychology, 21,* 1039-1044.

Williams, D. G. (1985). Gender, masculinity-femininity, and emotional intimacy in same-sex friendship. *Sex Roles, 12,* 587-600.

Youniss, J. (1980). *Parents and peers in social development: A Sullivan-Piaget perspective.* Chicago: University of Chicago Press.

5

Developmental Processes of Friendship

ROSEMARY BLIESZNER

Contemporary scholars who develop theory and conduct research on close relationships recognize that interactions with significant others develop and change over the course of time. Individuals meet, determine their level of attraction to each other, and decide whether to get to know one another better. If they choose in the affirmative, they continue to engage in conversation and various other joint activities during which they evaluate the benefits of deepening their level of involvement with each other. Relationship development proceeds according to the partners' desire to maintain the relationship at the current level of closeness, to increase its intimacy, to decrease its intimacy, or to terminate it. The objective of the present chapter is to examine aspects of friendship initiation, maintenance, and disengagement in the late adulthood years. Consideration of the needs and abilities of older adults that have an impact on their friendship behavior, and, reciprocally, the ways that friendship might affect individual development in the later years, informs this exploration.

INDIVIDUAL DEVELOPMENT
AND FRIENDSHIP

The Effects of Aging on Friendship

Features of both contemporary society and the aging process affect the opportunities of older adults to establish new friendships and their ability to continue existing ones. Several recent publications detail these features (Allan & Adams, this volume; Blieszner, 1988; Chown, 1981; Jerrome, 1981). Briefly put, loss of roles due to retirement and widowhood, diminished health and physical activity, reduced income, and residential mobility all may limit friend interaction in late adulthood. Changes in the health or life circumstances of either partner can have an impact on a friendship, and negative life events are more likely to occur in late adulthood than at any other period of life. The oldest old—those over 80 years of age—are most vulnerable to events and situations that can impede friendship. But the later years of life can also provide freedom from previous roles and restrictions, and attendant opportunities to make new friends (Adams, 1987; Shea, Thompson, & Blieszner, 1988).

In fact, numerous studies in social gerontology have revealed that the majority of older adults maintain and value their friendships throughout their lives. Research on personality and cognitive abilities has affirmed that elderly persons are certainly capable negotiating complex social behavior such as friendship. That is, individuals who possessed the requisite social skills to develop and maintain friendships during childhood and earlier adulthood are likely to retain those skills in the later years as long as their health and mental faculties remain intact. So, though the form and frequency of interaction may change with aging, the essential elements of friendship—equality, enjoyment, trust, assistance, respect, acceptance, spontaneity, understanding, affection (Davis & Todd, 1985)—can endure indefinitely.

Researchers have limited their direct examinations of the effects of aging on friendship to studies of sociological variables such as role loss and change in residence. One area of personality research that bears further exploration is the effects on friendship of the tendency toward increased introspection in late adulthood. Do the elderly use their closest friends to assist with their life review, seeking approval for previous accomplishments and support for coping with perceived failings? Or do they pursue the task of making sense of life independently of their confidants? Answers to these questions not only pertain to increased understanding of the life review process, but also hold implications for professionals who seek to enhance the psychological well-being of older adults.

The Effects of Friendship on Aging

Friends can serve as agents of socialization in old age just as at any other stage of life. People who have experienced role loss, health trauma, or other hazards of aging can assist their friends in learning how to manage similar events. Friends provide numerous resources to each other (Shea et al., 1988) that are both useful (e.g., information, a small loan) and emotionally supportive (e.g., affection, esteem). Because they tend to be age peers, friends enjoy a shared perspective and understanding that may not correspond to the viewpoints of other generations. In fact, older people may even feel more comfortable interacting with friends than with relatives because their ability to reciprocate each other's efforts is similar with friends but potentially more unbalanced with younger relatives (Allan & Adams, this volume; Arling, 1976). A fairly large body of work exists on the social support provided by friends to aged people (see Antonucci, 1985, and Crohan & Antonucci, this volume, for reviews) and on the connection between social relationships and psychological well-being among the elderly (e.g., Baldassare, Rosenfield, & Rook, 1984). It is clear that friends play a major role in the happiness of most older adults.

DEVELOPMENTAL PROCESSES
OF FRIENDSHIP

The focus of this section is friendship initiation, maintenance, and disengagement. Duck and Sants (1983, p. 31) argued that relationships are processes, not states, and that complete understanding of relationships requires study of their "adverbial properties." Researchers should investigate how partners interact with each other, not just the predictors and outcomes of interaction. Plath (1984) addressed the connection between individual development and relationships-as-processes when he noted that most research has focused on short-term interactions instead of lifelong patterns, yet it is continued engagements with others that contribute most to one's maturity.

Below, I provide a conceptual overview and discuss illustrative pieces of research from the social gerontology literature for each segment of the relationship process. Readers should note from the outset that very few investigators have conducted studies of older adult friendship from a relationship process perspective.

Friendship Initiation

Theory. Scholars have conceptualized the growth of close relationships within the framework of several psychological theories. Space does not permit examination of the myriad perspectives on attraction, impression formation, motivation, attributions, and the like. Instead, I present two key theoretical frameworks that have contributed to the understanding of relationships as processes, the reinforcement-social exchange-equity school and developmental principles.

According to reinforcement theories, individuals become friends with people who provide them with various sorts of rewards. If interactions between new acquaintances are reinforcing, they desire to repeat the interactions and develop positive feelings toward each other, which are rewarding and promote further interaction. Exchange and equity theorists take a slightly expanded perspective on reinforcement. They focus on the friends' evaluations of the benefits of interaction with each other in comparison to outcomes derived from past friendships and to those potentially available in other friendships. If the rewards of participating in this new friendship outweigh the costs and the partners' investments in it seem balanced, positive feelings toward the relationship result and interaction continues (see Roberto, this volume). Social penetration theorists place special emphasis on the exchange of information within developing relationships. Individuals find it rewarding to reveal to each other details about their personal lives, feelings, ideas about the future development of the friendship, and so on (Morton & Douglas, 1981; Perlman & Fehr, 1986, 1987).

Another perspective on friendship initiation exists in the writings of developmental theorists. Typically they identify stages of closeness ranging from mere awareness of the potential friend through acquaintanceship to most intimate friendship. Stage theorists posit that initial attraction depends on perceived similarities between the partners. As they get to know each other, new friends establish rapport and understanding, discover ways that they are compatible, and become committed to the relationship. Processes such as exchange and self-disclosure are involved in increased feelings of affection and enjoyment of the relationship.

Empirical tests of reinforcement, exchange, and social penetration theories have examined the very earliest stage of attraction to potential friends (e.g., see Byrne, 1971, Rusbult, 1980, and Altman & Taylor, 1973, respectively). It is likely that these processes continue to influence the course of personal relationships, but we do not know how any of them may differ as partners become close friends. In contrast, stage theorists (e.g., Levinger, 1980) assume that interaction processes vary over time and seek to explain not only characteristics of each level of closeness, but also causes of transition from one stage to another. More obvious in this approach than in the others is the possibility that relationships can deteriorate, not just escalate in a positive direction.

Perlman and Fehr (1987, pp. 31-32) provided a comprehensive list of changes that occur as partners move from initial acquaintance to close friendship:

(1) Interaction increases in terms of the frequency, duration, and number of settings in which it occurs.

(2) Individuals gain knowledge of the innermost being of their partner, the breadth and depth of knowledge exchanged expands, and partners develop personal communication codes.

(3) Individuals become more skilled at mapping and anticipating their partner's views and behaviors.

(4) Partners increase their investment in the relationship.

(5) The interdependence and the sense of "we-ness" experienced by partners increases.

(6) Partners come to feel that their separate interests are inextricably tied to the well-being and outcome of their relationship.

(7) The extent of positive affect (liking or loving) and the sense of caring, commitment, and trust increase.

(8) Attachment develops so that partners try to restore proximity if they are separated.

(9) Partners see the relationship as irreplaceable, or at least special.

This summary integrates elements from all the major theories of relationship initiation. Although the authors based the summary on research conducted with college students and young married couples, it points to a number of key variables that one can examine to increase understanding of friendship initiation among the elderly.

Research on late adulthood friendship initiation. Two recent reports on older adult friendship confirm that elderly persons make new friends. The first was by Matthews (1986a) who conducted biographical interviews using friendships as the guiding theme for examining the past, present, and future lives of the informants. She identified three styles of friendship behavior that reflected patterns that had emerged over the respondents' life course. Members of the "acquisitive" group were more likely than those in the other two groups to continue to make new friends in their later years. These individuals reported that their friend network increased in size as they passed through adulthood, often when they experienced events such as job change, relocation, or change in marital status.

Adams (1987) demonstrated changes in friend networks through a three-year study of older women. She discerned three independent dimensions of friend network change in the sample. The first represented a tendency toward expansion of the entire friend network in terms of increases in the number of friends and the frequency of interaction reported at Time 2. The second dimension represented contraction of the local friend network over time, including an increase in the percentage of nonlocal friends and a decrease in network density. The third change dimension reflected an increase in the percentage of friends who were emotionally distant to the respondents. The patterns of change varied among the different middle-class status groups represented in the sample. Nonetheless, a number of respondents reported having made new friends over the course of the study either by virtue of participating in local organizations or by traveling elsewhere.

The preceding researchers found that older adults do retain the ability and motivation to initiate friendships, but they did not address the processes by which aged people acquire the new friends. Other investigators have reported recently on several very informative studies of such processes among young adults (Berg, 1984; Hays, 1984, 1985). Whereas college freshman dormitory students provide new samples each fall, it is difficult to conduct such research with elderly persons because it is quite rare to find an entire group of older adults who are unacquainted, yet will be together long enough to form enduring friendships. Construction of a new retirement community in my town, however, afforded a unique opportunity to study friendship processes among older adults. Thus my colleague, Linda Thompson, and I developed a longitudinal study of the new residents' emerging friendships, as well as their old (continuing) ones.

The conceptual framework guiding our work was Foa and Foa's theory of resource exchange (Foa & Foa, 1974), which combines elements of both reinforcement and developmental approaches. Foa and Foa conceptualized friendship as a freely chosen bond based on mutually rewarding exchanges. All interpersonal encounters involve the exchange of six classes of resources: love, status (esteem), information, services, goods, and money. Foa and Foa suggested that in order for exchanges to take place, an individual must perceive a need for one or more resources and must believe both that the other person can provide needed resource(s) and that he or she also has resources to offer the other person. As relationships develop from acquaintance to friendship, people are likely to progress from exchanging only impersonal resources, such as goods and money, to exchanging personal resources, such as affection and esteem as well. Factors that facilitate exchange of the more personal and intimate resources are repetitive encounters, pair or small group interaction, and sufficient time to allow interactions to move beyond a superficial level.

Based on this model, we measured antecedents of resource exchange, conditions that facilitate resource exchange, the frequency of giving and of receiving resources in association with each target person, and consequences of resource exchange for the respondents' feelings about the friends. The sample consisted of a little over half the residents who were living in the community shortly after it opened. Five months after the first session, we contacted the participants for a second interview. A total of 27 residents (24 women and 3 men) provided complete data. The typical participant was a healthy widow, aged 70 years, with a high school education and an annual income under $10,000.

Respondents located their friends on a friendship circle diagram (Kahn & Antonucci, 1980). The diagram consisted of three concentric circles with the participant in the center. At the first interview, participants named one or two close friends for placement in the inner circle, placed their not quite so close friends in the middle circle, and named all acquaintances met since relocation with whom they wished to become friends in the outer circle. During the second interview, participants received a list of friend names from Time 1 and located each friendship on a blank concentric circle diagram. For two persons at each level of closeness (yielding a total of 162 friendships per time of interview), participants answered a series of questions concerning the antecedents, the frequency, and the consequences of resource exchange. They also answered open-ended questions about the meaning of resource exchange and reasons for change of closeness within each relationship.

We examined processes of relationship change by conducting a series of 2 (occasion) × 3 (friend type) repeated measures analyses of variance. The friend types were old friends, friends who became closer (i.e., respondents placed them nearer to the center of the circle diagram at Time 2 than they had been at Time 1), and friends who became less close (i.e., respondents placed them farther from the center of the circle diagram or moved them off the diagram at Time 2). Based on Foa and Foa's theory, we expected indicators of both emotional closeness and resource exchange to differentiate the long-term friendships and those that grew closer from the others. The findings confirmed the predictions and yielded insight into variables that appear to be important in moving relationships from acquaintanceship to friendship.

The Time 1 data showed a significant effect of friend type on trust, and post hoc analysis revealed that respondents trusted old friends significantly more than the new friends whom they categorized as less emotionally close by Time 2. The three groups of friends did not differ on liking, loving, or commitment to the future of the relationship at Time 1. At Time 2, however, respondents consistently rated the emotional indicators of trust, liking, and commitment higher for old friends and for friends who became closer than for friends who became less close.

We performed similar analyses for the relationship process variables concerning the likelihood and frequency of exchanging resources. At Time 1, the three groups of friends did not differ on perceived likelihood of giving the group of six resources to the various friends, nor on perceived likelihood of receiving resources, actual frequency of giving them, or frequency of receiving resources. But at Time 2, a significant effect of friend type occurred on three of the four variables: likelihood of receiving the six resources, frequency of giving resources, and frequency of receiving them. Follow-up comparisons of the significant effects indicated that, in each case, the old friends and those who became closer received higher scores than the friends who became more distant. Thus, though the respondents classified themselves as equally likely to provide resources to their target friends regardless of how close each friendship was, they believed that only their old friends and their close new friends were likely to give them resources in return. Their assessments of the actual frequency of giving resources showed that they did not really give much to the friends who were less close, even though they expressed willingness to do so. Their report on the frequency of receiving resources corresponded to their expectation: They received significantly more from their old friends and closer friends than from their less close friends. Looking across occasions, neither resource exchange nor affection differed with regard to the old friends, but both resource exchange and affection increased significantly between Time 1 and Time 2 for new friends. We reported more detailed results for individual resources elsewhere (Shea et al., 1988). Below are comments reflecting increases in the exchange of resources within the relationships that became closer. Respondents made these remarks in response to questions about how they and their friends exchanged resources and how the exchanges affected their friendships.

LOVE: We are closer than last summer. I think you need to show love and affection in order to be friends. I wouldn't feel comfortable with her if we did not show love and affection.

STATUS: I tell her I like her and I confide in her. I tell her she is my good friend. She tells me that she likes me. I am her good friend. She likes my handiwork. [We show respect and admiration] a little more because we see each other more often. I admire her very much and it is because I have spent more time with her and we've become closer.

SERVICES: The better we got to know each other, the more we did to help each other. I think it's wonderful to have friends to help you. That's an important part of friendship—having someone to depend on.

INFORMATION: She gives me advice about gossip, what to do. She fusses around me a lot. She gives me more advice than I give her. I don't like to be nosy or bothersome. It is important to share information.

GOODS: [We exchange goods] more often now that we're closer. It's good to know we can count on each other if we need to borrow something.

On the other hand, most respondents felt that the exchange of money was of little consequence to the development of their friendships:

MONEY: I haven't got any to spend. She doesn't either. Money is not important to our friendship.

Our findings support Foa and Foa's conceptualization of friendship development: Within five months of becoming acquainted, respondents differentiated among their friends on both subjective and behavioral measures. They reported more liking, loving, and commitment for friends who had grown closer than for those who became less close, and they exchanged resources more often with these people. These results suggest that both affective and behavioral variables are important contributors to the evolution of new friendships.

Friendship Maintenance

Theory. Few theoretical statements explicitly address continuity of relationships. Rather, the implicit assumption of the theories cited above is that individuals retain their friendships as long as they perceive them to be rewarding and enjoyable.

Commitment theory, as articulated by Johnson (1973, 1978), provides an explanation for relationship maintenance. Individuals are committed to continuing their friendships and other close relationships for both internal and external reasons. "Personal commitment" refers to a person's internal dedication to the friendship, and "structural commitment" describes external constraints against ending the friendship.

The elements of personal commitment include satisfaction with the relationship, definition of the self in terms of the relationship, and an internalized sense of moral obligation to maintain the relationship. On the other hand, the extent of irretrievable investments the person has made in the relationship, social pressures from others to maintain the relationship, the availability and attractiveness of alternative relational partners, and the ease or difficulty of ending the relationship determine the level of structural commitment. Because friendship is a fairly voluntary relationship, the effects of personal commitment are probably stronger influences on endurance than in relationships that are structurally determined.

Although Johnson did not directly address the processes by which personal and structural commitment develop, it is likely that commitment strengthens as relationships change from casual to close. Thus different patterns of relationship maintenance may be appropriate for different levels of commitment. Johnson (1978) found varying patterns of personal and structural constraint in a cross-sectional study of romantic relationships at several levels of involvement from casual dating to marriage. The closer relationships exhibited higher levels of both forms of commitment, and thus greater reluctance to terminate them and more perceived difficulty in doing so. Similarly, Rose and Serafica (1986) found, in a sample of young adults, that the strategies used to maintain friends varied by level of closeness. Maintenance of casual friendships as opposed to close or best friendships required more physical proximity but less affection, whereas maintenance of close and best friendships required at least some affection and a great deal of interaction.

Research on late adulthood friendship continuity. A study by Roberto and Kimboko (1989) confirmed the expectation that older adults sustain close friendships over the course of many years. Matthews (1986a) provided some insights into the processes involved in such continuity. She found that individuals maintained some friendships because of personal commitment, but others endured due to favorable social circumstances more than to the respondents' commitment and explicit maintenance efforts. Presumably individuals who actively maintained friendships through strategies such as letter writing, telephoning, and visiting made the effort because they were quite satisfied with their relationships. Less active attempts at friendship maintenance seemed to reflect different personality configurations and friendship style: the "discerning" type in Matthews's study had only a few friends over the life course and did not necessarily expect to have close friends in adulthood, so many of them did not make strong efforts to maintain friends. Among the informants who relied on social circumstances rather than personal efforts for ongoing friendships, some used events such as visits to their home town or school reunions as occasions to see old friends. Others selected a retirement community near their friends or arranged joint vacations with friends in order to maintain their ties. Still other respondents told of renewing friendships in old age that had been inactive for many years, often precipitated by a change in life circumstances (e.g., retirement, death of the friend's spouse). Matthews also found, parallel with other studies (Adams, 1986; Shea et al., 1988), that friendships could endure despite infrequent contact and geographic distance between the partners.

In our retirement community study, indicators of the relationship satisfaction dimension of personal commitment were the emotional closeness measures (trust, liking, love, commitment) and the resource exchange measures (likelihood and frequency of giving and receiving resources). Long-standing friendships were not negatively affected by the respondents' relocation, as indicated by stable patterns of resource exchange and affection across the duration of the study. Indeed, respondents expressed the expectation that the same level of intimacy and support within these friendships would continue well into the future. In some cases, they could remain in contact with their old friends by frequent visiting and other joint activities because their friends lived nearby. They used the telephone and cards or letters to contact out-of-town friends.

When we probed for specific maintenance behaviors in relation to each resource, we found that the respondents used different strategies for old than for new friendships (Shea et al., 1988). Expressions of love or affection were taken as givens in old friendships, whereas new ones required displays of affection to aid in their development and maintenance. Conveying status or esteem for each other was crucial to both ongoing and fairly new friendships. With regard to exchange of information, respondents valued advice from their old friends and engaged in reminiscing and self-disclosure with them, but the information shared between new friends focused more on current day-to-day events and impersonal topics. Old friends exchanged various forms of services and assistance as needed, and study participants appreciated the help and support old friends had provided them over the years. Exchange of services was not, however, a significant part of relationship maintenance between new friends, and those who did do favors for each other had a concern about reciprocity that was not evident in the discussions of old friendships. Exchanges of goods and money were relatively infrequent for both old and new friends.

A final consideration of factors that affect friendship continuity in the later years of life is social support, one of the most important functions of friendship. The exchange of social support between friends involves both personal and structural commitment, and both forms of commitment influence the continuation of the relationship. In terms of personal dedication, individuals not only derive satisfaction from assisting others, they may also define themselves as helpful persons and feel that the bonds of friendship obligate them to provide help when possible. Structural commitment is evident in the feelings friends have that they are willing to help each other because they have been friends for a long time and have invested a lot in the relationship, because others would be critical of them if they failed to help, or because they don't have any better alternative persons to befriend. Examination of these concepts in future research would enrich our knowledge of the processes by which older adults maintain their social ties.

Friendship Disengagement and Dissolution

Theory. Duck (1982) pointed out that many researchers implicitly assume that a steady, unlimited growth in intimacy is the norm for personal relationships such as friendship. He challenged this assumption, because obviously many relationships never get established and many ongoing relationships decline in intimacy and become more problematic over time (see Rook, this volume). Thus attention to the process of disengaging from close ties is a prerequisite to a comprehensive theory of relationships.

In Duck's (1982) model, a relationship begins to break down when either or both partners experience dissatisfaction with it. During the "intrapsychic phase" a cognitive process ensues, involving evaluation of the partner's behavior, the negative aspects of the relationship, and the positive aspects of other relationships. If the person concludes she or he would be justified in withdrawing from the relationship, there arises the "dyadic phase" requiring confrontation of the partner and decisions about attempting to repair the relationship or ending it. As the partners decide to reduce intimacy, they must negotiate face-saving and blame-placing stories within their larger social network ("social phase"). In the final "grave dressing phase" the former partners adjust to the dissolution by rationalizing the importance of the relationship in their previous lives and accounting for its demise.

Baxter (1985) reported a series of studies on communication strategies used in the dyadic phase of relationship disengagement. Individuals used direct or indirect approaches depending on the type of relationship (e.g., romantic versus friend), their own characteristics (age, personality), and their expectations concerning future contact with the partner. Disengagement strategies also varied on the extent to which the person attempted to protect the partner's feelings. These results demonstrate that disengagement follows no single pattern, and imply a need for more research on the circumstances that lead to various styles of terminating relationships.

Johnson (1982) interpreted relationship dissolution within the context of his commitment theory. Aspects of personal and structural commitment affect the steps that are involved in the decision about whether or not to end a close relationship, the difficulty of disengaging, the adjustment to loss of a relationship, and the effects of this relationship change on the partners and their larger social networks. If an individual becomes quite dissatisfied with a relationship, no longer identifies her- or himself as strongly attached to the partner, and does not feel obligated to maintain the interaction, personal commitment declines and the dissolution process becomes salient. The person must then enact the procedures required to disengage, which is less difficult in casual friendships than in very close friendships or romantic liaisons.

One must also come to terms with changes in the self-identity, loss of previous investments in the relationship, changes in the makeup of the social network, and the issue of finding substitute relationships—all of which also vary according to the type of relationship terminated.

A program of research by Rusbult (1987) showed that not all relationship stress results in disengagement. Rather, individuals can express dissatisfaction in a number of ways, summarized in the exit-voice-loyalty-neglect model. "Exit" refers to ending or threatening to end the relationship, "voice" signifies attempts to discuss and resolve problems or change one's behavior in a constructive way, "loyalty" connotes passively waiting for the relationship to improve, and "neglect" means passively allowing the relationship to whither. Rusbult and her colleagues found that partners' demographic characteristics, such as age and gender, and personality characteristics, such as sex-role orientation and self-esteem, affected their reactions to relationship dissatisfaction. But also, level of commitment to the relationship had an influence on the strategy employed. Individuals who were dissatisfied with the relationship, felt they had little to lose because they had invested little, and had good alternatives were those likely to exit in reaction to major relationship problems. In contrast, partners who were satisfied and who had invested a lot were more likely to try voice techniques when there were serious problems. Rusbult found that people used loyalty for resolution of minor problems when they were satisfied with the relationship and had invested a lot in it, whereas they chose neglect in cases of low satisfaction and low investment in the relationship.

Research on late adulthood friendship disengagement. The conceptualizations of relationship deterioration described above assume a fairly active stance on the part of partners who identify problems in their interaction. But studies of late-life friendship dissolution reveal that older persons rarely report actively ending friendships. Instead, they attribute their loss to external causes. Most of the respondents who had friendships that ended in Matthews's (1986a) study said that the friendships just "faded away" due to diverging life-styles and pathways. Because these relationships had not ended in disharmony, respondents felt they could revitalize them if circumstances should permit. This is not usually the aftermath expected after termination of dating or marriage relationships.

The friends who became less close to the respondents over the course of our retirement community study had been new friends at Time 1; no long-term friends became less close. In most cases, again, study participants did not actively terminate friendships. Rather, friendships deteriorated because one of the partners became too ill to assist the other or the friend moved out of the retirement community. Respondents cited as causes of decline in intimacy such events as failure of the friendship to grow close enough to be "self-maintaining" (Rose & Serafica, 1986) before geographic separation and lack of opportunities for self-disclosure and exchange of goods and services. In a few instances, however, respondents ended friendships due to violation of social norms (see Argyle & Henderson, 1984):

> She wanted me to lend her $100. Friends don't borrow money from each other. My husband told me never to lend or borrow [money]. I've tried to live that way. She didn't ask, she almost demanded it. If she needed it I would have given it. She made up stories and got huffy when I refused. Now we only say hi when we pass in the hall.

This quote also shows that dissolved relationships are not necessarily reduced to no interaction at all and suggests the need for information on the implications of this sort of superficial contact on the former friends' feelings and actions.

CONCLUSION

Summary of Relationship Process Issues

The research I reviewed in the sections on initiation, maintenance, and termination of friendships among elderly adults demonstrates that they employ the same processes as members of other age groups to accomplish their relationship goals. When seeking to establish new friendships, older adults begin with less personal and less intimate activities reflecting common interests among acquaintances, then move to more frequent and deeper forms of self-disclosure and expressions of affection and esteem. They retain their friendships by periodic contact, exchanges of gifts and favors, and continued communication of a personal nature. They tend to disengage from unsatisfactory friendships by letting them whither from neglect, unless a serious breach of norms calls for a more abrupt tactic.

In contrast, the context in which older adults carry out friendship behaviors differentiates their patterns from those of other age groups.

For one thing, life's exigencies may limit not only opportunities to establish new friendships but also candidates for the position. For another, maintenance and termination activities are not entirely under the individual's control, given that one cause of the demise of friendship is the person's disability or the friend's illness or death. Thus another age distinction is that old people are much more likely than young people to have nonage peers for friends, because persons younger than they make up the pool of potential friends (see Matthews, 1986b). Other chapters in this volume provide many details about the contextual variables that affect older adult's friendship opportunities and processes.

Recommendations for Future Research

Researchers have consistently demonstrated the importance of friendship in the lives of older adults, yet few have examined the strategies that these individuals use to begin and promote such relationships. More study of friendship as process would strengthen the knowledge base on social behavior in late life and yield insights into tactics that community practitioners might employ to assist lonely aged persons. The analysis provided in this chapter leads to several suggestions for future investigation.

With respect to the reciprocal influence of friendship and aging, the need for more research on the connection between late-life personality trends and friendship patterns is evident. Under what circumstances do friends assist with life review, and in what ways do they interfere? Do different configurations of personality traits have any impact on friendship styles? As aging adults become more introspective, does friendship take on new meaning, do elderly adults become more tolerant of friends' idiosyncrasies, do friends help them to prepare for death?

Earlier discussion in this chapter pointed to evidence for the operation of exchange theory principles in late-life friendship formation, but we need more data on how these and reinforcement and social penetration processes evolve over the course of friendship development. Likewise, it would be beneficial to know whether the kinds of changes summarized by Perlman and Fehr (1987)—increased interaction, self-disclosure, affect, sense of "we-ness," and so on—are prominent in late-life friendships, and whether these variables differ for relatively new versus long-term friends of older people.

The theory of commitment includes a number of concepts that researchers could operationalize to learn more about the processes, not just the outcomes, of friendship interaction. It would be interesting to know whether particular aspects of personal and of structural commitment come into play at different stages of friendship formation and maintenance, and, if so, how and why?

When friendships are problematic, what factors determine whether older people will use active or passive termination strategies? What implications does choice of strategy have for adjusting to decline in intimacy?

Perhaps a fourth stage of friendship development exists—adjusting to loss of significant friendships and filling the void in the social network. What processes do older adults use in this stage, and do they vary according to whether the friendship ended deliberately or because of a friend's relocation, illness, or death? How do older people manage the circumstance of withdrawing from a friendship with someone whom they are likely to continue seeing in their residential complex or social organizations?

Moreover, though the discussion above presented friendship process as though it is a linear phenomenon that inevitably leads to termination of the relationship and adjustment to the loss, this was for heuristic purposes only. In reality, friendship process is cyclical with ebbs and flows of contact and affection both within and across friendships. Thus it would be fruitful to study changes in friendship process that coincide with life events such as retirement and widowhood. Researchers should pay particular attention to the many stages and forms and styles of friendship maintenance that probably exist.

Research on old age friendship processes would be greatly enhanced by short-term and long-term longitudinal designs. A variety of data collection strategies, other than the typical one-shot interview or mail survey, exist. For instance, daily interaction records kept by participants for several weeks, frequent telephone calls by research staff to collect daily or weekly interaction data, and ongoing observations in residential or social group settings are all possibilities that friendship scholars might try. In addition, very long-term longitudinal studies of friendship would provide the data to enable us to determine whether retrospective accounts of friendship interaction over time are acceptable descriptions of stability and change. This last suggestion is ambitious, but investigators could accomplish it by teaming with researchers of other aspects of aging and development that also require longitudinal data.

REFERENCES

Adams, R. G. (1986). Emotional closeness and physical distance between friends: Implications for elderly women living in age-segregated and age-integrated settings. *International Journal of Aging and Human Development, 22,* 55-76.

Adams, R. G. (1987). Patterns of network change: A longitudinal study of friendships of elderly women. *The Gerontologist, 27,* 222-227.

Altman, I., & Taylor, D. A. (1973). *Social penetration: The development of interpersonal relationships.* New York: Irvington.

Antonucci, T. C. (1985). Personal characteristics, social support, and social behavior. In R. H. Binstock & E. Shanas (Eds.), *Handbook of aging and the social sciences* (2nd ed., pp. 94-128). New York: Van Nostrand Reinhold.

Argyle, M., & Henderson, M. (1984). The rules of friendship. *Journal of Social and Personal Relationships, 1,* 211-237.

Arling, G. (1976). The elderly widow and her family, neighbors and friends. *Journal of Marriage and the Family, 38,* 757-768.

Baldassare, M., Rosenfield, S., & Rook, K. (1984). The types of social relations predicting elderly well-being. *Research on Aging, 6,* 549-559.

Baxter, L. A. (1985). Accomplishing relationship disengagement. In S. Duck & D. Perlman (Eds.), *Understanding personal relationships* (pp. 243-265). London: Sage.

Berg, J. H. (1984). Development of friendship between roommates. *Journal of Personality and Social Psychology, 46,* 346-356.

Blieszner, R. (1988). Individual development and intimate relationships in middle and late adulthood. In R. M. Milardo (Ed.), *Families and social networks* (pp. 147-167). Newbury Park, CA: Sage.

Byrne, D. (1971). *The attraction paradigm.* New York: Academic Press.

Chown, S. M. (1981). Friendship in old age. In S. Duck & R. Gilmour (Eds.), *Personal relationships, Vol. 2: Developing personal relationships* (pp. 231-246). London: Academic Press.

Davis, K. E., & Todd, M. J. (1985). Assessing friendship: Prototypes, paradigm cases and relationship description. In S. Duck & D. Perlman (Eds.), *Understanding personal relationships* (pp. 17-37). London: Sage.

Duck, S. (1982). A topography of relationship disengagement and dissolution. In S. Duck (Ed.), *Personal relationships, Vol. 4: Dissolving personal relationships* (pp. 1-29). London: Academic Press.

Duck, S., & Sants, H. (1983). On the origin of the specious: Are personal relationships really interpersonal states? *Journal of Social and Clinical Psychology, 1,* 27-41.

Foa, U., & Foa, E. (1974). *Societal structures of the mind.* Springfield, IL: Charles C Thomas.

Hays, R. B. (1984). The development and maintenance of friendship. *Journal of Social and Personal Relationships, 1,* 75-98.

Hays, R. B. (1985). A longitudinal study of friendship development. *Journal of Personality and Social Psychology, 48,* 909-924.

Jerrome, D. (1981). The significance of friendship for women in later life. *Ageing and Society, 1,* 175-197.

Johnson, M. P. (1973). Commitment: A conceptual structure and empirical application. *Sociological Quarterly, 14*, 395-406.

Johnson, M. P. (1978, October). *Personal and structural commitment: Sources of consistency in the development of relationships.* Paper presented at the annual meeting of the National Council on Family Relations, Philadelphia.

Johnson, M. P. (1982). Social and cognitive features of the dissolution of commitment to relationships. In S. Duck (Ed.), *Personal relationships, Vol. 4: Dissolving personal relationships* (pp. 51-73). London: Academic Press.

Kahn, R. L., & Antonucci, T. C. (1980). Convoys over the life course: Attachment, roles and social support. In P. B. Baltes & O. G. Brim (Eds.), *Life span development and behavior* (Vol. 3, pp. 253-286). New York: Academic Press.

Levinger, G. (1980). Toward the analysis of close relationships. *Journal of Experimental Social Psychology, 16*, 510-544.

Matthews, S. H. (1986a). *Friendships through the life course.* Beverly Hills, CA: Sage.

Matthews, S. H. (1986b). Friendships in old age: Biography and circumstance. In V. W. Marshall (Ed.), *Later life: The social psychology of aging* (pp. 233-269). Beverly Hills, CA: Sage.

Morton, T. L., & Douglas, M. A. (1981). Growth of relationships. In S. Duck & R. Gilmour (Eds.), *Personal relationships, Vol. 2: Developing personal relationships* (pp. 3-26). London: Academic Press.

Perlman, D., & Fehr, B. (1986). Theories of friendship: The analysis of interpersonal attraction. In V. J. Derlega & B. A. Winstead (Eds.), *Friendship and social interaction* (pp. 9-40). New York: Springer-Verlag.

Perlman, D., & Fehr, B. (1987). The development of intimate relationships. In D. Perlman & S. Duck (Eds.), *Intimate relationships* (pp. 13-42). Newbury Park, CA: Sage.

Plath, D. W. (1984). Of time, love, and heroes. In V. Rogers (Ed.), *Adult development through relationships* (pp. 16-27). New York: Praeger.

Roberto, K. A., & Kimboko, P. J. (1989). Friendships in later life: Definitions and maintenance patterns. *International Journal of Aging and Human Development, 28*, 9-19.

Rose, S., & Serafica, F. C. (1986). Keeping and ending casual, close and best friendships. *Journal of Social and Personal Relationships, 3*, 275-288.

Rusbult, C. E. (1980). Satisfaction and commitment in friendships. *Representative Research in Social Psychology, 11*, 96-105.

Rusbult, C. E. (1987). Responses to dissatisfaction in close relationships: The exit-voice-loyalty-neglect model. In D. Perlman & S. Duck (Eds.), *Intimate relationships* (pp. 209-237). Newbury Park, CA: Sage.

Shea, L., Thompson, L., & Blieszner, R. (1988). Resources in older adults' old and new friendships. *Journal of Social and Personal Relationships, 5*, 83-96.

PART III

Social Process
and Friendship

6

Friends as a Source of Social Support in Old Age

SUSAN E. CROHAN
TONI C. ANTONUCCI

The purpose of this chapter is to review and integrate the literature on friends as a source of social support among older adults. We begin with a general discussion of the importance of social support to well-being and a review of one theoretical perspective on social support. We then consider how friendships differ from family relationships in important ways that influence both the amount and type of support each group provides as well as the impact of this support on well-being. Next we discuss the kinds of social support provided to and received from friends in old age in some detail. We then present empirical evidence from the Supports of the Elderly Study (Kahn & Antonucci, 1984) to explore the differential impact of friends and family on well-being. The chapter ends with suggestions for future research in the area.

The graying of America has created many pressing issues concerning the lives and care of older adults. In this light, the examination of the role of friends as social support providers assumes increased importance in current gerontological research as well as public policy (Kiesler, 1985; Peters & Kaiser, 1985). Research on social support has increased in recent years, with new theoretical and methodological advances occurring rapidly. At the same time, the field is plagued by certain definitional and measurement problems that make the study of friends as social support providers difficult. How investigators conceptualize and operationalize social support has constrained what we know about friends as support providers, just as how they define friendships limits what we know about friendships in general (see Adams, this volume).

Many of the problems that apply to the study of friendship and aging also apply to the study of friendship and social support. Researchers have defined social support in more than one way, so the measures and approaches used to study the concept differ from study to study. Another problem in the support literature is that the processes and mechanisms by which social support operates are still unclear, although researchers have begun to address these issues (e.g., Antonucci & Jackson, 1987). Most researchers have not distinguished between friends and neighbors as support providers or between qualitative and quantitative measures of support (see Cantor, 1979, and Israel & Antonucci, 1987, for exceptions). For example, researchers sometimes use the frequency of interaction with friends or the number of friends as measures of social support, paying little attention to the quality of the interaction or what partners actually do together. Some researchers have suggested that the quality of the interaction, rather than its quantity, is what matters to psychological well-being (e.g., Connor, Powers, & Bultena, 1979; Sandler & Barrera, 1984; Strain & Chappell, 1982), and others have indicated that structural or quantitative measures of interaction are the best predictors (e.g., Berkman & Syme, 1979; House, Robbins, & Metzner, 1982). Furthermore, the majority of studies have been cross-sectional ones of biased samples (e.g., studies including only white, middle-class, or institutionalized respondents or studies based on nonrandom, nonprobability samples).

One recent study had the advantage of including multiple racial groups but illustrates other problems often found in this field. Creecy and Wright (1979) examined the relationship between social support and well-being among blacks and whites. They found that informal activity with friends was positively related to morale among white but not among black elderly respondents. The authors explained this finding by suggesting that blacks define friends in a less restrictive manner than whites, considering people with whom they have not achieved intimate relations as friends. Thus the frequency of activity with these "friends" was not related to greater happiness or satisfaction among blacks because they defined friends too inclusively.

The data did not sustain this explanation if one closely examines the actual measures used in this study. Creecy and Wright (1979) assessed frequency of activity with friends, but made assumptions about the quality of the interaction in explaining the results. In addition to this problem, other explanations are equally appropriate to the data. For example, one might argue that blacks are more discriminating with respect to informal relationships than whites, and, therefore, only informal, close, or intimate contacts have a positive effect on well-being for blacks. Alternatively, it may be that although the relationship between the quality of support with friends and well-being is the same for both blacks and whites, the overlap between quality and quantity is greater for whites than blacks. Given that this study examined only measures of the quantity of support, these explanations may account for the differential results for blacks and whites. Clearly, before drawing conclusions, research needs to examine the consequences of qualitative and functional dimensions of friendship for the elderly among both blacks and whites. For more detailed discussions of the methodological and conceptual problems in the study of social support, see Antonucci (1985) and House and Kahn (1985).

In this chapter, we adopt the definition Kahn and Antonucci (1980) offered, and define social support as "interpersonal transactions that include one or more of the following key elements: affect, aid and affirmation." "Affective transactions" are expressions of emotional support, including expressions of liking, admiration, respect, or love; "aid" refers to transactions that provide information and practical assistance; and "transactions of affirmation" include expressions of agreement or acknowledgment of the appropriateness of some act or statement of another. These transactions act to validate the individual's feelings of self-worth.

THE CONVOY MODEL
OF SOCIAL SUPPORT

The convoy model (Kahn & Antonucci, 1980) is one theoretical approach to social support that attempts to overcome several of the conceptual and methodological problems in the field. Kahn and Antonucci (1980) derived the model from a social-developmental framework and postulated that each person moves through the life cycle surrounded by a convoy, a set of other people to whom he or she is related by the giving or receiving of social support. The model allows for the examination of both the structural (age, sex, relationship to focal person, frequency of contact) and functional (type of supports provided and received) characteristics of a person's network. It is a dynamic model; the specific people who make up an individual's social network may change over time, as properties of the person (such as age, sex, and health) and situational forces (such as finances, residential mobility, role changes, and role losses) interact to shape the convoy. These properties also jointly determine a person's requirements for social support at any given time and the adequacy of the support provided by the convoy. This person-centered convoy determines, in part, an individual's well-being and helps the individual to adapt and develop over the life course. There is both stability and change in convoy memberships and relationships. Whereas role changes may parallel age, relationship styles and expectations are likely to show continuity and stability over the life course.

Convoy membership initially develops through the performance of roles (i.e., people's neighbors, children, coworkers, friends, and spouses may be in their convoys) and therefore is vulnerable to the role changes associated with the aging process. As Atchley (1980, p. 364) asserted, however, "long after the roles of worker, organization member, or even spouse are lost, the friend role remains." For this reason, research on the social support that friends can and do provide in old age is crucial.

SOCIAL SUPPORT
AND WELL-BEING

The central proposition of the convoy model is that social support is an important determinant of well-being for both its direct contribution and its ability to moderate the effects of stress. Empirical evidence from several studies using a variety of support and well-being measures has supported this proposition (Leavy, 1983; Lin, Ensel, Simeone, & Kuo, 1979; Schaefer, Coyne, & Lazarus, 1981; Turner, 1981; Williams, Ware, & Donald, 1981). Social support can reduce morbidity and mortality (Berkman & Syme, 1979), aid adaptation to and recovery from physical illness (Wortman & Conway, 1985), and buffer the effects of stress on mental and physical health (Bankoff, 1983; House, 1981; Krause, 1986; Lowenthal & Haven, 1968; Sandler & Barrerra, 1984). In addition, researchers have found social support to be associated with low depression and high morale (Schaefer et al., 1981) and with the performance of preventive health behaviors (Abella & Heslin, 1984; Langlie, 1977).

Researchers have documented a positive relationship between social support provided by friends and mental and physical well-being. Simply having friends and, therefore, being a friend helps the life satisfaction and morale of the elderly (Arling, 1976; Chown, 1981; Mancini, 1980; Strain & Chappell, 1982; Wood & Robertson, 1978). In one study, for example, Adams (1986a) found that the number of emotionally close, local friends reported by elderly women was positively related to well-being. Similarly, Bankoff (1983) found that support provided by friends (defined as emotional support, intimacy, and contact) was particularly important to the well-being of widows. Ferraro, Mutran, and Barresi (1984) found that the frequency of friendship support (defined as intimacy and feelings of belonging provided by friends) was causally related to a positive change in physical health over the course of a year for both widows and nonwidows.

Before examining the support functions performed by friends more closely, we consider the differences between friends and family relationships and the implications that these differences have for the types of social support provided by each group.

FRIEND AND
FAMILY RELATIONSHIPS

For the most part, researchers have shown that friendships are more important than family relations to morale and well-being in old age. For example, Arling (1976) found that the number of friends in one's social network was related to less loneliness and worry and to feelings of greater usefulness and respect within the community for elderly widows, but neither the number of family members nor the frequency of contact with them was related to morale. Similarly, Spakes (1979) reported that the number of close friends and satisfaction with the frequency of contact with friends each were related to the life satisfaction of the elderly, but neither frequency of nor satisfaction with family contacts was related to life satisfaction. In addition, Wood and Robertson (1978) found that the number of and frequency of activities with friends was related to morale among elderly grandparents, yet involvement with grandchildren was not. Finally, Elwell and Maltbie-Crannell (1981) reported that the frequency of socializing with friends and neighbors was related positively to life satisfaction among elderly women and men. For men, the frequency of family participation was not related to well-being, whereas for women, friendship participation was a better predictor of satisfaction than family participation. The findings are not totally consistent, however. Essex and Nam (1987), for example, suggested that the relationships that are most important in determining the frequency of loneliness for older women vary according to their marital status.

Given this evidence, it becomes important to explore the differential impact that support provided by friends and family has on the well-being of the elderly. The fundamental differences between friendships and family relations, especially in old age, is a critical issue.

Older friends tend to be highly homogeneous in terms of age and sex, and thus researchers have described friendships in old age as based upon common interests and life-styles, as developing voluntarily, and as characterized by an equal ability to exchange assistance. On the other hand, the family bond in old age, largely because of cultural norms or the financial and health needs of the elderly, may result in a sense of formal obligation on the part of family members toward their elderly relatives (Bengtson, Cutler, Mangen, & Marshall, 1985). The needy older persons may experience something of a role reversal with their children, exacerbated by feelings of dependency. Emotional ties between older persons and their kin can become problematic as dependency increases. Differences due to age, interests, life-styles, or unresolved conflicts can result in estranged family relationships (Wood & Robertson, 1978).

In addition, investigators have shown that family and friendship relations are separate dimensions of social involvement. Friendships foster feelings of attachment that are based on equalitarianism, consensus, and the sharing of good times. Thus friends appear to be most significant to older adults as a source of enjoyment, and, as such, tend to have their greatest impact on the older adults' sense of immediate well-being (Larson, Mannell, & Zuzanek, 1986). On the other hand, people sustain family relations through formal kinship norms and prescribed roles (Adams, 1986b; Antonucci, 1985; Arling, 1976; Wood & Robertson, 1978).

In friendship, partners offer social support voluntarily, with the relationship being defined by the mutual gratification that comes from interaction. As old people lose roles and relationships, friends can fill the void to some degree. Because friends have more in common than family members due to their shared cohort experiences, life-styles, and interests, they often serve to involve older persons in the larger society more than family relationships do (Atchley, 1980; Hess, 1972).

It is precisely because friendships are voluntary, not obligatory, that they may be more important to the well-being of the elderly than kin relationships. The freedom of choice in picking one's friends is important for feelings of autonomy in old age (Adams, 1986b). Friendship minimizes older adults' sense of obligation toward each other because the demands of the friend role are flexible and adjustable to elderly individuals' capability in terms of health and energy (Atchley, 1980). Antonucci (1985) hypothesized that people judge friends and family by different standards and hence use different standards to evaluate their relative effectiveness as support providers. Family members provide a minimal level of support without which one would suffer. Support from friends, however, is optional, not obligatory. For family members then, a relatively strict code of expectations operates such that support not provided has a very negative impact on the well-being of the older person. On the other hand, there are few, if any, obligations or expectations regarding support from friends. Given this, when friends give support, people evaluate it positively and it affects well-being in a positive way. When friends do not provide support, however, there are fewer negative repercussions in the sense of unmet obligations (see Suls, 1982, for a more detailed discussion of the role that expectations play in peoples' evaluations of their social support).

THE IMPACT OF FRIEND
SUPPORT ON WELL-BEING

Cantor (1979) and Litwak (1985) each proposed a model of the informal support system that examines the differential support functions performed by family and friends. Briefly, Litwak's (1985) task-specific model places emphasis on the nature of the task and the characteristics of the various support elements in hypothesizing who is best suited to provide help (see Litwak, this volume, for a more detailed discussion of this model). According to this model, kin fulfill tasks involving long-term commitment and intimacy (such as long-term sick care); neighbors perform tasks requiring speed of response, knowledge of resources, and geographical proximity; and friends deal with problems involving peer group status and similarity of experience and history. As a result of demographic similarities, friends are best with helping people learn new or altered roles (Bankoff, 1983; Peters & Kaiser, 1985). According to this model, they are potentially important sources of affective and emotional support, because they transcend the obligations of kin as well as the legitimate claims made on each other by neighbors.

In contrast, Cantor (1979) has proposed a hierarchical-compensatory model of social support that postulates an order of preference in the choice of the support element. Cantor argued that the primacy of the relationship of the support giver to the recipient is more important than the nature of the task. According to this model, kin are the support source of choice, followed by nonkin, and last by formal organizations. If the first choice is not available or accessible to a person who needs support, Cantor argued that the other support elements are drawn in to compensate for this lack. In a similar manner, Shanas (1979) offered a principle of substitution in social support. According to this principle, people have a hierarchy of preferred support providers, but the availability of these choices is critical in determining whom to ask to provide support (see Chatters, Taylor, & Jackson, 1986; Johnson & Catalano, 1981).

Researchers attempting to assess the validity of both of these models have found support for elements of each. In one study, for example, Cantor (1979) presented hypothetical situations of need to a sample of elderly adults and assessed their choices for support agents. For both affective and instrumental assistance, elderly people picked kin, especially children, as the support element most often. This was especially true, as Litwak's (1985) model predicts, for instrumental assistance (such as sick care, financial aid, and help with tasks of daily living). Cantor argued that the elderly see kin as the appropriate source of help in times of need, but that a compensatory mechanism also operates among the elderly with no children or with children who are not immediately available. For these groups, friends and neighbors are the most important support elements.

Chatters et al. (1986) recently replicated this finding. They asked a nationally representative sample of older blacks (55 years and above) who would help them in the event of sickness or disability. They found that, in general, respondents nominated kin (especially children) before friends and that certain sociodemographic and social-psychological characteristics predicted who they nominated. Separated and widowed individuals were more likely than married individuals to name friends. Respondents who reported that their families were emotionally close to them and respondents who had children were less likely to name friends. The authors interpreted their results by the principle of substitution that, like Cantor's (1979) hierarchical-compensatory model, suggests that when support from a spouse or children is unavailable, individuals turn to nonkin for support. Similarly, Stoller and Earl (1983) reported that marital status and the number of children and other relatives living within an hour's drive predicted assistance from friends with daily living and personal care for older adults. Unmarried individuals and individuals not proximal to family members were more likely to turn to friends for assistance.

In summary, these theorists have argued that one of the most important functions of friends, especially during crises or times of need, appears to be compensatory; that is, they stand in for kin when kin are nonexistent or unavailable and thus are an important adjunct to family in the support networks of the elderly (Cantor, 1979; Peters & Kaiser, 1985). Yet the nature of the support task, cultural norms, and personal expectations also affect the probability of someone looking to their friends as a source of support. In contrast to the family's normative obligation to help, Adams (1986b) argued that the norm governing help from friends is that they are not called on unless the request causes no inconvenience and the person has no alternative. As Antonucci (1985) suggested, if people do receive help from friends under these circumstances, they especially appreciate it and consider it nonobligatory. Below, we consider the relative effectiveness of different classes or types of social support and explore the assumption of reciprocity across the life span.

Types of Support

Researchers have found that emotional intimacy and companionship are the types of support provided by friends most often (Atchley, 1980; Chown, 1981). The elderly often turn to friends when they are worried or lonely (Cantor, 1979). Friends often provide emotional support by exchanging confidences, advice, or comfort (Chown, 1981) and often serve as confidants (Adams, 1986a; Reisman, 1981). The presence of a confidant in one's support network is related to good mental health and high morale and appears to act as a buffer to lessen anxiety and tension when stressful life events occur (Arling, 1976; Cantor, 1979; Lowenthal & Haven, 1968; Strain & Chappell, 1982). Additionally, interaction with friends can be an important mechanism for social integration into the community and broader society (Atchley, 1980; Bankoff, 1983; Hess, 1972; Peters & Kaiser, 1985; Spakes, 1979).

A recent study by Bankoff (1983) demonstrated the multifaceted, emotional support functions provided by friends, in this case to widows. Bankoff hypothesized that transition-phase widows (19-35 months after bereavement) benefit most from the support of their peers in the same life stage who can facilitate their role transitions from married to single persons. She found that widowed, single friends were the most important source of support for widows in the transition group. In the transition phase of widowhood, women needed to reestablish a social life, so their peers became especially important. Peers provided instrumental support such as information and new social contacts for the widows' new lives as single people. Also important to the well-being of the widows, friends provided emotional support such as guidance, comfort, and intimacy. This study illustrated how friends can help reintegrate older people into the community and may be most helpful when an individual is confronting role losses or changes, especially those that frequently accompany age.

In sum, friends tend to play their largest role in the arenas of socialization and the provision of day-to-day companionship. Although friends are less likely to be involved in the provision of instrumental support than family members, some researchers have specifically explored the types of instrumental support that friends provide.

Researchers have shown that friends often provide short-term emergency service and help with certain tasks (Cantor, 1979; Mercier & Powers, 1984). In an examination of the sources of instrumental support for older people with varying functional capacity, Stoller and Earl (1983) found that friends provide support primarily with certain tasks of daily living, such as shopping and light chores. Similarly, Adams (1986a) assessed the percentages of elderly women who received help from friends with several different tasks. Of the 70 respondents, 67% had at least one friend who helped them with at least one task. These tasks ranged from receiving help with transportation or shopping and errands to receiving help during sickness and with emergencies other than sickness. In general, friends who were emotionally close to the respondent were significantly more likely to help, regardless of the physical distance between them. Similarly, Stephens and Bernstein (1984) found, in a study of elderly residents of planned housing, that relationships that involved intimate conversation also involved the exchange of more material and service resources than relationships not involving this form of intimacy.

Friendships also may serve as the principal avenue for ego testing and the reaffirmation of self-worth in old age (Atchley, 1980; Cantor, 1979; Chown, 1981). Friends can shield the elderly from negative self-evaluation by making them feel competent, liked, and needed (Mancini, 1980). Friendships can convey status and position (Candy, Troll, & Levy, 1981). Research also has suggested that perceiving oneself as a good friend is important for morale in old age. Mancini (1980) found a positive relationship between feeling competent in the friend role (in terms of companionship, counsel, aid in times of physical problems, and empathy) and morale among older adults. In addition, feeling that one could help a physically ill peer, if needed, was the most important contributor to the morale of the women and men in Mancini's (1980) study.

Theorists have maintained that feeling needed is crucial to the elderly person's well-being. When older people define themselves as important to the welfare of a peer, their own ability to adapt to old age is enhanced (Atchley, 1980). Furthermore, Wood and Robertson (1978, p. 370) argued that this affirmation may be most important if it comes from a friend: "After widowhood and retirement, old people need relationships with others who appreciate them and share their needs and interests; roles that can be filled only by their contemporaries." The voluntary and mutual nature of friendship serves to sustain a person's sense of self-worth. Because people can choose their friends, being selected as a friend and maintaining a friendship can make people feel good about their own values and actions. Also, in older age, giving support to friends can be gratifying, because it allows people to feel that they can make a contribution to others and suggests that support will be available for them when they need it.

Reciprocity

The discussion of the self-validating functions of friendship highlighted the importance of reciprocity in the friendships of the elderly. Peters and Kaiser (1985) suggested that it is more relevant to see how the elderly are involved in "systems of exchange" with friends rather than just examining the amount and kind of support older people receive from significant others. Reciprocity in the exchange of support may be particularly important in defining the responsibility of nonkin for one another (Wentowski, 1981). Roberto (this volume) reviewed the expanding literature on exchange and equity in elderly friendship and showed that a high degree of reciprocity in the pattern of exchange is evident and important to the well-being of the elderly. Because people gain feelings of independence and self-worth from the ability to reciprocate support, it may be that friendship support is beneficial only to well-being in those relationships where the potential of reciprocation is present. Some of our recent work (Akiyama, Antonucci, & Campbell, in press; Antonucci & Israel, 1986; Ingersoll-Dayton & Antonucci, 1988) has specifically focused on the empirical investigation of reciprocity. To summarize these findings briefly, we have found that (a) an individual's perception of reciprocity with another person was more important to his or her well-being and satisfaction with support than mutual agreement concerning reciprocity; (b) there were distinctive cultural differences in the norms of reciprocity within Japanese and American three-generation triads; and (c) perceived reciprocity was higher among intimate relationships than among less intimate relationships.

Another issue of great importance is whether adults presume that reciprocity in friendships can be long-term or whether it must be immediate. Some researchers suggested that participation in balanced exchanges over long time periods is the major means of guaranteeing security in old age (Akiyama et al., in press; Antonucci, 1985; Wentowski, 1981). Antonucci (1985), for example, proposed the idea of a "support bank" to emphasize this enduring aspect of interpersonal relationships. She suggested that individuals use a generalized accounting system in their support exchanges. In a manner analogous to a savings account at a local bank, individuals strive to maintain a balance between what they deposit and what they withdraw, but the development of a support reserve is most desirable. Wentowski (1981, p. 608) suggested that in old age "independence is interdependence"; one must accept support from the network in which one invested over a lifetime. Researchers need to examine whether the norms of friendship allow for such "saving for a rainy day." A recent examination of this question (Antonucci & Jackson, in press) suggested that functional disability or illness rather than age is the turning point from deposits to withdrawals in the support bank.

Empirical Evidence from the
Supports of the Elderly Study

The Social Networks in Adult Life survey (Kahn & Antonucci, 1984) was a national study conducted by the Survey Research Center of the University of Michigan. The study focused on the social support networks and support relationships of 718 American adults aged 50-95 (227 aged 65-74 and 158 aged 75-95). In the analyses we report here, we examine two issues: the relative impact of family and friends on respondents' psychological well-being and the role of family and friends in respondents' assessments of network quality.

The first set of analyses investigated the relative impact of quantity and quality of support on well-being. We conducted multiple regression analyses that included two quality variables (satisfaction with friends, satisfaction with family) and four quantity variables (the presence of a spouse in network, a child in network, other family in network, a friend in network). We used age as a control variable and conducted analyses separately by sex. We report results from the analyses using life satisfaction here, but we obtained identical results using happiness as the outcome variable. Significant regression analyses indicated that quality of support is a more consistent predictor of life satisfaction than quantity, although some sex differences were apparent, indicating that certain quantity variables were important for women. The responses of both men and women indicated that satisfaction with family and with friend relationships was important to their life satisfaction. Women, however, were also likely to indicate that having a spouse and a friend in their network were significant predictors of their life satisfaction. In these analyses age was not significantly related to life satisfaction.

When we combined men and women and separated the analyses by age, that is, conducted one analysis with respondents 50-64 years of age and a second with respondents 65 years of age and over, the results for younger people were identical to those reported above for women. The analyses conducted with the older half of the sample replicated only the quality aspect, however, not the quantity aspects of the previous analyses. For the older group, being satisfied with family and friendship relationships was significantly related to life satisfaction, but the presence of either a spouse or friend in the support network was not significantly related to well-being.

A second set of analyses examined the relationships between quality and quantity of support from family and friends and individuals' assessments of their social networks. Two measures of the perceived adequacy of the social network were available: the extent to which the members of the network got on the individual's nerves and how often the network members were too demanding. The results of the two sets of analyses were similar, but not identical. We focus here on perceptions of network demand because this variable is most similar to others reported in the literature. We used the same predictors as those presented above in the next two sets of analyses.

The results indicated that satisfaction with friends was unrelated to assessments of network demand for either men or women. For both men and women, however, satisfaction with family was negatively related to perceptions of the network as too demanding. Age was also negatively related to the perception of the network as demanding, with older respondents reporting less demanding networks. Finally, for men, having a child in the network was positively related to perceptions of the network as too demanding.

We found fewer significant predictors of network quality when repeating the regression analysis for each of the two age groups. For respondents in both age groups, the perception of the network as too demanding was negatively related to satisfaction with family life and positively associated with the presence of a child in the network. Only among older respondents was the presence of a spouse in the network positively associated with the perception of a demanding network.

The most interesting aspect of these findings is that satisfaction with friends, or lack thereof, was not related to the perception of the network as demanding, whereas satisfaction with family was negatively related. This suggests, as postulated above, that friends can have a positive effect on individuals' perceptions of and satisfaction with their network, but are much less likely to have a negative effect. The opposite was true for family relationships. A lack of satisfaction with family was predictive of individuals' perceptions of their network as too demanding. On the other hand, both family and friends had a positive impact on the older person's well-being, as indicated by the finding that satisfaction with family and friends were both positively related to life satisfaction.

These results seem to support Antonucci's hypothesis that friends can have a positive impact on well-being, but are much less likely to be related to perceptions of negativity. With family, the situation is reversed. Respondents who were not satisfied with their family relationships were more likely to assess their networks negatively. This was not true when respondents were unsatisfied with friend relationships. These data clearly support the notion that older adults evaluate family and friends differently and that family and friends differentially affect respondents' perceptions of network adequacy and personal well-being.

SUMMARY AND SUGGESTIONS FOR FUTURE RESERACH

Our review of the literature and our own empirical work suggest that friends and family members as support providers, although potentially substitutable one for the other, are usually governed by different norms, values, and expectations. Our empirical evidence also suggests that there are sex differences, and perhaps age differences, in the relationships between support provided by friends versus family and well-being. Clearly, additional research needs to explore norms about social support from friends; expectations for friends, both behavioral and affective; and what it means when friends violate these expectations (either in a positive or negative way). Such research would begin to clarify some of the issues raised in this chapter. Investigators should also delineate the circumstances under which support from friends has a greater impact on well-being than support from family. As suggested, this effect may hinge on the issue of reciprocal exchange.

Finally, as the social support field advances, researchers should study different ethnic and racial groups and use multimethod ways of assessing social support from friends and family. In order to gain an understanding of the role that friends play as sources of social support in old age, we must move beyond categorizing all nonkin as friends and begin distinguishing among neighbors, casual acquaintances, and more intimate relationships. We can then begin to understand why and how these relationships influence the individual's quality of life.

REFERENCES

Abella, R., & Heslin, R. (1984). Health, locus of control, values, and the behavior of family and friends: An integrated approach to understanding health behavior. *Basic and Applied Social Psychology, 5*, 283-293.

Adams, R. G. (1986a). Emotional closeness and physical distance between friends: Implications for elderly women living in age-segregated and age-integrated settings. *International Journal of Aging and Human Development, 22*, 55-76.

Adams, R. G. (1986b). A look at friendship and aging. *Generations, 10*, 40-43.

Akiyama, H., Antonucci, T. C., & Campbell, R. (in press). Rules of support exchange among two generations of Japanese and American women. In J. Sokolovsky (Ed.), *Growing old in different societies*. Belmont, CA: Wadsworth.

Antonucci, T. C. (1985). Personal characteristics, social support, and social behavior. In R. H. Binstock & E. Shanas (Eds.), *Handbook of aging and the social sciences* (pp. 94-128). New York: Van Nostrand Reinhold.

Antonucci, T. C., & Israel, B. A. (1986). Veridicality of social support: A comparison of principal and network members' responses. *Journal of Consulting and Clinical Psychology, 54*, 432-437.

Antonucci, T. C., & Jackson, J. S. (1987). Social support, interpersonal efficacy and health. In L. Cartensen & B. A. Edelstein (Eds.), *Handbook of clinical gerontology* (pp. 291-311). New York: Pergamon.

Antonucci, T. C., & Jackson, J. S. (in press). Successful aging and life course reciprocity. In A. Warnes (Ed.), *Human aging and later life: Multidisciplinary perspectives*. London: Hodder & Soughton Educational.

Arling, G. (1976). The elderly widow and her family, neighbors, and friends. *Journal of Marriage and the Family, 38*, 757-768.

Atchley, R. C. (1980). *The social forces in later life*. Belmont, CA: Wadsworth.

Bankoff, E. A. (1983). Social support and adaptation to widowhood. *Journal of Marriage and the Family, 45*, 827-839.

Bengtson, V. L., Cutler, N. E., Mangen, D. J., & Marshall, V. W. (1985). Generations, cohorts, and relations between age groups. In R. H. Binstock & E. Shanas (Eds.), *Handbook of aging and the social sciences* (pp. 304-338). New York: Van Nostrand Reinhold.

Berkman, L. S., & Syme, S. L. (1979). Social networks, host resistance, and mortality: A nine year follow-up study of Almeda County residents. *American Journal of Epidemiology, 109*, 186-204.

Candy, S. G., Troll, L. E., & Levy, S. G. (1981). A developmental exploration of friendship functions in women. *Psychology of Women Quarterly, 5*, 456-472.

Cantor, M. (1979). Neighbors and friends: An overlooked resource in the informal support system. *Research on Aging, 1*, 434-463.

Chatters, L. M., Taylor, R. J., & Jackson, J. S. (1986). Aged blacks' choices for an informal helper network. *Journal of Gerontology, 41*, 94-100.

Chown, S. M. (1981). Friendship in old age. In S. W. Duck & R. Gilmour (Eds.), *Personal relationships, Vol. 2: Developing personal relationships* (pp. 231-246). London: Academic Press.

Connor, K. A., Powers, E. A., & Bultena, G. L. (1979). Social interaction and life satisfaction: An empirical assessment of late-life patterns. *Journal of Gerontology, 34*, 116-121.

Creecy, R. F., & Wright, R. (1979). Morale and informal activity with friends among black and white elderly. *The Gerontologist, 19*, 544-547.

Elwell, F., & Maltbie-Crannell, A. D. (1981). The impact of role loss upon coping resources and life satisfaction of the elderly. *Journal of Gerontology, 36*, 223-232.

Essex, M. J., & Nam, S. (1987). Marital status and loneliness among older women: The differential importance of close family and friends. *Journal of Marriage and the Family, 49*, 93-106.

Ferraro, K. F., Mutran, E., & Barresi, C. M. (1984). Widowhood, health, and friendship support in later life. *Journal of Health and Social Behavior, 25*, 245-259.

Hess, B. (1972). Friendship. In M. W. Riley, M. Johnson, & A. Foner (Eds.), *Aging and society* (Vol. 3, pp. 357-393). New York: Russell Sage.

House, J. S. (1981). *Work stress and social support.* Reading, MA: Addison-Wesley.

House, J. S., & Kahn, R. L. (1985). Measures and concepts of social support. In S. Cohen & S. L. Syme (Eds.), *Social support and health* (pp. 83-108). New York: Academic Press.

House, J. S., Robbins, C., & Metzner, H. L. (1982). The association of social relationships and activities with mortality: Prospective evidence from the Tecumseh community health study. *American Journal of Epidemiology, 116*, 123-140.

Ingersoll-Dayton, B., & Antonucci, T. C. (1988). Non-reciprocal social support: Another side of intimate relationships. *Journal of Gerontology, 43*(3), 65-73.

Israel, B. A., & Antonucci, T. C. (1987). Social network characteristics and psychological well-being: A replication and extension. *Health Education Quarterly, 14*, 461-481.

Johnson, C. L., & Catalano, D. J. (1981). Childless elderly and their family supports. *The Gerontologist, 21*, 610-618.

Kahn, R. L., & Antonucci, T. C. (1980). Convoys over the life course: Attachment, roles, and social support. In P. B. Baltes & O. Brim (Eds.), *Life-span development and behavior* (Vol. 3, pp. 253-286). New York: Academic Press.

Kahn, R. L., & Antonucci, T. C. (1984). *Supports of the elderly: Family, friends, professionals* (Final report to the National Institute of Aging). Washington, DC: Government Printing Office.

Kiesler, C. A. (1985). Policy implications of research on social support and health. In S. Cohen & S. L. Syme (Eds.), *Social support and health* (pp. 347-364). New York: Academic Press.

Krause, N. (1986). Social support, stress, and well-being among older adults. *Journal of Gerontology, 41*, 512-519.

Langlie, J. L. (1977). Social networks, health beliefs, and preventive health behavior. *Journal of Health and Social Behavior, 18*, 244-260.

Larson, R., Mannell, R., & Zuzanek, J. (1986). Daily well-being of older adults with friends and family. *Psychology and Aging, 1*, 117-126.

Leavy, R. L. (1983). Social support and psychological disorder: A review. *American Journal of Community Psychology, 11*, 3-21.

Lin, N., Ensel, W. M., Simeone, R. S., & Kuo, W. (1979). Social support, stressful life events, and illness: A model and an empirical test. *Journal of Health and Social Behavior, 20*, 108-119.

Litwak, E. (1985). *Helping the elderly: The complementary roles of informal networks and formal systems.* New York: Guilford.

Lowenthal, M. F., & Haven, C. (1968). Interaction and adaptation: Intimacy as a critical variable. *American Sociological Review, 33*, 20-30.

Mancini, J. A. (1980). Friend interaction, competence, and morale in old age. *Research on Aging, 2*, 416-431.

Mercier, J. M., & Powers, E. A. (1984). The family and friends of rural aged as a natural support system. *Journal of Community Psychology, 12*, 334-346.

Peters, G. R., & Kaiser, M. A. (1985). The role of friends and neighbors in providing social support. In W. Sauer & R. Coward (Eds.), *Social support networks and the care of the elderly: Theory, research, practice, and policy* (pp. 123-158). New York: Springer.

Reisman, J. M. (1981). Adult friendships. In S. W. Duck & R. Gilmour (Eds.), *Personal relationships, Vol. 2: Developing personal relationships* (pp. 205-230). London: Academic Press.

Sandler, I. N., & Barrera, M. (1984). Towards a multimethod approach to assessing the effects of social support. *American Journal of Community Psychology, 12*, 37-52.

Schaefer, C., Coyne, J. C., & Lazarus, R. S. (1981). The health-related functions of social support. *Journal of Behavioral Medicine, 4*, 381-406.

Shanas, E. (1979). Social myth as hypothesis: The case of the family relations of old people. *The Gerontologist, 19*, 3-9.

Spakes, P. R. (1979). Family, friendship and community interaction as related to life satisfaction of the elderly. *Journal of Gerontological Social Work, 1*, 279-293.

Stephens, M. A., & Bernstein, M. D. (1984). Social support and well-being among residents of planned housing. *The Gerontologist, 24*, 144-148.

Stoller, E. P., & Earl, L. L. (1983). Help with activities of everyday life: Sources of support for the noninstitutionalized elderly. *The Gerontologist, 23*, 64-70.

Strain, L. A., & Chappell, N. L. (1982). Confidants: Do they make a difference in quality of life? *Research on Aging, 4*, 479-502.

Suls, J. (1982). Social support, interpersonal relations, and health: Benefits and liabilities. In G. S. Sanders & J. Suls (Eds.), *Social psychology of health and illness* (pp. 255-277). Hillsdale, NJ: Lawrence Erlbaum.

Turner, R. J. (1981). Social support as a contingency in psychological well-being. *Journal of Health and Social Behavior, 22*, 357-367.

Wentowski, G. J. (1981). Reciprocity and the coping strategies of older people: Cultural dimensions of network building. *The Gerontologist, 21*, 600-609.

Williams, A. W., Ware, J. E., & Donald, C. A. (1981). A model of mental health, life events, and social supports applicable to general populations. *Journal of Health and Social Behavior, 22*, 324-336.

Wood, V., & Robertson, J. F. (1978). Friendship and kinship interaction: Differential effect on the morale of the elderly. *Journal of Marriage and the Family, 40*, 367-375.

Wortman, C. B., & Conway, T. L. (1985). The role of social support in adaptation and recovery from physical illness. In S. Cohen & S. L. Syme (Eds.), *Social support and health* (pp. 281-302). New York: Academic Press.

7

Exchange and Equity in Friendships

KAREN A. ROBERTO

One element of friendship is exchange. Almost every working definition of friendship alludes to its importance. For example, Hess (1972, p. 359) defined a friendship as "a dyadic relationship that involves the sharing of affect, concerns, interests, and information." Four out of seven variables in Wright's (1969, 1974, 1982) conceptual and measurement model of friendship reflect the benefits or direct rewards partners provide for one another in their daily interaction. Weiss and Lowenthal (1975) identified six descriptors of friendship of which reciprocity, the balance of giving and receiving, was one. Candy, Troll, and Levy (1981) found intimacy-assistance to be one of three most important functions of friendships for women throughout adulthood.

Each of these definitions implies that without a mutual sense of give-and-take a friendship would not exist. Theoretical explanations of this assumption emerge from the work of Homans (1961), Blau (1964), and Adams (1965). Each developed an exchange theory based on the premise that in order for a relationship to be successfully maintained, the cost of the relationship (what is given) cannot outweigh the rewards of the relationship (what is received).

The purpose of this chapter is to review the literature that focuses on the exchange component of later-life friendships. I begin by identifying the types of things commonly exchanged between friends. Next, I describe the theories that seem to contribute most to understanding the importance of balanced or equitable exchanges in relationships. In the third section, I examine factors that may work to influence the equity of exchanges. In the final section, I explore the consequences of equity or inequity for maintaining friendships in later life.

EXCHANGES BETWEEN FRIENDS

Exactly what friends exchange depends on the persons involved and the situation. Generally, there are two groups of exchanges: instrumental and affective. Instrumental exchanges are nonpersonal and provide a materialistic type of assistance, such as transportation, help with tasks, economic support, running errands, and so forth. Affective exchanges are more personal in nature, and provide comfort, sharing of problems and ideas, and special time together. The empirical literature contains validation for the existence and importance of both types of exchanges in friendships throughout the adult life cycle.

For young adults, the sharing of affection, ideas, and time (companionship) predominate (Ashton, 1980; Hays, 1984; Knapp & Harwood, 1977). Gender, however, influences the importance friends place on what they exchange. For example, in a study of college undergraduates, shared interests were more important for male friends than for female friends, whereas females viewed boosting each other's egos as a more salient characteristic of friendship than males did (Ashton, 1980).

In later-life friendships, researchers observe a combination of instrumental and affectional exchanges. In two studies, investigators assessed the type and frequency of exchanges between members in the social networks of older adults using Foa and Foa's (1974, 1980) resource classification system that groups exchanges into six classes: love, status, information, money, goods, and services (Blieszner, 1982; Shea, Thompson, & Blieszner, 1988). The older individuals in these studies described their exchanges with very close persons, casual friends, and acquaintances. The data indicated that, across the three relationships, friends gave money extremely infrequently and status and love had the highest frequencies. The exchange of goods, services, and information fell in between. The pattern for receiving resources was similar.

In a study of the friendship patterns of older women, respondents indicated how many times in the past year they had received help from or given it to a close friend in the following areas: transportation, minor household repair, housekeeping, shopping, yard work, taking care of the car, assistance when ill, making important decisions, legal aid, and financial aid (Roberto & Scott, 1984). The most common types of help exchanged were transportation, assistance when ill, and making minor household repairs. The areas where help was least likely to occur were financial aid, legal aid, and housekeeping.

Neighbors also provide assistance to one another, however, the type of help tends to be more instrumental than affective. An analysis of the giving and receiving patterns among older adult neighbors showed that the major types of exchanges involved tangibles and personal and domestic upkeep (Goodman, 1985). These accounted for over one-half of the exchanges named. Those studied reported other types of exchanges, including, in descending order, social initiation, providing vigilance, informing, and focused listening.

Background characteristics of older persons can influence the type of exchanges found in their friendships. As in young adulthood, gender has an impact on the types of exchanges between older friends (Wright, this volume). In friendships between older women, intimacy or the sharing of confidences is more predominant than in the friendships of older men (Hess, 1979; Roberto & Scott, 1986a). When older men report affectional exchanges in their friendships, they are less frequent and at a more superficial level than is the case for women (Roberto & Scott, 1986a). Other factors such as marital status, living arrangements, and income also influence the type of exchanges between older friends (Blau, 1981; Crohan & Antonucci, this volume; Roberto & Scott, 1984, 1987). 1987).

THEORETICAL FRAMEWORK
FOR EXCHANGES

In spite of the general consensus about the importance and prevalence of exchange in older adult friend relationships, researchers have done little theoretical examination of this component of friendship. They have based most of their conceptualizing upon the principles of exchange theory in general and a more recent derivation, equity theory.

Equity theory deals with the question of fairness within a relationship. Its basic assumption is that a person experiencing inequity encounters a tension state, which then motivates the person to diminish the inequity (West & Wicklund, 1980). Central to equity theory is the notion that equity lies in the eye of the beholder. Within this framework, individuals assess the equity of exchanges in a relationship by determining their own and their partner's inputs to and outcomes from the interactions. Therefore, equity in a relationship does not necessarily exist in any objective sense independent of the perceptions of the people involved.

The initial statement of equity theory developed from the exchange theories of Homans (1961) and Blau (1964) and from Adams's (1963, 1965) theory of inequity. Their work provided the impetus for a large volume of research in the 1960s and 1970s and the context within which others have developed subsequent theoretical statements (Cohen & Greenberg, 1982). The following provides a brief discussion of each of their theories.

Distributive Justice

Homans (1961, 1974) proposed an exchange theory based on the rules of distributive justice. This theory is psychological in orientation. Homans based the propositions that define the fundamental determinants of exchange on the principles of behavior set forth by Skinnerian behavioral psychologists (McClintock & Keil, 1982). Homans's (1961, 1974) theory focuses primarily on the actual social behavior of individuals who are in direct contact with one another, where each person is both giving and receiving rewards from the other. Homans assumed that persons base equity on a learned expectancy that outcomes to self and others will conform to the "rule of distributive justice." According to Homans (1961, 1974), the fundamental rule of distributive justice states that an individual in an exchange relationship with another has two expectations: (a) that the rewards of each will be proportional to the costs of each and (b) that net rewards or profits will be proportional to investments. When an individual does not receive the expected outcome, he or she is likely to display what Homans called "emotional behavior": anger, if the actual receipt is less valuable than expected, or guilt, if the actual receipt is more valuable than that expected (Homans, 1974). People experience guilt less often than anger, and guilt is less often the basis for future actions. Individuals who find themselves at an unjust disadvantage learn to complain, but individuals who find they have done better for themselves than they ought to have done are less apt to make a prominent display of their guilt (Homans, 1961). Instead, they (i.e., the beneficiaries) more often manage to discover good reasons why they are not profiteers at all, but merely getting what they deserve (Homans, 1974).

Norms of Fairness

Taking a more eclectic approach than Homans, Blau (1964) relied heavily on sociological arguments in describing his theory of exchange. While Blau (1964) accepted Homans's definition of distributive justice, he asserted that rather than being derived from the principles of operant conditioning, it is normatively given (McClintock & Keil, 1982). He argued that justice or fairness represents a social norm that prescribes just treatment as a moral principle. In other words, a norm is reinforced initially by society, and may subsequently be internalized by an individual, thereby producing feelings of guilt if violated. Blau discussed fairness by pointing to the importance of expectations for the experience of satisfaction in social relationships. People base the expectations on past individual experience and on acquired reference standards, each of which results partly from benefits individuals have obtained in the past and partly from learning about the benefits received by others in comparable situations (Cohen & Greenberg, 1982). Although Blau (1964) distinguished between three types of expectations concerning social rewards (i.e., general, particular, and comparative), comparative expectations or the profits an individual expects to achieve in social associations (i.e., their rewards minus their costs) are the most important to Blau's discussion of justice.

Absence of Equity

Unlike the work of Homans and Blau, Adams's (1963, 1965) theory focuses on the causes and consequences of the absence of equity in human exchange relationships. Drawing on Homans's concept of distributive justice, the major components of Adams's (1963, 1965) theory are "inputs" and "outcomes". He described inputs as what a person perceives as his or her contributions to the exchange for which he or she expects a just return. Outcomes are an individual's receipts from the exchange, including such factors as pay and intrinsic satisfaction. To function as inputs or outcomes in any particular situation, their possessor must recognize such factors and consider them relevant to the exchange. According to Adams (1963, 1965), inequity exists whenever a person perceives that the ratio of his or her outcomes to his or her inputs and the ratio of other's outcomes to other's inputs are unequal. The result of the perceived inequity is tension, which exists in proportion to the magnitude of inequity and that motivates individuals to reduce it.

Equity Theory

Walster and her colleagues developed what is probably the most popular version of an equity theory derived from the works of Homans, Blau, and Adams (Walster, Walster, & Berscheid, 1978a). The main purpose of their work has been to predict when individuals will perceive themselves to be unjustly treated and how they will react to the perception. Their theory integrates the insights of reinforcement theory, cognitive consistency theory, psychoanalytic theory, and exchange theory (Walster, Walster, & Traupmann, 1978b). It retains most of the basic features of Adams's (1963, 1965) theory but also extends the formulation in many ways.

According to Walster et al. (1978a), an equitable relationship exists if a person scrutinizing the relationship concludes that all participants are receiving equal relative gains from the relationship. The scrutineer is simply the person who is examining any given relationship in order to determine if it is fair or unfair. The scrutineer may be an outside observer or either of the participants (Walster et al., 1978a). Within this framework, individuals can assess the equity of a relationship by determining their own and their partners' inputs to and outcomes from the relationship. Walster et al. (1978a) defined inputs as the participant's positive and negative contributions to the exchange, which a scrutineer sees as entitling him or her to rewards or costs. They defined outcomes as both positive and negative consequences that a scrutineer perceives a participant has incurred in his or her relationship with another. Participants' net gains (or losses) are their perceived outcomes from the relationship minus their perceived inputs to the relationship. From the sign and the magnitude of the net gains measure, the scrutineer can determine how profitable a relationship is to each of the participants. Overbenefited individuals perceive their relative gains from the relationship to be greater than their partner's, and underbenefited individuals perceive their relative gains to be less than their partner's. An equitable relationship exists for an individual when he or she perceives relative gains to be equal for self and partner.

Individuals who find themselves participating in inequitable relationships experience distress (Walster et al., 1978a). The distress engendered by being overbenefited may take the form of guilt or shame. The distress engendered by being underbenefited derives from a sense of exploitation. Participants in inequitable relationships can move to restore equity in either of two general manners. People can restore actual equity by altering their own or their partners' relative gains. People can restore psychological equity to relationships by perceptually distorting and convincing themselves that apparent inequitable relationships are in fact fair. The primary determinant in the selection of an equity restoring technique is cost. As with the exchange theories, the greater the cost, the less popular an option becomes.

WHEN IS EQUITY IMPORTANT?

Few equity theorists have believed that the equity norm is always applicable. Factors such as cognitive acknowledgment and perception, the personality of the individual, the length of the relationship, and the type of relationship can influence the importance of equity in friendships.

Cognition and Perception

Persons' cognitive abilities influence their perceptions of equity. According to equity theory (Walster et al., 1978a), to determine if a situation is equitable, the individual must form and compare ratios of outcomes to inputs for each interaction. In their review of the literature, Hook and Thomas (1979) found that the proportional equity response predicted by equity theory was entirely absent in studies of children under 13 years of age. Citing studies based upon Piaget's concept of logico-mathematical structure, the authors suggested a three-step development of proportional thought corresponding roughly to Piaget's sequential stages of cognitive development: preoperations, concrete operations, and formal operational thought. According to this model, proportional thought is not fully developed until a person reaches the formal operations stage. Researchers have suggested, however, that not everyone reaches this final level of development (Flavell, 1977; Papalia & Bielby, 1974; Tomlinson-Keasey, 1972), and others have shown a decline in the abilities of older adults to perform tasks indicative of formal operations (Papalia, 1972; Papalia, Salverson, & True, 1973;

Storck, Looft, & Hooper, 1972). Hence the older person's level of cognitive functioning can govern the perceptions of equity in friendships.

Egocentric bias can also alter a person's perceptions of equity. That is, in making a judgment as to the relative contributions in a relationship, individuals claim more responsibility for the exchanges that go on than their partners usually attribute to them (Ross & Sicoly, 1979). The cause of this bias is differential retrieval of information (Ross & Sicoly, 1979; Thompson & Kelley, 1981). According to Thompson and Kelley (1981, p. 476):

> Individuals focus on their own activity to make a judgment of relative contribution which logically requires considering both information about the self and information about the partner. This may occur because people find it difficult or time consuming to retrieve two separate pieces of information and combine them to produce a single judgment. . . . It is quicker and easier to access just one's own contributions and to use that as an estimate of relative contribution.

A person's perception or evaluation of his or her friend's capability may also have an impact on how important equity is in the relationship. Roberto and Scott (1986a, p. 246) suggested that the older individual's perception of his or her own and the friend's "equity potential" may influence satisfaction and willingness to maintain involvement in the relationship. A person's equity potential reflects the resources available to him or her (e.g., health, adequate income, availability of support networks). When individuals perceive themselves as having a higher (or lower) equity potential than their friend they may not expect equity.

Personality

An individual's personality can influence the importance attributed to equity in friendships. For instance, people vary in the degree to which they believe equity of exchange should characterize their relationships. Murstein, Cerreto, and MacDonald (1977) found that high exchange-oriented individuals feel uncomfortable when someone does them a favor and they cannot repay it in some way, but nonexchange-oriented persons are not at all concerned with keeping a mental record of exchanges. Friendships in which the investigators categorized both members as being high exchange oriented were significantly stronger more intense relationships than those in which the partners were both nonexchange oriented or were of opposite orientations (Murstein et al., 1977).

Adults who are nonconventional (i.e., desire to influence change, seek pleasure, exert more control over their lives, and report overall satisfaction with life) differ from more conventional individuals (i.e., people at the opposite pole with regard to these characteristics) in terms of their definition of friendship (Bell, 1981). The majority of nonconventional men and women felt that what makes a good friend is being supportive, understanding, caring, and willing to share. The conventional men and women also valued helping one another, but placed greater emphasis on the negotiable and external aspects of friendships rather than the internal and emotional components (Bell, 1981).

Motivational differences can also influence interactions with friends. For example, McAdams, Healy, and Krause (1984) examined the association between involvement with friends and two personality motives, intimacy and power. High-power individuals tended to experience friendship in an hierarchical manner, seeing them as opportunities to take on dominant, controlling, organizational roles. Persons high in intimacy motivation reported more self-disclosure with friends, often taking on the role of the listener.

Specific information regarding the influence of personality on friendships in later life is not available. Recent data from several longitudinal studies, however, have suggested an overall stability of personality over time (Eichhorn, Clausen, Haan, Honzik, & Mussen, 1981; Leon, Gillum, Gillum, & Gouze, 1979; McCrae & Costa, 1984; Siegler, George, & Okun, 1979). If people maintain their basic disposition as they age, then the personality factors that influence friendships in young adulthood should continue to influence these relationships in old age.

Length of Relationship

The length of time individuals have known each other may also influence equity within a relationship. Altman (1973, p. 10) hypothesized that the social "norm of reciprocity"—the perceived obligation to reciprocate disclosure—plays a more important role in the early stages of a social bond than in the later stages. For example, patterns of reciprocity in dyads of female college students composed of strangers or close friends revealed greater reciprocity in the stranger condition, particularly when the students discussed intimate topics (Derlega, Wilson, & Chaikin, 1976). This type of response may occur either because strangers pose no threat to each other because it is unlikely they will meet again or in order to build trust in hopes of continuing the relationship. As friendships grow and become more intimate, an immediate balance of inputs to outcomes becomes less salient (Holt, 1982).

Strangers and friends also differ in their readiness to perceive inequity and their reactions to it (Traupmann, 1975, cited in Walster et al., 1978a). College women who were either strangers or friends participated as partners in a verbal learning experiment and evaluated each other in terms of cooperativeness, creativity, ability to learn quickly, and consciousness. Regardless of the actual outcome, the researchers told the women that they had received very low ratings by their partners. Although both strangers and friends felt their partner had rated them unfairly, strangers were far more distressed by their low evaluations and were more likely to then give their partners lower personal evaluations. Friends were more likely to give their partners fair evaluations of their performance. Walster et al. (1978a) suggested that strangers are unwilling to tolerate imbalances in relationships and respond to the inequity in a vindictive manner. Friends, on the other hand, respond in such a way as not to damage the relationship.

An investigation of old and new friendships in later life revealed a stability in resources exchanged between long-standing friends, whereas exchanges increased in newly formed friendships (Shea et al., 1988). Both types of friendships involved the exchange of love, status, information, and service, but differed in the degree to which they showed the various resources. For example, study participants reported the exchange of advice and personal information more often in old than new relationships. Accountability of exchanges was also a more salient factor in new friendships. New friends placed a greater emphasis on the prompt reciprocity of aid than long-term friends did.

Type of Relationship

Although researchers have tended to agree that equity principles prevail in most casual relationships, they have been reluctant to apply it to more intimate types of relationships. Recent research challenges the contention of Walster and associates (1978a) that equity considerations also shape more intimate relationships such as close friendships.

A series of experiments have demonstrated the difference between two kinds of relationships in which persons are receiving and giving benefits (Clark, 1981, 1984; Clark & Mills, 1979; Clark, Mills, & Powell, 1986). In these studies, Clark and her colleagues defined a benefit as anything a person can choose to give to another person that is of use to the person receiving it. In exchange relationships, people give benefits with the expectation of receiving a benefit in return. In communal relationships, each person has concern for the welfare of the other. The receipt of a benefit does not create a specific debt to return a comparable benefit. Communal relationships are typically personal, hence friendships fall into this category. The research based upon this distinction has indicated that individuals perceive friendships to be at a more intimate level when benefits are noncomparable than when they are comparable. This suggests that to give benefits directly comparable to benefits recently received implies a preference for a less valued (i.e., exchange) type of relationship than a more valued (i.e., communal) one (Clark, 1981). In addition, record keeping is more predominant in exchange than in communal relationships (Clark, 1984). A person is more likely, however, to keep track of the other's needs in an existing or potential communal relationship than in an exchange relationship (Clark et al., 1986).

In later life, the type of friendship being examined has implications for the importance of equity. Roberto and Scott (1986a) explored the relationship between perceived equity of exchanges and friendship satisfaction for older individuals and two members of their friend network: their best friend and one other friend. Equity and friendship satisfaction were not related significantly in the case of the best friend, but had a curvilinear relationship for the other friend. These findings are consistent with Clark's (1984) distinction between communal and exchange relations if we define best friends as communal relationships and other friends as exchange relationships. In terms of equity theory, overbenefited individuals in exchange relationships are concerned with what they have to return in order to achieve equity. Older adults with limited resources may perceive this expectation as stressful and thus experience less satisfaction in friendships (Roberto & Scott, 1986a). The history of best friend relationships may account for the differences found.

> In a best-friend relationship, a specific part of their total friendship may be inequitable for a certain period, but at the same time, the overall

relationship may be very satisfying. Although the other, less intimate friendship also has a history, the exchanges between the two friends may actually provide the basis for the total relationship. (Roberto & Scott, 1986a, p. 107)

Shea and her colleagues' (1988) finding that older men and women were more aware of the day-to-day exchange of love with newer friends than with old friends provides additional support for this contention.

CONSEQUENCES OF EXCHANGE

According to equity theory, in order for individuals to continue with relationships, they must perceive them as equitable. Although research suggests that what partners give and receive does not have to be the same, both partners must perceive a balance of inputs and outcomes or negative feelings such as anger or guilt occur (Walster et al., 1978a).

In previous research, a colleague and I found that differences in the morale of older women varied according to the equity of instrumental helping behaviors with their friend (Roberto & Scott, 1984). Congruent with equity theory, women in equitable friendships had higher morale scores than overbenefited women, suggesting that the women's inability to reciprocate created adverse feelings about themselves. Contrary to the theory, however, the underbenefited women did not differ from equitably benefited women, and they had higher morale scores than the overbenefited women. A similar finding occurred in relationship to friendship satisfaction between less intimate friends in later life (Roberto & Scott, 1986a). Equitable friendships were most satisfying when compared to overbenefiting relationships, but were not more satisfying than underbenefiting friendships.

To determine if older people react to inequity differently depending upon the particular aspect of the friendship being studied, we examined the amount of distress reported in the overall friend relationship, the helping aspect of the friendship, and the affective component of the relationship for older individuals in equitable versus inequitable friendships (Roberto & Scott, 1986b). Individuals who perceived their relationship to be equitable expressed less distress with all three aspects of their friendships than those who perceived their friendships as inequitable. The type of distress that respondents in the inequitable group reported with regard to their overall friendship was contrary to the propositions of equity theory, however. Specifically, overbenefited older adults reported feeling a greater amount of anger than under-benefited individuals. We found a similar result for respondents' affective relationships. The overbenefited reported significantly more anger and less contentment with this aspect of their friendship than the underbenefited. We suggested that not being able to reciprocate resources undermined the older person's sense of independence, and although most older adults accept the fact they may need to rely more on others for both instrumental and emotional support, feelings of discontentment and anger can persist.

Loneliness may also be a consequence of inequitable relationships in later life. Rook (1987) found that older women who were overbenefited or underbenefited in their overall relationship with members of their social network (i.e., children and friends) expressed greater feelings of loneliness than women whose social exchanges were balanced. She suggested that loneliness resulting from inequitable relationships may have reflected a lack of intimacy or quality in the women's social interactions. Examination of specific relationships revealed a positive relationship between the average number of reciprocal exchanges and friendship satisfaction, but no relationship between reciprocal ex-changes and satisfaction with adult children. In fact, older mothers were more satisfied with their relationship with their children when they received more instrumental assistance from them than they gave. The nature of the relationships studied may affect these results. Parent-child relationships start out and remain unbalanced, at least in terms of instrumental exchanges, for several years. Mothers in the later stages of the life cycle, however, may feel it is now their children's turn to repay them for past debts or assistance (Beckman, 1981). Friendships, on the other hand, tend to develop on the basis of mutual exchange, and although there may be periods of inequity, most people seek balanced friendships.

Loss of power is another potential result of older persons having unbalanced social relationships (Dowd, 1975). As people grow older, they may experience decreasing resources (i.e., income, health, mobility) that lead to increasing difficulty in maintaining equitable relationships. An inability to reciprocate gives power to one partner while the other becomes more dependent. This power advantage can be gratifying for underbenefited older persons when they perceive themselves as being in a position to provide support for a friend who may be of a comparable age, yet in greater need. For the overbenefited older adult, however, greater reliance on others may result in lowered self-esteem, especially if the underbenefited partner abuses his or her power.

Termination of a friendship may be the ultimate result when partners view exchanges as inequitable. Partners base the decision to end a relationship, however, not only on the inequity of the situation, but also on the cost of leaving and the perceived alternatives to the relationship (Blieszner, this volume; Thibaut & Kelley, 1959). For example, if college students perceived the available alternatives as equal or superior to the satisfaction with the current relationship, they were more likely to report that they ended a relationship rather than trying to maintain it (Holt, 1982). In later life, the relative scarcity of similar-age peers may limit the available alternatives for developing new friendships, hence making it too costly for an older person to end a friendship even if it is not equitable (Roberto & Scott, 1984).

SUMMARY AND SUGGESTIONS FOR FURTHER RESEARCH

The literature I reviewed in this chapter confirms the significance of exchange between friends in later life. What friends exchange and the balance of exchanges depends upon the degree of friendship that exists and on situational factors. When exchanges in later-life friendships are equitable, both partners view the relationship as positive and very satisfying. Inequitable friendships, however, can have either positive or negative consequences depending upon which person's perspective one evaluates.

It is difficult to determine if patterns of exchange are similar or different across adulthood. Although the basic categories of exchange (instrumental and affective) are evident in the friendships of both young and older adults, methodological differences limit the generalizability of the findings. Studies that examine exchanges in friendships of young adults are primarily laboratory experiments using college students. Researchers rarely base these studies on actual friendships, but rather simulate a friend situation that the observer must judge. Information concerning exchanges between friends in later life tends to focus on existing relationships, asking respondents, either by questionnaires or by personal interviews, to discuss what they give and receive in their friendships. In these studies, the researchers often impose the definition of friend in order to establish consistency across respondents. Thus they force respondents to discuss only the friendship that meets with the given criteria. When respondents generate their own definition, issues of generalizability across samples arise (see Adams, this volume).

Another problem in trying to determine exchange patterns between friends in later life is that most studies examine only one component of the friend relationship. The most common information obtained is the frequency of these exchanges, usually within a given time frame (e.g., during the past year). Investigators must take a broader perspective to determine the extent of exchanges as well as the quality and meaning of the exchanges for the participants. We need both longitudinal and cross-sectional studies to determine the similarity of exchanges between adult friends at different points in their lives and to identify variables that influence these exchange patterns over time.

Equity, or a balance of exchange, is common in the friendships of older adults. Perhaps more than age, factors such as cognition, perceptions, personality characteristics, and the length and type of friendship influence the perceived importance of equity. Although investigators have based studies of exchanges within friendships on samples of the well-elderly, variation in their respondents' cognitive abilities and perceptions may influence their calculation of equity. Probing respondents about the method they use to assess the balance of exchange in their friendships would provide us with greater insight into the most typical ways older adults determine equity.

The relationship between personality traits and the importance of equity in young adult friendships suggests that these same traits might affect the significance of equity in later-life relationships, particularly if the notion of basic stability in personality across the adult life cycle continues to be upheld. Research that includes personality variables in the study of late-life friendship is necessary to confirm this relationship.

The length and type of friendship being examined are the two most common factors researchers have discussed with regard to the importance of equity. It seems clear that in less intimate friendships, the principles of equity theory hold true. In more meaningful or communal friendships, however, they are not as rigidly followed. Perhaps equity between the closest of friends is not really necessary or is determined differently due to their past history and the nature of their relationship. We need more studies that examine the development of friendships and changes in the needs of the friends to explore these differences.

Older adults do react contrary to the propositions of equity theory when they perceive themselves as being in inequitable friendships.

Researchers have sometimes found that underbenefited persons were just as happy or satisfied with their friendship as individuals in equitable friendships. They have not encountered the feelings of resentment predicted by the theory. Overbenefited older adults seemed to stay in these friendships even though they are less satisfying and are related to feelings of lower morale and loneliness. Termination of inequitable friendships does not seem to be an option for these older adults. Future research is necessary to explore reactions to inequity in actual friendships of young, middle-aged, and older adults in order to determine if older adults are unique in their reactions.

A general issue that friendship scholars need to address is how to determine equity statistically within friendships of older adults. There is little consistency throughout the literature. Researchers often impose the concept of equity by simply subtracting the amount of what persons report receiving from their friends from what they claim to give. Very few studies use the more sophisticated mathematical formulae proposed by Walster et al. (1978a), or more recently by Harris (1983), to calculate equity in relationships. Although one can argue in favor of either approach, the lack of a standard formula makes it difficult to generalize the findings across studies. We need additional work with samples sufficiently large enough to permit testing and comparing different formulae.

Researchers must explore further and refine our understanding of the importance of the equity of exchanges between friends in later life. Investigations that more thoroughly examine the issues I have reviewed in this chapter would provide greater insight into this component of friendship. Such research is necessary to strengthen the support for equity theory as a general theory of social behavior.

REFERENCES

Adams, J. (1963). Toward an understanding of inequity. *Journal of Abnormal and Social Psychology, 67,* 422-436.

Adams, J. (1965). Inequity in social exchange. In L. Berkowitz (Ed.), *Advances in experimental social psychology* (Vol. 2, pp. 267-299). New York: Academic Press.

Altman, I. (1973). Reciprocity of interpersonal exchange. *Journal for the Theory of Social Behavior, 3,* 249-261.

Ashton, N. (1980). Exploratory investigation of perceptions of influences on best-friend relationships. *Perceptual and Motor Skills, 50,* 379-386.

Beckman, L. (1981). Effects of social interaction and children's relative inputs on older women's psychological well-being. *Journal of Personality and Social Psychology, 41*, 1075-1086.

Bell, R. (1981). Friendships of women and of men. *Psychology of Women Quarterly, 5*, 402-417.

Blau, P. (1964). *Exchanges and power in social life.* New York: John Wiley.

Blau, Z. (1981). *Aging in a changing society* (2nd ed.). New York: Franklin Watts.

Blieszner, R. (1982, October). *Expected and actual reciprocity of resource exchanges in the social networks of elderly women.* Paper presented at the annual meeting of the National Council on Family Relations, Washington, DC.

Candy, S., Troll, L., & Levy, S. (1981). A developmental exploration of friendship functions in women. *Psychology of Women Quarterly, 5*, 456-472.

Clark, M. (1981). Noncomparability of benefits given and received: A cue to the existence of friendship. *Social Psychology Quarterly, 44*, 373-381.

Clark, M. (1984). Record keeping in two types of relationships. *Journal of Personality and Social Psychology, 47*, 549-557.

Clark, M., & Mills, J. (1979). Interpersonal attraction in exchange and communal relationships. *Journal of Personality and Social Psychology, 37*, 12-24.

Clark, M., Mills, J., & Powell, M. (1986). Keeping track of needs in communal and exchange relationships. *Journal of Personality and Social Psychology, 51*, 333-338.

Cohen, R., & Greenberg, J. (1982). The justice concept in social psychology. In J. Greenberg & R. Cohen (Eds.) *Equity and justice in social behavior* (pp. 1-41). New York: Academic Press.

Derlega, V., Wilson, M., & Chaikin, A. (1976). Friendships and disclosure reciprocity. *Journal of Personality and Social Psychology, 34*, 578-582.

Dowd, J. (1975). Aging as exchange: A preface to theory. *The Gerontologist, 3*, 584-594.

Eichhorn, D., Clausen, J., Haan, N., Honzik, M., & Mussen, P. (1981). *Present and past in middle life.* New York: Academic Press.

Flavell, J. (1977). *Cognitive development.* Englewood Cliffs, NJ: Prentice-Hall.

Foa, E., & Foa, U. (1980). Resource theory: Interpersonal behavior as exchange. In K. Gergen, J. Greenberg, & R. Willis (Eds.), *Social exchange: Advances in theory and research* (pp. 77-101). New York: Plenum.

Foa, U., & Foa, E. (1974). *Societal structures of the mind.* Springfield, IL: Charles C Thomas.

Goodman, C. (1985). Reciprocity among older adult peers. *Social Service Review, 59*, 269-282.

Harris, R. (1983). Pinning down the equity formula. In D. Messick & K. Cook (Eds.), *Equity theory: Psychological and sociological perspectives* (pp. 207-242). New York: Praeger.

Hays, R. (1984). The development and maintenance of friendship. *Journal of Social and Personal Relationships, 1*, 75-98.

Hess, B. (1972). Friendship. In M. Riley, M. Johnson, & A. Foner (Eds.), *Aging and society* (pp. 358-393). New York: Russell Sage.

Hess, B. (1979). Sex roles, friendship, and the life course. *Research on Aging, 1*, 494-515.

Holt, R. (1982). Perceptions of the equity and exchange processes in dyadic social relationships. *Perceptual and Motor Skills, 54*, 303-320.

Homans, G. (1961). *Social behavior: Its elementary forms.* New York: Harcourt Brace & World.

Homans, G. (1974). *Social behavior: Its elementary forms* (2nd ed.). New York: Harcourt Brace & World.

Hook, J., & Thomas, C. (1979). Equity theory and the cognitive ability of children. *Psychological Bulletin, 86,* 429-445.

Knapp, C., & Harwood, B. (1977). Factors in the determination of intimate same-sex friendship. *Journal of Genetic Psychology, 31,* 83-90.

Leon, R., Gillum, G., Gillum, R., & Gouze, M. (1979). Personality stability over a thirty-year period—middle-age to old age. *Journal of Consulting and Clinical Psychology, 23,* 245-259.

McAdams, D., Healy, S., & Krause, S. (1984). Social motives and patterns of friendship. *Journal of Personality and Social Psychology, 47,* 828-838.

McClintock, C., & Keil, L. (1982). Equity and social exchange. In J. Greenberg & R. Cohen (Eds.), *Equity and justice in social behavior* (pp. 337-387). New York: Academic Press.

McCrae, R., & Costa, P. (1984). *Emerging lives, enduring dispositions and personality in adulthood.* Boston: Little, Brown.

Murstein, B., Cerreto, M., & MacDonald, M. (1977). A theory and investigation of the effect of exchange-orientation on marriage and friendship. *Journal of Marriage and the Family, 39,* 543-548.

Papalia, D. (1972). The status of several conservation abilities across the life-span. *Human Development, 15,* 229-243.

Papalia, D., & Bielby, D. (1974). Cognitive functioning in middle and old age adults. *Human Development, 17,* 424-443.

Papalia, D., Salverson, S., & True, M. (1973). An evaluation of quantity conservation performance during old age. *International Journal of Aging and Human Development, 4,* 103-109.

Roberto, K., & Scott, J. (1984). Friendship patterns of older women. *Journal of Aging and Human Development, 19,* 1-10.

Roberto, K., & Scott, J. (1986a). Friendships of older men and women: Exchange patterns and satisfaction. *Psychology and Aging, 1,* 103-109.

Roberto, K., & Scott, J. (1986b). Equity considerations in the friendships of older adults. *Journal of Gerontology, 41,* 241-247.

Roberto, K., & Scott, J. (1987). Friendships in later life: A rural-urban comparison. *Lifestyles, 8,* 146-156.

Rook, K. (1987). Reciprocity of social exchange and social satisfaction among older women. *Journal of Personality and Social Psychology, 52,* 145-154.

Ross, M., & Sicoly, F. (1979). Egocentric biases in availability and attribution. *Journal of Personality and Social Psychology, 37,* 322-336.

Shea, L., Thompson, L., & Blieszner, R. (1988). Resources in older adults' old and new friendships. *Journal of Social and Personal Relationships, 5,* 83-96.

Siegler, I., George, L., & Okun, M. (1979). Cross-sequential analysis of adult personality. *Development Psychology, 15,* 350-351.

Storck, P., Looft, W., & Hooper, F. (1972). Interrelationships among Piagetian tasks and traditional measures of cognitive abilities in mature and aged adults. *Journal of Gerontology, 27,* 461-465.

Thibaut, J. W., & Kelley, H. (1959). *The social psychology of groups.* New York: John Wiley.

Thompson, S., & Kelley, H. (1981). Judgments of responsibility for activities in close relationships. *Journal of Personal and Social Psychology, 41,* 469-477.

Tomlinson-Keasey, C. (1972). Formal operations in females from eleven to fifty-six years of age. *Developmental Psychology, 6,* 364.

Walster, E., Berscheid E., & Walster, G. (1973). New directions in equity research. *Journal of Personality and Social Psychology, 2,* 151-176.

Walster, E., Walster, G., & Berscheid, E. (1978a). *Equity: Theory and research.* Boston: Allyn & Bacon.

Walster, E., Walster, G., & Traupmann, G. (1978b). Equity and premarital sex. *Journal of Personality and Social Psychology, 26,* 82-92.

Weiss, L., & Lowenthal, M. (1975). Life-course perspectives on friendship. In M. Lowenthal, M. Thurher, & D. Chiriboga (Eds.), *Four stages of life* (pp. 48-61). San Francisco: Jossey-Bass.

West, S., & Wicklund, R. (1980). *A primer of social psychological theories.* Monterey, CA: Brooks/Cole.

Wright, P. (1969). A model and a technique for studies of friendship. *Journal of Experimental Social Psychology, 5,* 295-308.

Wright, P. (1974). The delineation and measurement of some key variables in the study of friendship. *Representative Research in Social Psychology, 5,* 93-96.

Wright, P. (1982). Men's friendship, women's friendships and the alleged and inferiority of the latter. *Sex Roles, 8,* 1-20.

8

Strains in Older
Adults' Friendships

KAREN S. ROOK

It is prudent to pour the delicate oil of politeness on the machinery of friendship. (Collette)

Friendships can be fragile—vulnerable to dissolution in the wake of perceived or real slights, as this comment by the French novelist Collette suggests. Unlike kin and marital relationships, formal bonds do not sustain friendships (Allan & Adams, this volume; Litwak & Szelenyi, 1969; Wood & Robertson, 1978). No societal or contractual mechanisms exist to ensure the maintenance of friendships or to encourage reconciliation should rifts occur (Wiseman, 1986). Rather, friendships emerge voluntarily from shared affection and interests (Cooley, 1964; Simmel, 1949) and are self-maintaining themselves (Wiseman, 1986). These differences give rise to dual and sometimes conflicting tendencies in friendships. On the one hand, friendships are particularly conducive to interactions characterized by spontaneity, playfulness, permissiveness, and candor (Adams, 1967; Blau, 1973; Hess, 1972; Simmel, 1949), and interactions of this sort tend to make the greatest contributions to feelings of happiness (Blau, 1973; Larson, Mannell, &

AUTHOR'S NOTE: Preparation of this chapter was supported by a grant from the National Institute on Aging, AG03975-03.

Zuzanek, 1986; Lee, 1979). Yet, as compared with kin relationships, disagreements or other negative exchanges may threaten the stability of friendships more precisely because friendships are voluntary and lack cultural mechanisms to support their maintenance.

Despite recognition of the dual nature of friendship (Homans, 1974; Thibaut & Kelley, 1959), most research has focused on the positive aspects of friendship. Researchers have only recently begun to focus explicitly on the problems that arise in friendships and in other social relationships.[1] This new emphasis is evident in studies of the impact of negative exchanges on physical and mental health (e.g., Pagel, Erdly, & Becker, 1987; Rook, 1984; Stephens, Kinney, Ritchie, & Norris, 1987), of social support attempts that fail (e.g., Wortman & Lehman, 1985), and of friendship dissolution itself (e.g., Baxter, 1985; Rose, 1984; Rose & Serafica, 1986; Rusbult, 1987).

The problematic aspects of friendship ties merit greater attention for several reasons. First, longitudinal studies indicate that, as social relationships develop, both rewarding exchanges and troublesome exchanges become more frequent (e.g., Braiker & Kelley, 1979; Hays, 1985). Second, evidence suggests that when problematic exchanges between friends occur, they can be surprisingly potent. Indeed, the adverse impact of problematic exchanges may exceed the beneficial impact of supportive exchanges (see reviews by Pagel et al., 1987, and Rook & Pietromonaco, 1987). Thus to overlook such negative interactions, even if they are comparatively infrequent, yields a false picture of the impact of friendship ties on older adults' emotional health.

Third, friendship strains may be quite salient to the elderly. Widowhood, retirement, and other social role losses that affect the elderly make friendship a particularly important context for social involvement (Blau, 1973; Hess, 1972). Moreover, some have argued that old age is a period of life in which people are free to exercise greater control over their leisure time and social contacts (e.g., Adams, 1987). If older adults do indeed have greater discretionary control over friendship contacts, they should be particularly attentive to the potential costs and benefits of various friendships as they decide which friends to interact with (or whether to interact with others at all). Other theorists have argued that old age is a time of more rather than of fewer constraints (c.g., Rosow, 1976) and that control over one's social world accordingly shrinks. If so, older adults have fewer opportunities to protect themselves from interactions with others that are ill-timed or otherwise problematic. These two perspectives differ in major respects, but they converge in postulating that older adults may be highly attuned to the potential for strains in their friendships.

The study of problematic aspects of older adults' friendships also lends itself nicely to analyses of specific theoretical questions. For example, research on friendship formation among young adults has demonstrated that negative aspects of friendships increase in quantity and salience over time (Hays, 1985). We know little about the balance of positives and negatives in friendships that have endured for years or even decades, as have the friendships of many older adults. Investigating the dual aspects of older adults' friendships, therefore, would complement and extend previous studies and would also contribute to the development of a knowledge base that might aid in the design of interventions to enhance older adults' social lives.

The purpose of this chapter is to contribute to understanding of the kinds of negative exchanges or experiences that detract from older adults' friendships. The chapter is organized in four parts. In the first part, I examine different types of problematic interactions that occur in older adults' friendships, considering both the manifest content of conflicts and the latent themes that such conflicts represent. In the second part, I consider the causes of tension between elderly friends, including individual, interpersonal, and situational factors that contribute to strained friendships. In the third section, I address the consequences of such problematic exchanges for the friendship itself, for other relationships in the older person's social network, and for the older person's psychological health. Throughout the chapter, I attempt to identify gaps in the existing knowledge base and directions for further research. Finally, I urge an appropriate perspective on the negative aspects of older adults' friendships and caution against exaggerating the prevalence and impact of such friendship strains.

Before turning to the first section, two definitional issues warrant attention. First, what do I mean by the term *friend*? In this chapter, I knowingly sidestep the complexities involved in differentiating among alternative definitions (see Matthews, 1986, and Adams, this volume) and rely instead upon the subjective definitions of participants in the studies that I describe. That is, a friend is whomever the individual regards as a friend. This indiscriminate definition has obvious limitations (Adams, this volume), but I hope that it is adequate to the task of providing a broad-gauged perspective on friendship strain in late life.

Second, what do I mean by problematic or conflictual exchanges between friends? In this chapter, I emphasize actions by one member of a friend dyad that cause the other member to experience psychological distress (e.g., anger, resentment, guilt, sadness) and reservations about the friendship itself. This definition excludes the conventional costs of friendship that have been discussed in social exchange theories (Homans, 1974; Thibaut & Kelley, 1959), such as the time, money, and material goods that may be required to maintain a friendship or the displacement of opportunities to engage in other kinds of social involvement. The current definition also excludes actions by friends that may be irritating but that do not cause lingering distress because one can attribute them to good intentions, such as efforts to prompt one to stop smoking. Instead, I emphasize those actions by friends that older adults specifically regard as misdeeds or transgressions and that cause emotional distress. This definition includes acts of omission (e.g., failing to repay a loan from a friend or forgetting a friend's birthday) as well as acts of commission.

Finally, in this chapter I emphasize the friendships of community-residing older adults. Other authors have discussed the friendships of older adults who live in special settings, such as nursing homes (Retsinas & Garrity, 1985), inner-city areas and single-room occupant hotels (Cohen, this volume; Sokolovsky & Cohen, 1981), and isolated rural areas (Antonucci, 1985; Lawton, 1980). In addition, space constraints preclude a discussion of variations in the nature, causes, and consequences of friendship strains among demographically diverse subgroups of the elderly population (such as men versus women, the young-old versus the old-old, and those of higher versus lower socioeconomic status). I hope that by providing a general overview of some of the major questions and issues that arise in studying friendship strains in later life, this chapter stimulates more refined analyses that reflect the considerable heterogeneity that exists in the elderly population.

TYPES OF FRIENDSHIP STRAINS

Researchers have studied conflicts and problematic interactions more extensively in the context of family relationships and romantic relationships than in the context of friendships. Nevertheless, some researchers have attempted to identify the types of strains that occur in friendships (Parlee, 1979; Rose, 1984; Wiseman, 1986), and a small number have focused specifically on strains that occur in older adults' relationships (Fiore, Becker, & Coppel, 1983; Pagel et al., 1987; Rook, 1984; Stephens et al., 1987).

Peterson (1983) noted in discussing efforts to categorize conflicts in marital relationships that one could base such classification either on the manifest content of conflicts or on the latent issues expressed by conflicts. A similar distinction characterizes theoretical and empirical efforts to categorize strains in friendships. Some researchers have concentrated primarily on the manifest actions and exchanges that cause friction between friends, whereas others have concentrated on the underlying themes or issues reflected in conflicts.

Manifest Content of Problematic
Exchanges Between Friends

Most studies of strains in older adults' social relationships have presented respondents with lists or categories of problematic exchanges developed on an a priori basis by the investigator(s). For example, I (Rook, 1984) asked elderly widowed women whether individuals in their social networks invaded their privacy, tended to take advantage of them, failed to provide promised help, consistently provoked conflicts or feelings of anger, and consistently caused problems for them. Stephens et al. (1987) asked recovering geriatric stroke victims to indicate how often friends and family members provided unwanted or unneeded instrumental support and emotional support, such as offering unwanted advice or unneeded assistance with self-care tasks. In two studies, respondents who were caring for someone with Alzheimer's disease rated how upsetting or helpful members of their social networks were on five dimensions: socializing, self-disclosure, cognitive guidance, emotional support, and tangible aid (Fiore et al., 1983; Pagel et al., 1987).

None of these researchers sought to map the full range of problematic exchanges that can mar older adults' social relationships; rather, they investigated specific sets of exchanges that appeared likely to influence such important outcomes as life satisfaction (Rook, 1984), depression (Fiore et al., 1983; Pagel et al., 1987), and cognitive functioning (Stephens et al., 1987). As a result, the studies do not provide a comprehensive picture of the types of strains that occur most commonly and have the greatest impact on older adults' friendships. Research of an open-ended, descriptive nature would complement previous research in documenting the range of problems that older adults experience in their friendships. Descriptive studies would allow elderly participants themselves to volunteer examples of the kinds of interactions that jeopardize their friendships.

Notably, each of the above studies included transactions involving aid as a potential source of problems in older adults' social relationships. Indeed, some have argued that exchanges of aid (particularly those involving money, material goods, and services) represent areas of special sensitivity and potential difficulty in older adults' friendships (Allan, 1986). Wortman and her colleagues (Lehman, Ellard, & Wortman, 1986; Wortman & Dunkel-Schetter, 1979; Wortman & Lehman, 1985) have provided insightful empirical and theoretical analyses of the reasons why efforts to provide support sometimes backfire (see also Morgan, 1986; Shinn, Lehmann, & Wong, 1984; Walker, MacBride, & Vachon, 1977). Researchers should further investigate whether transactions involving aid cause greater strain in older adults' friendships than do other kinds of transactions and whether older adults' friendships are, in fact, singularly vulnerable to such stress.

Latent Themes Underlying
Problematic Exchanges Between Friends

Most efforts to categorize the themes that underlie problematic exchanges between friends share the basic assumption that, through repeated interaction (and partly through cultural prescriptions), the members of a close relationship come to develop implicit rules and expectations that guide their behavioral exchanges and interpretations of relationship events. Duck (1986), for example, referred to "social formulae," and Argyle and Henderson (1984) discussed relationship rules that apply specifically to friendship. From this perspective, seemingly disparate misdeeds may elicit a similar response because they violate the same implicit rule.

Perhaps the most hurtful and puzzling actions by friends are those that appear to reflect willful violation of highly valued, if rarely discussed, norms that have evolved over the course of the relationship (Wiseman, 1986). A breach of confidence, nonreciprocated affection or self-disclosure, invasion of privacy, and critical or competitive remarks represent examples of actions that violate implicit norms of trust, respect, reciprocity, and status equality. These norms seem to be at the heart of most friendships (Argyle & Henderson, 1984). Resentment may also stem from violations of norms that are idiosyncratic to a particular friendship, such as the conviction that friends should not probe painful or humiliating areas of each other's past, that strongly conflicting values or beliefs represent taboo topics of conversation, that friends should refute each other's self-disparaging comments, that responsibility for initiating and planning joint activities should alternate between friends, and so forth.

Empirical evidence supports the view that many conflicts in close relationships arise from such perceived violations of relationship norms or rules. Wiseman (1986) conducted in-depth interviews about friendship strains with 80 men and women aged 18-80 and analyzed essays written by 150 college students about problems that had threatened or severed a close friendship. Most of the specific problems reported were either "originating" or "reactive" in nature. Originating problems reflected "an apparent character change or unseemly act of a friend," whereas reactive problems reflected "an apparent lack of understanding that a friend has shown in reaction to some infraction" caused by oneself (p. 194). Originating problems essentially centered on the question, "How could (s)he have done that to me?" Reactive problems centered on the question, "How could (s)he fail to understand why I did that?" Originating problems were more common than reactive problems in the samples that Wiseman (1986) studied, although both types of friendship problems appeared in respondents' accounts.

Braiker and Kelley (1979) asked 100 young couples to describe the kinds of conflicts they had experienced. Although this study did not focus on friendships, the findings underscored the importance of perceived violations of relationship norms and identified additional issues that underlie many interpersonal conflicts. The enormous diversity of the roughly 400 conflicts described by the couples defied classification into homogeneous clusters on the basis of content. The conflicts did differ systematically, however, in terms of the level of generality at which couples defined their problems. Braiker and Kelley distinguished four such levels. The most concrete level consisted of conflicts about specific behaviors, such as failing to perform a particular household chore or refusing to participate in a leisure activity desired by the partner. The next level consisted of conflicts about norms. These conflicts focused not on specific misdeeds but, rather, on violations of general responsibilities and implicit agreements about the extent or intensity of interaction. Conflicts about the partner's personality characteristics and motives made up the next level of generality. Such conflicts tended to involve accusations about global traits (such as selfishness, passivity, or lack of self-discipline) and motives (such as competitiveness or disloyalty). A fourth kind of conflict focused on the couple's conflict behavior itself. That is, even in the process of trying to resolve their differences, couples sometimes found new things to argue about, such as spiteful comments made during the conflict or withdrawal by one of the partners. This fourth category would appear to subsume Wiseman's (1986) concept of reactive complaints in the sense that reactive complaints reflect a friend's dissatisfaction with the process of trying to resolve a disagreement.

This differentiation of four levels of generality provides a useful framework for investigating the kinds of conflicts and strains that older adults experience in their friendships. Some older adults may identify and attempt to rectify perceived misdeeds at the time of their occurrence, so that frustrations do not accumulate and thereby invite expression at more general levels (i.e., disputes about norms or personal characteristics). Others may be less able or willing to broach discussion with their friends of specific irritations or disagreements, perhaps preferring to view such specific problems as potential evidence of more general or more enduring patterns. To the extent that cognitive complexity declines with advanced age (e.g., Hess & Slaughter, 1986; Ludwig, 1982), the elderly may be more likely than other age groups to construe their complaints in general terms. Moreover, as I discuss in a subsequent section, factors inherent in the "culture of friendship" (Wiseman, 1986) may encourage friends to construe complaints about each other in general rather than specific terms. Any such generalizing tendencies bode ill for the friendship because conflicts that involve complaints and accusations at general levels are apt to be more upsetting and more difficult to resolve than those that involve more narrowly defined concerns (Braiker & Kelley, 1979; Orvis, Kelley, & Butler, 1976). Thus the level of generality at which older adults define their difficulties with friends should have important implications for the survival of the friendship.

CAUSES OF FRIENDSHIP STRAINS

Friendship strains have numerous origins as well as numerous forms. Although relatively little research has explicitly addressed the causes of estrangement between friends, several recurring themes appear in existing theoretical accounts and empirical studies. I discuss these themes below and, wherever possible, highlight work that has focused specifically on the elderly.

Hazards of Social Penetration

Social interaction in developing relationships gradually progresses from superficial to intimate exchanges (Altman & Taylor, 1973; Levinger, 1983). Such social penetration facilitates the growth of intimacy in the relationship but also increases the risk of disapproval or rejection through revelation of potentially embarrassing material (e.g., admissions of past failings, personal flaws, or private fantasies). Moreover, communication norms that facilitate discussion of superficial topics do not apply to discussion of highly personal material (Altman & Taylor, 1973). Rather, people must rely on their own intuitions in deciding how to disclose intimate material or how to respond to intimate disclosures by others (Altman & Taylor, 1973).

Little empirical evidence exists to indicate how often self-disclosure creates dilemmas in emerging or established friendships in old age. Dickson-Markman (1986) found that, as compared with younger age groups, older adults reported disclosing more personal information of a negative nature to their close friends. This hints at the possibility that disclosing potentially uncomfortable material to friends may not be particularly problematic in old age. Alternatively, such disclosures may pose problems primarily in the early stages of friendship formation, perhaps deflecting some relationships from further development. Indeed, older adults may monitor would-be friends' responsivity to trial disclosures as a means of deciding whether to continue investing in the relationship. We need to learn more about the pivotal conditions under which the content and processes of self-disclosure either strengthen or sour potential friendships in old age.

Tension Between Spontaneity and Responsibility

Some friendship strains in late life may result from an uneasy tension between spontaneity and responsibility that appears to exist unnoticed in most friendships. According to Wiseman (1986) the voluntary nature of friendship itself fosters a sense of naturalness or unself-conscious spontaneity about the emotions and events experienced with one's friends. Although gratifying, such seeming naturalness can cause problems because it appears to obviate the "need for clarification and/or negotiation of [friends'] mutual attraction and [relationship] status" (Wiseman, 1986, p. 95). People develop unstated expectations that their close friends will continue to exhibit the desirable behaviors and character traits that inspired formation of the friendship bond (Wiseman, 1986). That is, people implicitly assume that their close friends have a responsibility to behave in a desirable, stable fashion, but they rarely communicate which behavioral patterns are most important.

Indeed, the very idea of discussing mutual obligations with a friend appears to be at odds with the value attached to freedom and spontaneity in friendship (Wiseman, 1986). Members of other kinds of relationships (such as romantic partners or coworkers) more frequently engage in explicit discussion and decision making regarding the nature of the relationship and attendant commitments and responsibilities (Levinger, 1983). Disappointment and resentment may result when friends cannot maintain the necessarily delicate balance in their relationship between the value attached to spontaneity and freedom from obligation and the value attached to mutual, if unspoken, responsibility.

The applicability of Wiseman's (1986) analysis to friendships in late life merits investigation. For example, the inherent tension that she described would be less problematic to the extent that older adults assign substantially greater importance to one value than to the other. Increased needs for social support might lead many older adults to attribute greater significance to mutual responsibility as a guide for proper conduct in the friendship. Alternatively, older adults who can rely exclusively upon kin for support may attach much significance to spontaneity and freedom from obligation in their interactions with friends. Research on older adults' views of the responsibilities entailed in friendship and of the kinds of interactions with friends that they prize most highly would be helpful in testing the relevance of Wiseman's (1986) analysis.

Actor-Observer Biases

Actor-observer biases that develop in close relationships may also contribute to problematic exchanges between elderly friends. For example, people often have a clear notion of the specific traits and behaviors that they wish their friends to preserve, and they assume that their friends can correctly intuit these personal preferences. At the same time, they tend to have only a vague idea of the traits and behaviors that their friends expect of them (Wiseman, 1986). Members of a friend dyad probably rarely recognize this bias in their respective perspectives, thus providing fertile ground for misunderstanding and resentment.

Studies of marital conflict (e.g., Orvis et al., 1976) have documented an additional tendency for people to attribute their own transgressions to temporary, situational factors (such as time pressures, bad mood, or illness), but to attribute transgressions by their partners to enduring, dispositional factors (such as selfishness, insensitivity, or incompetence). People may similarly tend to infer that their friends' misdeeds reflect personal failings, whereas their own misdeeds reflect the press of circumstance (see Watson, 1982). Such systematically biased inferences regarding the causes of events that occur in the friendship could obviously provoke conflict and might additionally interfere with efforts to resolve a disagreement (Orvis et al., 1976). Whether older adults exhibit these or similar biases and, if so, whether such biases contribute to problems in their friendships represent worthy topics for research.

Social Skills and
Personality Characteristics

Research has frequently implicated deficient social skills and problematic personality characteristics in the deterioration or demise of friendships as well as in the failure of emerging friendships to develop to their full potential (Duck, 1982; see also a discussion of relational competence by Hansson, Jones, & Carpenter, 1984). Nonetheless, only scant and generally indirect evidence bears on these factors as they affect older adults' relationships specifically. In a study of 158 elderly Canadians, lonely subjects tended to endorse ineffective strategies in response to hypothetical interpersonal dilemmas and also exhibited limited sensitivity to social rules regarding appropriate self-disclosure (Perlman, Gerson, & Spinner, 1978). Shyness was associated with measures of social fear and anxiety in another study of 200 older adults (Hansson, 1986a). Of course, loneliness and shyness in old age may reflect a failure to establish meaningful friendships rather than distress caused by problems within existing friendships; in this sense, the above findings only implicate deficient social skill and personality factors as contributors to friction in late-life friendships.

Researchers have made much progress recently in the development of refined instruments for measuring social skills (e.g., Levenson & Gottman, 1978; Riggio, 1986). In addition, researchers studying young adults have begun to identify the specific skills or clusters of skills that correlate most strongly with having satisfying social ties (e.g., Buhrmester, Furman, Wittenberg, & Reis, in press; Wittenberg & Reis, 1985). Gerontologists could adapt the measurement strategies and conceptual insights suggested by this work to investigations of the impact of deficient social skills on older adults' friendships. Hansson (1986b) argued, though, that the association between interpersonal competence and social involvement may be more complex in late life than in young adulthood and cautioned against overly simplistic translation of models developed from studies of young adults.

Researchers have also developed sophisticated accounts of the role of personality factors in various interpersonal problems (Coyne, 1976; Hansson et al., 1984; McAdams, 1985; Shaver, Furman, & Buhrmester, 1985). These theoretical perspectives may prove useful in efforts to understand how problematic personality characteristics undermine older adults' efforts to establish or maintain satisfying friendships. To consider just one example, Horowitz (1983) recently offered an interesting analysis of how ineffective social behaviors sometimes reflect efforts to protect fragile self-esteem. Because social interaction is a centrally important source of feedback about the self (Cooley, 1964; Rosenberg, 1981), people with low self-esteem sometimes adopt dysfunctional interpersonal strategies in an effort to minimize the risk of negative feedback. Horowitz (1983) described three dysfunctional strategies: (a) excessive compliance with the wishes of others, apparently as a means of avoiding criticism and social rejection, (b) rebellion, as a means of invalidating others as a source of negative feedback, and (c) social withdrawal, as a means of reducing the threat of rejection by eliminating social contact altogether. Interestingly, these strategies correspond closely to three dysfunctional interpersonal strategies identified by Bowlby (1977): compulsive caregiving, emotional detachment, and compulsive self-reliance.

This analysis suggests a possible motivational basis for certain imbalances in patterns of giving and receiving that investigators have documented in studies of the reciprocity of older adults' exchanges and have found to be associated with greater loneliness and psychological distress (Roberto & Scott, 1986; Rook, 1987). More generally, analyses such as the one developed by Horowitz (1983) not only call attention to specific personality factors that may be implicated in problematic social relationships, including those of the elderly, but also provide theoretical insights about the role of such personality factors in inspiring, maintaining, and channeling patterns of dysfunctional interpersonal behavior.

Role Complementarity with Other Social Network Members

A different perspective on the sources of friendship strain in late life comes from considering friendship within the broader context of an older adult's social network. Specifically, the degree to which different groups within a focal person's social network perform complementary functions or roles may influence the likelihood of experiencing strain in a given friendship or set of friendships.

Considerable research on the elderly suggests that friends and kin perform somewhat dissimilar functions (e.g., Litwak, this volume). The clearest differences emerge in the areas of instrumental support and companionship. Kin tend to function as the primary providers of instrumental support (material goods and services), whereas friends appear to be particularly important as companions for leisure activities (Adams, 1967; Allan, 1986; Hill, Foote, Aldous, Carlson, & MacDonald, 1970; Stoller & Earl, 1983; Troll, Miller, & Atchley, 1979). Although researchers should not exaggerate these differences (some friends do provide instrumental support and some kin do provide satisfying companionship), such differences appear to reflect older adults' preferences (Hill et al., 1970; Rundall & Evaschwick, 1982; Shanas, 1979) as well as inherent characteristics of kin and friend relationships that make them particularly well-suited to specific functions (Allan, 1986; Litwak, 1985, this volume). Moreover, empirical evidence of task differentiation between kin and friends is consistent with the general argument of both Litwak (1985) and Weiss (1974) that individuals or groups often specialize in the basic functions they perform for others. Weiss (1974) argued from this perspective that, to fulfill a range of common social needs, people must form multiple relationships that complement each other with respect to the functions they perform.

Friendships embedded in social networks that depart from normative patterns of role specialization and complementarity, therefore, may be more vulnerable to strain. For example, older adults who lack kin or whose kin are unable or unwilling to provide instrumental support may be forced to turn to friends for such support. This would violate normative patterns, particularly if the aged individuals need extensive support (Allan, 1986), and might contribute to feelings of resentment, guilt, or other problematic sentiments within the friendship (Rook, 1987).

Disruptive External Events

External events may also jeopardize friendships, perhaps particularly the friendships of older adults. Some events threaten the friendship by decreasing the participants' similarity (Duck, 1982). Changes in health, income, or marital status, for example, may dramatically alter the opportunities available to two friends to engage in formerly valued activities or may lower the motivation to engage in such activities (Antonucci, 1985). Ample evidence has documented the changes in friendships that occur following mid- or late-life divorce (Berardo, 1982), death of a spouse (Lopata, 1979), residential relocation (Lawton, 1980), and other disruptive events (Antonucci, 1985).

In addition to threatening friends' compatibility, external events may strain an older person's friendships by introducing new stresses or demands. Events such as accidents, illnesses, and bereavement often create demands for a level of support that exceeds the resources of a social network or for types of assistance that well-intentioned supporters simply do not know how to provide (Wortman & Lehman, 1985). Allan (1986) argued that, although friends readily provide short-term aid in a crisis, efforts to incorporate friends into long-term provision of care undermine the friendships themselves. People base friendship on sociability and enjoyment, rather than assistance (Allan, 1986). In addition, because friendships are founded on the premise of equality, they suffer from events that create asymmetrical patterns of need and aid (Allan, 1986). Allan (1986) suggested that researchers and policy-makers sometimes confuse two types of caring—"caring about," or an expression of generalized concern for another person, and "caring for," or tending to another person's routine needs. Friendship normally involves the former but not the latter.

I have discussed various causes of friendship strain in old age as if they operated independently of one another. Such single-cause explanations, however, probably do not reflect the reality of most older adults' social worlds (see Duck, 1982). Instead, causal factors undoubtedly combine in complex ways to affect the likelihood of older adults' experiencing difficulties in their dealings with friends. Researchers have shown that environmental and personal factors influence young adults' loneliness through complex interactions (e.g., Shaver et al., 1985). Gerontologists should similarly examine interactive models in studies of older adults' conflicts with friends.

CONSEQUENCES OF FRIENDSHIP STRAIN

One can consider the consequences of rifts in older adults' friendships from a variety of different perspectives. In this section, I discuss effects of rifts on the course of the friendship itself, on other relationships in the social network, and on the friends' psychological well-being.

Effects on the Course of the Friendship

Severe strains may cause dissolution of the relationship, whereas less severe strains may prompt implicit or explicit renegotiation of at least some aspects of the relationship, such as the level of intimacy or frequency of contact. Moreover, as I discuss below, conflicts between friends do not inevitably have negative consequences; the processes of conflict resolution and reconciliation sometimes strengthen friendships.

Renegotiation of the friendship. Partial disengagement from the friendship probably represents the most common response to conflicts that do not cause sufficient distress to sever the bond (see Blieszner, this volume, for a review of research on friendship disengagement). For example, people may alter their investment in a friendship by reducing the amount of contact with the friend, expectations for receipt of support from the friend, or strength of affective tie to the friend. People may also protectively avoid disclosure of intimate material that they normally would have discussed with the friend whose trustworthiness has come into question (see Altman & Taylor's, 1973, discussion of social depenetration).

Not all friendships, of course, deteriorate in the wake of disputes and perceived transgressions; some actually emerge rejuvenated from such events. Indeed, theorists have argued that conflicts are both inevitable and essential to the growth of intimacy in close relationships (Bach & Wyden, 1968; Simmel, 1950; Waller & Hill, 1951). The manner of handling conflicts determines whether they serve to bolster or despoil the relationship (Altman & Taylor, 1973; Lloyd & Cate, 1985; Peterson, 1983). Constructive handling of conflicts allows members of a relationship to gain a better understanding of each other's values and needs, to discover how to undo any harm they may have caused, and to reaffirm the basic value of the relationship (Simmel, 1950). Whether conflicts between friends actually achieve these hypothesized positive outcomes may depend upon each person's investment in the friendship (Rusbult, 1987) and upon the processes that unfold during efforts to come to terms with the disagreement (Duck, 1982; Peterson, 1983).

Most empirical evidence of beneficial outcomes of conflict stems from studies of premarital and marital relationships (e.g., Lloyd & Cate, 1985; Rausch, Barry, Hertel, & Swain 1974). As Levinger (1983) noted, marital relationships differ from other relationships (including friendships) in their goals, duration, strength, exclusiveness, degree of interdependence, and in the existence of socially structured norms that guide interactions and expectations. The meaning of and response to conflicts undoubtedly also differ in marital relationships and friendships. Thus the postulated positive outcomes of conflict, which appear to be rare enough in marriages (Peterson, 1983), may be even rarer in friendships.

Many questions exist about the dynamics of conflict management between elderly friends. For example, under what circumstances do older adults actually confront their friends about perceived misdeeds? Alternatively, when do they simply try to forgive friends' upsetting actions or reappraise the actions as insufficiently consequential to warrant confrontation (see Rusbult, 1987)? Do such unilateral strategies succeed in restoring good feelings about the friendship, or does the aggrieved person who uses such strategies continue to keep a tacit ledger of the friend's wrongdoings? When older adults express dissatisfaction to their friends, do they generally do so on an episodic basis as specific disagreements occur (which many therapists prescribe as a key to successful conflict management; Jacobson & Margolin, 1979), or do they more often allow disagreements to accumulate before registering their dissatisfaction? What factors might be associated with each of these two different styles? How do older adults attempt to redress their own wrongdoings toward friends—what kinds of direct or indirect conciliatory gestures do they make? Research on these and related questions would help to shed light on the factors that lead some friendships to deteriorate in response to conflicts whereas others either persevere relatively unchanged or emerge renewed.

Dissolution of the friendship. Highly distressing conflicts or significant declines in attraction toward a friend prompt termination of the friendship (Duck, 1982). Termination may occur either through abrupt cessation or gradual erosion of contact (see review by Blieszner, this volume). Research has suggested that termination of older adults' friendships typically takes the latter form (Blieszner, this volume). Relatively few older adults in studies by Adams (1985), Blieszner (this volume), and Matthews (1986) reported actively terminating their friendships; instead, they reported that friendships simply withered from lack of interest or deteriorated in response to external events, such as illness or geographic separation.

Several factors may help to explain why older adults' friendships tend to terminate gradually rather than abruptly. Slow fading permits the status of the friendship to remain vague and leaves open a possible renewal of the friendship in the future (Blieszner, this volume). Gradual erosion probably also causes less trauma than sudden breaks between friends, and it may afford greater flexibility in the construction of face-saving accounts to explain the decline of the friendship (Duck, 1982; McCall, 1982). Moreover, cultural norms regarding friendship appear to discourage friends from explicitly discussing the status of their relationship (Levinger, 1983; Wiseman, 1986). Thus dramatic declarations that a friendship has terminated (or has been established, for that matter) would seem gauche (Wiseman, 1986). Finally, the kinds of transgressions that occur between elderly friends may rarely be so severe as to warrant abrupt termination of the friendship.

Longitudinal studies would increase our understanding of the circumstances that lead to a slow withering versus abrupt cessation of older adults' friendships. The question of how these two different forms of friendship termination affect older adults' emotional health also invites research. It is worth noting in this regard that the formation and maintenance of a friendship require the participation of both individuals, whereas only one individual may precipitate termination (Levinger, 1983). Thus the psychological distress that normally would accompany deterioration of a friendship may be more pronounced when one person exercises far greater control over the course of dissolution. How older adults cope with mutually versus nonmutually desired fading of their friendships merits investigation.

Effects on Other Relationships
in the Social Network

Conflicts between friends may affect not only the friendship itself but other relationships as well (McCall, 1982). As Jaffe and Kanter (1976) observed, third parties may act as "potential audiences, interveners, and allies" (p. 177). Rifts between friends may prompt changes in their respective social networks, just as divorce often prompts realignments of allegiances in the social networks of former spouses (Berardo, 1982). Intense pressures for such realignments may develop in congregate housing, where conflicts are apt to be more visible and where the smaller size of the available friendship pool may increase the importance of clarifying allegiances among residents (e.g., Hochschild, 1973).

Such shifting allegiances can pose problems for these third parties. For example, researchers have documented the strains that third parties feel in attempting to remain neutral in marital disputes, particularly in disputes that lead to divorce (Spanier & Casto, 1979). Public rifts between friends might similarly create feelings of awkwardness and conflicting loyalties among members of their social networks. We know little, however, about the extent to which older adults perceive tensions in their friends' relationships and how such awareness affects their own interactions with the friends. Techniques of network analysis may be useful in identifying characteristics of social networks that make older adults most vulnerable to competing demands for their loyalties and in charting structural realignments that occur in response to interpersonal conflicts (e.g., Wellman, 1983; see Morgan, 1986, for an illustrative analysis of social network changes precipitated by widowhood).

Of course, a rift between a pair of friends does not inevitably create problems of allegiance for members of the friends' social networks. Ironically, such disputes may provide an occasion for a third party to strengthen his or her own relationship with one of the participants in the dispute. A third party may step forth to provide support or companionship that one of the aggrieved individuals perceived to be deficient in the friendship in question, confirming the aggrieved individual's doubts about the friendship and simultaneously enhancing the third party's attractiveness (see Levinger, 1983). Indeed, the existence of attractive alternatives to the current friendship may serve to accelerate the dissolution of the friendship (Duck, 1982; see Thibaut & Kelley's [1959] concept of comparison level for alternatives).

Effects on Older Adults' Psychological Well-Being

Rifts between elderly friends may also have consequences for the participants' psychological well-being. In this section, I examine how large an impact friendship strains have on older adults' emotional health and reasons why negative social exchanges appear to be quite potent.

Magnitude of effects of friendship strains on psychological well-being. Three recent studies (Fiore et al., 1983; Pagel et al., 1987; Rook, 1984) indicated that negative interpersonal experiences often have rather substantial effects on older adults' mental health. Each study contrasted the relative effects of supportive and problematic social exchanges on older adults' psychological well-being. Although the studies differed with respect to the specific populations sampled and the means of operationalizing supportive and problematic exchanges, the findings nonetheless converged in suggesting that the detrimental impact of negative social exchanges exceeds the beneficial impact of positive social exchanges (see Rook & Pietromonaco, 1987, for a review of similar findings from studies of other age groups). The results converged further in demonstrating that positive social exchanges made weak and generally nonsignificant contributions to the psychological health of the individuals studied.

The findings of Pagel et al. (1987) are particularly persuasive because the researchers made use of a short-term longitudinal design that permitted statistical controls for respondents' initial levels of depression. Changes in the level of negative social exchanges predicted changes in the level of depression, controlling for initial depression levels as well as for age, sex, and health status. This finding addressed the concern that the "negativity effect" documented in the three studies could have been a mere artifact of respondents' state of psychological adjustment. Moreover, the negativity effect did not appear merely to reflect restricted variability or lower reliability of the measures of positive interactions (Pagel et al., 1987).

The results of a study of recovering geriatric stroke victims (Stephens et al., 1987) departed somewhat from the pattern described above because both positive and negative social exchanges proved to be important but for different aspects of respondents' psychological health. Controlling for respondents' status upon discharge from the hospital, negative interactions were associated with lower morale and more psychiatric symptoms, whereas positive interactions were unrelated to these two outcomes. Positive interactions, in contrast, were related to better cognitive functioning (e.g., fewer memory problems, less disorientation and confusion), but negative exchanges were unrelated to cognitive functioning. Although these results did not demonstrate that negative social exchanges outweigh positive exchanges in impact, they did provide further evidence of the adverse impact of negative exchanges on the emotional health of older adults, particularly of frail older adults.

Each of these studies assessed negative exchanges that occurred in the elderly participants' social networks in general and did not focus specifically on negative exchanges involving friends. Nevertheless, friends appeared to be a significant source of such conflictual exchanges. For example, I (Rook, 1984) found that friends constituted 38% of those with whom elderly respondents had problematic interactions. Pagel et al. (1987) reported that 57% of the individuals in networks characterized by a high degree of negativity were kin; presumably a sizable proportion of the remaining network members were friends.

Reasons for strong impact of negative exchanges. Several factors help to explain why negative social exchanges appear to have such strong effects and, indeed, why they often appear to have substantially stronger effects than positive social exchanges (Rook & Pietromonaco, 1987). The explanations I discuss below do not focus specifically on transactions between friends. Nor do they focus on older adults per se. Nevertheless, the explanations appear relevant to a range of close relationships, including friendships, and no basis exists for questioning their applicability to the elderly.

The first explanation traces the potency of negative social exchanges to their comparative rareness and, as a result, to their greater salience. Studies have shown that positive social interactions occur much more frequently than do negative social interactions (Abbey, Abramis, & Caplan, 1985; Pagel et al., 1987; Rook, 1984; Stephens et al., 1987; see also studies of marital interaction, e.g., Jacobson, Follette, & McDonald, 1982). For example, in my study (Rook, 1984), supportive relations outnumbered problematic relations 6 to 1. Positive exchanges accordingly may form a general backdrop against which the comparatively infrequent negative exchanges appear quite salient. Indeed, the substantially greater frequency of positive events allows individuals to take them for granted to some extent (Berscheid, 1983). Positive exchanges with others appear to be assimilated to a mere baseline level of expectation. As Wiseman (1986) argued, people tend to develop expectations that their friends will exhibit desired behaviors stably and predictably. Behaviors that conform to such expectations elicit little reaction; behaviors that depart from such expectations, in contrast, appear puzzling or even shocking and may prompt ruminative scrutiny.

Indirect evidence that the comparative rareness of negative interactions helps to account for their disproportionate impact comes from studies of relationship satisfaction. Jacobson et al. (1982), for example, had married couples keep daily records of positive, negative, and neutral actions by their spouses as well as daily ratings of their satisfaction with the marital relationship. Reactivity to negative spouse behaviors was inversely related to the frequency of the behaviors: The rarer the negative behaviors, the more they were associated with lower marital satisfaction. Reactivity to positive behaviors by the spouse, in contrast, was unrelated to the frequency of such behaviors. Pagel et al. (1987) found a similar pattern when they tested interactions between network members' helpful and upsetting behaviors in predicting elderly respondents' overall network satisfaction. Among respondents whose networks were characterized by a generally high level of helpfulness, upsetting behaviors strongly predicted lower network satisfaction. Among respondents whose networks were characterized by a generally low level of helpfulness, upsetting behaviors exhibited only a weak association with network satisfaction. Thus consistent with the frequency-salience argument, a pattern of predominantly positive interactions with network members appeared to be a precondition for negative interactions to have much impact. As I noted earlier, this pattern characterizes the social networks of many older adults.

Another closely related explanation for the often disproportionate impact of unpleasant social exchanges emphasizes the cognitive processing that follows positive versus negative encounters with others (Pagel et al., 1987; Rook & Pietromonaco, 1987). Attribution theorists have argued that only counternormative behavior permits confident inferences about other people's motives (Jones & Davis, 1965; Kelley, 1967). Expected actions by friends, such as expressions of sympathy during a crisis or ordinary gestures of support, convey little information about friends' motives (Suls, 1982). To the extent that such actions stimulate attributional processing at all, people may be uncertain whether the actions reflect genuine caring or merely feelings of obligation to behave supportively. Negative behaviors by friends, in contrast, present no such attributional ambiguity (Suls, 1982). It is counternormative to withhold help from friends, to insult or exploit them, or otherwise to upset them. People may readily attribute such behaviors to malice or at least insufficient caring, which would help to explain their strong adverse effects.

A third reason why negative and positive social exchanges often have dissimilar consequences stems from the idea that they differ in adaptive significance. In trying to interpret negativity effects that have appeared in studies of diverse topics, Kanouse and Hanson (1972) argued that humans may have an innate tendency to be more vigilant to potential threats or risks than to potential pleasures or benefits.[2] Berscheid (1983, p. 145) commented in this regard that the human "emotional system appears to be a 'trouble-shooting' system." Such vigilance to threats makes people quite reactive to negative events. This basic predisposition may have aided human survival during periods when people were regularly forced to cope with many tangible threats from the environment.

A related explanation suggests that many negative experiences have the power to spoil the pleasure of positive events, whereas comparatively few positive experiences can cancel the misery of negative events (Kanouse & Hanson, 1972). For example, a single heated exchange during the course of an otherwise pleasant dinner party may spoil the experience; in contrast, a single pleasant exchange in the midst of an evening marred with strife has little power to restore tranquility (Rook & Pietromonaco, 1987). Because of such differences in reversibility, along with potential differences in adaptive significance, it is not surprising that people appear to be more sensitive to negative inter-personal exchanges than to positive ones, even though such an orientation at times has emotional costs.

The explanations I have discussed do not exhaust the possible reasons why negative social encounters appear to be quite potent. This topic needs further theoretical work and, even more important, empirical work that seeks to test specific explanations. For example, researchers could adapt methods of assessing daily interaction used in research on marital satisfaction (e.g., Jacobson et al., 1982) to study how the relative frequency of positive and negative exchanges between elderly friends influences mood and friendship satisfaction. Investigators could also assess older adults' attributions for positive and negative actions by friends to determine whether negative actions invite different causal attributions and whether certain kinds of attributions evoke the strongest emotional reactions (see Weiner, 1986). Studies of attri-butional processes might also yield useful information about the kinds of positive and negative behaviors by friends that older adults consider normative or nonnormative. The adaptive significance explanation may be more difficult to study directly, but analysts might devise methods for studying differential vigilance to positive versus negative outcomes in varying social contexts. Such vigilance would have important moti-vational implications if researchers found that older adults base their decisions about whether to participate in various social activities more on perceptions of potential risks than on perceptions of potential benefits (e.g., Pietromonaco & Rook, 1987). Thus researchers should consider not only why older adults react differently to positive and negative interpersonal events but also how older adults proactively seek to regulate the occurrence of such events in their lives (Lawton, 1988).

CONCLUSION

In this chapter, I have focused on the kinds of strains that occur in older adults' friendship and on the causes and consequences of such strains. I chose this focus because most previous work has examined only the positive aspects of older adults' friendships and because tensions inherent in the nature of friendship itself seemed likely to make people particularly sensitive to disagreements and other negative exchanges involving their friends.

At the same time, one should exaggerate neither the prevalence nor the impact of strains in older adults' friendships. Interactions among elderly friends are probably quite positive most of the time, and being able to spend time with friends appears to mean a great deal to the elderly. Fairly consistent evidence has indicated, for example, that contact with friends enhances older adults' morale to a greater extent than does contact with adult children and other family members (Lee & Ishii-Kuntz, 1987). Indeed, some investigators have found that contact with kin has only a weak or even negative relationship to morale (e.g., Lee, 1979). The fact that relatively few older adults report having experienced explosive or otherwise abrupt termination of their friendships further testifies to the general absence of turmoil in their dealings with friends.

Nor should readers take the focus of this chapter to imply that older adults are more susceptible to troubled friendships than other age groups. In fact, evidence has suggested that the opposite is true. As compared with younger age groups, the elderly generally report higher levels of friendship satisfaction, are less likely to wish that they had more friends, and report fewer negative feelings about members of their social networks (Antonucci, 1985).

A balanced perspective on older adults' friendships requires acknowledgment of the enormous benefits provided by friendships as well as recognition that problems can arise in friendships. Precisely because of the great significance of friendships to the elderly, we need to learn more about the kinds of problems they sometimes encounter with their friends, what factors increase their vulnerability to such problems, how they attempt to manage friendship difficulties, and how such problems affect their lives. Little systematic knowledge about these issues exists, and many types of inquiry would help to fill gaps in the literature. What seems needed most urgently, however, is conceptually grounded, longitudinal research that addresses the dynamics of friendship strain in late life and that incorporates the perspectives of both partners in the relationship. Such research would substantially enrich our current understanding of the pleasures and problems of friendship in the lives of older adults.

NOTES

1. A longer tradition of work exists on family relationships that are pathogenic (e.g., Croog, 1970; Jacob, 1975). Because this chapter focuses on friendships, I have not examined that literature.

2. See Taylor and Brown (in press) for a different perspective on sensitivity to potential threats.

REFERENCES

Abbey, A., Abramis, D. J., & Caplan, R. D. (1985). Effects of different sources of social support and social conflict on emotional well-being. *Basic and Applied Social Psychology, 6*, 111-129.

Adams, B. (1967). Interaction theory and the social network. *Sociometry, 30*, 64-78.

Adams, R. G. (1985, November). *The permeable boundaries of friendship: A longitudinal study of elderly women*. Paper presented at the 38th Annual Meeting of the Gerontological Society of America, New Orleans.

Adams, R. G. (1987). Patterns of network change: A longitudinal study of friendships of elderly women. *The Gerontologist, 27*, 222-227.

Allan, G. (1986). Friendship and care for elderly people. *Ageing and Society, 6*, 1-12.

Altman, I., & Taylor, D. A. (1973). *Social penetration: The development of interpersonal relationships*. New York: Irvington.

Antonucci, T. C. (1985). Personal characteristics, social support, and social behavior. In R. H. Binstock & E. Shanas (Eds.), *Handbook of aging and the social sciences* (2nd ed., pp. 94-128). New York: Van Nostrand Reinhold.

Argyle, M., & Henderson, M. (1984). The rules of friendships. *Journal of Social and Personal Relationships, 1*, 211-237.

Bach, G. R., & Wyden, P. (1968). *The intimate enemy: How to fight fair in love and marriage*. New York: Avon.

Baxter, L. A. (1985). Accomplishing relationship disengagement. In S. Duck & D. Perlman (Eds.), *Understanding personal relationships* (pp. 243-265). London: Sage.

Berardo, D. H. (1982). Divorce and remarriage at middle age and beyond. *Annals of the American Academy of Political and Social Science, 464*, 132-139.

Berscheid, E. (1983). Emotion. In H. H. Kelley, E. Berscheid, A. Christensen, J. H. Harvey, T. L. Huston, G. Levinger, E. McClintock, L. A. Peplau, & D. Peterson (Eds.), *Close relationships* (pp. 110-168). New York: Freeman.

Blau, Z. (1973). *Old age in a changing society.* New York: Viewpoints.

Bowlby, J. (1977). The making and breaking of affectional bonds. I. Aetiology and psychopathology in the light of attachment theory. *British Journal of Psychiatry, 130*, 201-210.

Braiker, H., & Kelley, H. H. (1979). Conflict in the development of close relationships. In R. L. Burgess & T. L. Huston (Eds.), *Social exchange in developing relationships* (pp. 135-167). New York: Academic Press.

Buhrmester, D., Furman, W., Wittenberg, M. T., & Reis, H. T. (in press). Five domains of interpersonal competence in peer relations. *Journal of Personality and Social Psychology*.

Cooley, C. H. (1964). *Human nature and the social order.* New York: Scribner. (Original work published in 1902)

Coyne, J. C. (1976). Depression and the response of others. *Journal of Abnormal Psychology, 85*, 186-193.

Croog, S. H. (1970). The family as a source of stress. In S. Levine & N. A. Scotch (Eds.), *Social stress* (pp. 19-53). Chicago: Aldine.

Dickson-Markman, F. (1986). Self-disclosure with friends across the life-cycle. *Journal of Social and Personal Relationships, 3*, 259-264.

Duck, S. (1982). A topography of relationship disengagement and dissolution. In S. Duck (Ed.), *Personal relationships, Vol. 4: Dissolving personal relationships* (pp. 1-29). London: Academic Press.

Duck, S. (1986). *Human relationships: An introduction to social psychology.* London: Sage.

Fiore, J., Becker, J., & Coppel, D. (1983). Social network interactions: A buffer or a stress? *American Journal of Community Psychology, 11*, 423-439.

Hansson, R. O. (1986a). Shyness and the elderly. In W. H. Jones, J. M. Cheek, & S. R. Briggs (Eds.), *Shyness: Perspectives on research and treatment* (pp. 117-129). New York: Plenum.

Hansson, R. O. (1986b). Relational competence, relationships, and adjustment in old age. *Journal of Personality and Social Psychology, 50*, 1050-1058.

Hansson, R. O., Jones, W. H., & Carpenter, B. N. (1984). Relational competence and social support. In P. Shaver (Ed.), *Review of Personality and Social Psychology* (Vol. 5, pp. 265-384). Beverly Hills, CA: Sage.

Hays, R. B. (1985). A longitudinal study of friendship development. *Journal of Personality and Social Psychology, 48*, 909-924.

Hess, B. (1972). Friendship. In M. Riley, M. Johnson, & A. Foner (Eds.), *Aging and society, Vol. 3: A sociology of age stratification* (pp. 357-393). New York: Russell Sage.

Hess, T. M., & Slaughter, S. J. (1986). Aging effects on prototype abstraction and concept identification. *Journal of Gerontology, 41*, 214-221.

Hill, R. N., Foote, J., Aldous, R., Carlson, R., & MacDonald, R. (1970). *Family development in three generations.* Cambridge, MA: Schenkman.

Hochschild, A. R. (1973). *The unexpected community.* Berkeley: University of California Press.

Homans, G. G. (1974). *Social behavior* (2nd ed.). New York: Harcourt Brace Jovanovich.

Horowitz, L. M. (1983). *The toll of loneliness: Manifestations, mechanisms, and means of prevention* (Technical advisory report). Washington, DC: National Institute of Mental Health, Office of Prevention.

Jacob, T. (1975). Family interaction in disturbed and normal families: A methodological and substantive analysis. *Psychological Bulletin, 18*, 35-65.

Jacobson, N. S., Follette, W. C., & McDonald, D. W. (1982). Reactivity to positive and negative behavior in distressed and nondistressed married couples. *Journal of Consulting and Clinical Psychology, 50*, 706-714.

Jacobson, N. S., & Margolin, G. (1979). *Marital therapy*. New York: Brunner/Mazel.

Jaffe, D. T., & Kanter, R. M. (1976). Couple strains in communal households: A four-factor model of the separation process. *Journal of Social Issues, 32*, 169-191.

Jones, E. E., & Davis, K. E. (1965). From acts to dispositions: The attribution process in person perception. In L. Berkowitz (Ed.), *Advances in experimental social psychology* (Vol. 2, pp. 219-266). New York: Academic Press.

Kanouse, D. E., & Hanson, L. R. (1972). Negativity in evaluations. In E. E. Jones, D. E. Kanouse, H. H. Kelley, R. E. Nisbett, S. Valins, & B. Weiner (Eds.), *Attribution: Perceiving the causes of behavior* (pp. 47-62). Morristown, NJ: General Learning Press.

Kelley, H. H. (1967). Attribution theory in social psychology. In D. Levine (Ed.), *Nebraska symposium on motivation* (Vol. 2, pp. 192-238). Lincoln: University of Nebraska Press.

Larson, R., Mannell, R., & Zuzanek, J. (1986). Daily well-being of older adults with friends and family. *Psychology and Aging, 1*, 117-126.

Lawton, M. P. (1980). *Environment and aging*. Monterey, CA: Brooks/Cole.

Lawton, M. P. (1988, February). *Environmental proactivity and affect in older people*. Paper presented at the Fifth Annual Claremont Symposium on Applied Social Psychology, Claremont, CA.

Lee, G. R. (1979). Children and the elderly: Interaction and morale. *Research on Aging, 1*, 335-360.

Lee, G. R., & Ishii-Kuntz, M. (1987). Social interaction, loneliness, and emotional well-being among the elderly. *Research on Aging, 9*, 459-482.

Lehman, D. R., Ellard, J. H., & Wortman, C. B. (1986). Social support for the bereaved: Recipients' and providers' perspectives on what is helpful. *Journal of Consulting and Clinical Psychology, 54*, 438-446.

Levenson, R. W., & Gottman, J. M. (1978). Toward the assessment of social competence. *Journal of Consulting and Clinical Psychology, 46*, 453-462.

Levinger, G. (1983). Development and change. In H. H. Kelley, E. Berscheid, A. Christensen, J. H. Harvey, T. L. Huston, G. Levinger, E. McClintock, L. A. Peplau, & D. Peterson (Eds.), *Close relationships* (pp. 315-359). New York: Freeman.

Litwak, E. (1985). *Helping the elderly: The complementary roles of informal networks and formal systems*. New York: Guilford.

Litwak, E., & Szelenyi, I. (1969). Primary group structures and their functions: Kin, neighbors, and friends. *American Sociological Review, 34*, 465-481.

Lloyd, S. A., & Cate, R. M. (1985). The developmental course of conflict in dissolution of premarital relationships. *Journal of Social and Personal Relationships, 2*, 179-194.

Lopata, H. Z. (1979). *Women as widows*. New York: Elsevier.

Ludwig, T. E. (1982). Age differences in mental synthesis. *Journal of Gerontology, 37*, 183-189.

Matthews, S. H. (1986). *Friendships through the life course.* Beverly Hills, CA: Sage.

McAdams, D. P. (1985). Motivation and friendship. In S. Duck & D. Perlman (Eds.), *Understanding personal relationships* (pp. 85-105). London: Sage.

McCall, G. J. (1982). Becoming unrelated: The management of bond dissolution. In S. Duck (Ed.), *Personal relationships, Vol. 4: Dissolving personal relationships* (pp. 211-231). London: Academic Press.

Morgan, D. L. (1986). Personal relationships as an interface between social networks and social cognitions. *Journal of Social and Personal Relationships, 3*, 403-422.

Orvis, B. R., Kelley, H. H., & Butler, D. (1976). Attributional conflict in young couples. In J. H. Harvey, W. J. Ickes, & R. E. Kidd (Eds.), *New directions in attribution research* (Vol. 1, pp. 353-386). Hillsdale, NJ: Lawrence Erlbaum.

Pagel, M. D., Erdly, W. W., & Becker, J. (1987). Social networks: We get by with (and in spite of) a little help from our friends. *Journal of Personality and Social Psychology, 53*, 793-804.

Parlee, M. B. (1979, October). The friendship bond. *Psychology Today, 13*, 43-54.

Perlman, D., Gerson, A. C., & Spinner, B. (1978). Loneliness among senior citizens: An empirical report. *Essence, 2*, 239-248.

Peterson, D. R. (1983). Conflict. In H. H. Kelley, E. Berscheid, A. Christensen, J. H. Harvey, T. L. Huston, G. Levinger, E. McClintock, L. A. Peplau, & D. Peterson (Eds.), *Close relationships* (pp. 360-396). New York: Freeman.

Pietromonaco, P. R., & Rook, K. S. (1987). Decision style in depression: The contribution of perceived risks versus benefits. *Journal of Personality and Social Psychology, 52*, 399-408.

Rausch, H. L., Barry, W. A., Hertel, R. K., & Swain, M. A. (1974). *Communication, conflict, and marriage.* San Francisco: Jossey-Bass.

Retsinas, J., & Garrity, P. (1985). Nursing home friendships. *The Gerontologist, 25*, 376-381.

Riggio, R. E. (1986). Assessment of basic social skills. *Journal of Personality and Social Psychology, 51*, 649-660.

Roberto, K. A., & Scott, J. P. (1986). Equity considerations in the friendships of older adults. *Journal of Gerontology, 41*, 241-247.

Rook, K. S. (1984). The negative side of social interaction: Impact on psychological well-being. *Journal of Personality and Social Psychology, 46*, 1097-1108.

Rook, K. S. (1987). Reciprocity of social exchange and social satisfaction among older women. *Journal of Personality and Social Psychology, 62*, 145-154.

Rook, K. S., & Pietromonaco, P. (1987). Close relationships: Ties that heal or ties that bind? In W. H. Jones & D. Perlman (Eds.), *Advances in personal relationships* (Vol. 1, pp. 1-35). Greenwich, CT: JAI.

Rose, S. (1984). How friendships end: Patterns among young adults. *Journal of Social and Personal Relationships, 1*, 267-277.

Rose, S., & Serafica, F. C. (1986). Keeping and ending casual, close, and best friendships. *Journal of Social and Personal Relationships, 3*, 275-288.

Rosenberg, M. (1981). The self-concept: Social product and social force. In M. Rosenberg & R. H. Turner (Eds.), *Social psychology: Sociological perspectives* (pp. 593-624). New York: Basic Books.

Rosow, I. (1976). Status and role change through the life span. In R. H. Binstock & E. Shanas (Eds.), *Handbook of aging and the social sciences* (pp. 457-482). New York: Van Nostrand Reinhold.

Rundall, T., & Evashwick, C. (1982). Social networks and help-seeking among the elderly. *Research on Aging, 4,* 205-226.

Rusbult, C. E. (1987). Response to dissatisfaction in close relationships: The exit-voice-loyalty-neglect model. In D. Perlman & S. Duck (Eds.), *Intimate relationships* (pp. 209-237). Newbury Park, CA: Sage.

Shanas, E. (1979). The family as social support system in old age. *The Gerontologist, 19,* 169-174.

Shaver, P., Furman, W., & Buhrmester, D. (1985). Transitions to college: Network changes, social skills, and loneliness. In S. Duck & D. Perlman (Eds.), *Understanding personal relationships: An interdisciplinary approach* (pp. 193-219). London: Sage.

Shinn, M., Lehmann, S., & Wong, N. W. (1984). Social interaction and social support. *Journal of Social Issues, 40,* 55-76.

Simmel, G. (1949). The sociology of sociability. *American Journal of Sociology, 55,* 254-261.

Simmel, G. (1950). *The sociology of Georg Simmel* (K. H. Wolf, Trans.). New York: Free Press.

Sokolovsky, J., & Cohen, C. I. (1981). Measuring social interaction of the urban elderly: A methodological synthesis. *International Journal of Aging and Human Development, 13,* 233-244.

Spanier, G. B., & Casto, R. F. (1979). Adjustment to separation and divorce: A qualitative analysis. In G. Levinger & O. C. Moles (Eds.), *Divorce and separation* (pp. 211-227). New York: Basic Books.

Stephens, M.A.P., Kinney, J. M., Ritchie, S. W., & Norris, V. K. (1987). Social networks as assets and liabilities in recovery from stroke by geriatric patients. *Psychology and Aging, 2,* 125-129.

Stoller, E. P., & Earl, L. L. (1983). Help with activities of everyday life: Sources of support of the noninstitutionalized elderly. *The Gerontologist, 22,* 526-531.

Suls, J. (1982). Social support, interpersonal relations, and health: Benefits and liabilities. In G. S. Sanders & J. Suls (Eds.), *Social psychology of health and illness* (pp. 255-277). Hillsdale, NJ: Lawrence Erlbaum.

Taylor, S. E., & Brown, J. D. (in press). Illusion and well-being: A social psychological perspective on mental health. *Psychological Bulletin.*

Thibaut, J. W., & Kelley, H. H. (1959). *The social psychology of groups.* New York: John Wiley.

Troll, L. E., Miller, S., & Atchley, R. (1979). *Families of late life.* Belmont, CA: Wadsworth.

Walker, K. N., MacBride, A., & Vachon, L. S. (1977). Social support networks and the crisis of bereavement. *Social Science and Medicine, 11,* 35-41.

Waller, W., & Hill, R. (1951). *The family.* New York: Holt, Rinehart, & Winston.

Watson, D. (1982). The actor and observer: How are their perceptions of casuality different? *Psychological Bulletin, 92,* 682-700.

Weiner, B. (1986). *An attributional theory of motivation and emotion.* New York: Springer-Verlag.

Weiss, R. S. (1974). The provisions of social relationships. In Z. Rubin (Ed.), *Doing unto others* (pp. 17-26). Englewood Cliffs, NJ: Prentice-Hall.

Wellman, B. (1983). Network analysis: Some basic principles. In R. Collins (Ed.), *Sociological theory 1983*. San Francisco: Jossey-Bass.

Wiseman, J. P. (1986). Friendship: Bonds and binds in a voluntary relationship. *Journal of Social and Personal Relationships, 3*, 191-211.

Wittenberg, M. T., & Reis, H. T. (1985). Loneliness, social skills, and social perceptions. *Personality and Social Psychology Bulletin, 12*, 121-130.

Wood, V., & Robertson, J. F. (1978). Friendship and kinship interaction: Differential effect on the morale of the elderly. *Journal of Marriage and the Family, 40*, 367-375.

Wortman, C., & Dunkel-Schetter, C. (1979). Interpersonal relationships and cancer: A theoretical analysis. *Journal of Social Issues, 35*, 120-155.

Wortman, C., & Lehman, D. R. (1985). Reactions to victims of life crises: Support attempts that fail. In I. G. Sarason & B. R. Sarason (Eds.), *Social support: Theory, research and application* (pp. 463-489). The Hague, Netherlands: Martinus Nijhof.

PART IV

Social Status
and Friendship

9

Gender Differences in Adults' Same- and Cross-Gender Friendships

PAUL H. WRIGHT

Social scientists from several disciplines have devoted a considerable amount of research to gender differences in adults' same-gender friendships. They have devoted appreciably less to gender differences in cross-gender friendships, and still less to such differences at different stages of adulthood. All told, empirical studies have emphasized gender differences in general. Relatively few studies have focused upon the combined and presumably interacting influence of gender and adult developmental stages. Even so, when we piece together the strands of research that are currently available, we encounter the paradoxical adage, "The more things change, the more they stay the same."

The adage seems particularly applicable to gender differences in the friendships of old age. This is not to say that the patterning of differences is identical to that of earlier years. It is to say, however, the findings suggest a continuity indicating that gender differences in the friendships of old age are consistent with, and perhaps an exacerbation of, those observable throughout adulthood. This continuity is merely suggested, not clearly demonstrated. Almost all of the relevant studies have been correlational, and almost none has been longitudinal. In any case, my task in the present chapter is to move toward an integrative summary of two essentially independent bodies of research bearing on gender differences in the friendships of adults at varying life stages, highlighting those characteristic of the friendships of old age.

Because relevant research comes from different disciplines employing a variety of methodologies and conceptual foci, I begin with an overall perspective based on a few orienting concepts suggested by Fischer and Oliker (1983). Then I summarize research on same- and cross-gender friendships apart from an explicit consideration of age differences. Following this, I summarize research with implications for the ways, if any, in which global gender differences are eliminated or modified in various stages of adult development, particularly in old age. This summary is organized around a tentative framework based on the work of Hess (1972).

AN OVERALL PERSPECTIVE

The perspective begins with a broad but essential distinction between dispositional and structural approaches to studying gender differences in friendship (Fischer & Oliker, 1983). Dispositional explanations are those that emphasize gender differences in internalized and presumably stable individual characteristics such as the kinds of motives underlying friendship, the different adaptive or adjustive functions sought from or provided to friendships, and personal preferences concerning the form or content of the interaction that takes place. Structural explanations are those that emphasize "the different positions women and men typically occupy in the social system, and their differing access to economic, political and ideological sources of power or privilege" (p. 124). Structural factors represent the "direct, uninternalized effects of social structure" (p. 124), and include normative constraints, role demands, and sometimes simply the availability or accessibility of certain kinds of potential partners.

According to Fischer and Oliker (1983, p.124), "dispositional explanations have been the most frequent approaches to gender contrast in social relations." Let us modify this assessment slightly. Friendship research exploring gender differences in general has overwhelmingly favored the dispositional approach. Friendship research exploring gender differences in relation to adult development has predominantly used the structural approach.

In broad anticipation of the outcome of my review, it appears that dispositional differences between women as a group versus men as a group are basic influences in their friendships, resulting in modal differences that tend to persist over the adult life cycle. At the same time, structural factors influence the forms that friendships may take, the propriety of particular kinds of friendships, and sometimes the sheer possibility of relevant social contacts. Different structural factors are operative at different stages of adulthood and, for any given stage, may either maximize or minimize overall gender differences based on dispositional factors. We have already noted that more of the relevant research has emphasized the dispositional approach. All things considered, it appeared most parsimonious to deal first with gender differences in general and to treat them as superordinate, and then to deal with structural and age-related differences.

GENDER DIFFERENCES IN SAME-GENDER FRIENDSHIPS

A Cautionary Note

The modal pattern of differences in women's and men's friendships is both clear and robust. Like most social research yielding global differences between groups or categories, however, these differences are easy to interpret in exaggerated and sometimes misleading ways. I have dealt with this problem in detail elsewhere (Wright, 1988). For our purposes, it is sufficient to maintain a moderate stance in assessing the practical magnitude and pervasiveness of gender differences in friendship by keeping a few simple points clearly in view.

Most important, the same kinds of experiences and interactions take place, albeit in varying degrees, in virtually all close friendships, whether those friendships are composed of female, male, or mixed dyads. When researchers have found gender differences, those differences have been matters of averages and degrees, that is, qualities or characteristics that are more typical or average in the friendships of women than of men, or vice versa. They have not been matters of polar opposites or contrasting categories. Moreover, considerable numbers of women and men do not conform to the modal pattern. Hence, although overall gender differences in friendship are important with respect to both theory and application, let us avoid thinking about those differences in either dichotomous or overgeneralized terms.

The Modal Pattern

Various authors have attempted to epitomize the modal pattern of gender differences in friendship with expressions that are virtually identical in connotation. Booth (1972) described women's friendships as affectively richer than those of men. Weiss and Lowenthal (1975) used the terms reciprocity versus commonality to characterize the differing emphases in women's and men's friendships. Reisman (1981) concluded from his review that women are more likely to have friendships that are reciprocal while men are more likely to have those that are associative. Elsewhere (Wright, 1982), I suggested that women's friendships tend to be face-to-face while men's friendships tend to be side-by-side. Currently, it appears to be common to follow Bakan's (1966) terminology and label women's modal kind of friendships as "communal" and men's modal kind as "agentic."

The foregoing expressions summarize a variety of specific findings. With one notable exception, these findings identify characteristics that women's friendships exhibit more frequently or in greater degrees than those of men. The exception is that men usually place greater emphasis on structured activities. In contrast, women place greater emphasis upon a variety of interrelated characteristics.

Personalism, confiding, and emotional supportiveness. Studies typically reveal that women place relatively greater emphasis upon confiding and emotional supportiveness in friendships than do men. Booth (1972) and Booth and Hess (1974) reported this finding for samples of men and women aged 45 years and older, as did Weiss and Lowenthal (1975) for subjects ranging in age from adolescence through preretirement. The men in the Weiss and Lowenthal sample were more likely to report friendships characterized by similar patterns of activity and shared interests. Yoon (1978) reported similar findings for a sample of young adults. Wright and Crawford (1971) found that pairs of men indicated stronger friendships and considered one another more stimulating if they agreed on their preferences for specific, day-to-day activities. Pairs of women indicated stronger friendships and considered one another more stimulating if they agreed on their personal values. Hill and Stull (1981) reported strikingly corroborative findings.

A sample of college women studied by Davidson and Packard (1981) indicated that their closer same-gender friendships were not only important sources of emotional support, but also helped them change behavior in positive ways and grow personally. Moreover, these women made a clear distinction between their best and casual friends in this regard. Wright (1985) found that women rated their same-gender friends as higher on ego support value, self-affirmation value, and utility value than did men and, perhaps more important, also made a clearer distinction on these variables between their best versus their less close friends. The foregoing findings, based on various forms of self-report, are consistent with at least one study using observations of reactive behavior in a contrived but realistic stress situation (Winstead & Derlega, 1984).

"Mere talk" and self-disclosure. Enlarging upon the fact that talk is the essential medium of emotional support, Johnson and Aries (1983) pointed out that women, unlike men, give talk a prominent place in friendship. They concluded from comprehensive interviews with 20 women that "talk creates for female friends an elaborate and ongoing mosaic of non-critical listening, mutual support, enhancement of self-worth, relationship exclusiveness, and personal growth and self-discovery" (p. 358). In a comparison of middle-aged women and men, Aries and Johnson (1983) found that women friends discussed doubts and fears, personal and family problems, and intimate relationships more frequently and deeply than did men. They made a point of noting that male friends did discuss such topics, but with less frequency and depth. Caldwell and Peplau (1982) reported similar findings for a two-part study involving questionnaire responses and role-played telephone conversations.

Investigators usually interpret findings of the foregoing kind in terms of a specific subset of conversational content, that is, self-disclosure. Implicit in the observation that the conversations of women friends are more personalized than those of men is that women tend to be more self-disclosing, and that their self-disclosures are more intimate. Additional research dealing specifically with self-disclosure appears to support the second of these implications, but not necessarily the first (see, e.g., Hacker, 1981; Walker & Wright, 1976).

Affective quality and complexity. In addition to the above, I (Wright, 1982) summarized over a decade of research suggesting that women are more sensitive than men to the overall affective quality of their friendships. For example, women are more likely to confront and attempt to work through sources of tension or strain whereas men are more likely to disregard and work around them. Also, women are more likely to react to their friends in a holistic and multifaceted way whereas men are more likely to react to their friends with respect to distinct, relatively isolated attributes. This suggestion is consistent with findings indicating that women perceive more complexity in their friendships than men (Weiss & Lowenthal, 1975), and that men are more likely to have special purpose friendships than women (Block, 1980).

Exceptions to the Modal Pattern

Although the modal pattern of gender differences in friendship appears to be impressively consistent, studies in which the researchers did not find the usual differences have occurred with sufficient frequency to warrant serious attention. Rose (1985) found no appreciable gender differences in either the functions, formation, or maintenance of same-gender friendships. Caldwell and Peplau (1982) reported no gender difference in the preference for having intimate versus good or casual friends. Werner and Parmalee (1979) found similarity of activity preferences to be a better predictor of friendship for both female and male undergraduates than was similarity of attitudes. Comparing friendship conceptions of university students and alumni, Tesch and Martin (1983) found several age differences but only negligible gender differences. Studies of conceptions of a best friend among both undergraduates (Ashton, 1980) and college-educated men (Wall, Pickert, & Paradise, 1984) revealed that both women and men emphasized communication, intimacy, trust, and interpersonal qualities in a manner characteristic of the modal pattern for women. In a study of widows and widowers over 60 years old, Candy-Gibbs (1982) found a gender difference on only one of seven friendship variables.

It should come as no surprise that findings concerning gender and friendship have not been more consistent. In fact, considering some of the difficulties associated with research in this area, it is somewhat surprising that investigators have observed the modal pattern so consistently. Three specific problems are especially prominent. First, relevant research has varied widely in conceptual focus, methodology, and analytic approach (see Adams, this volume). Second, the conceptual status of dispositional influences is extremely unsettled. Precisely what the dispositional differences are and how they differentially affect women's and men's friendships is not at all clear.[1] Third, research involving gender—a subject variable—is difficult to interpret with confidence. More specifically, the modal pattern of gender differences in friendship sometimes has been attenuated or overridden by factors that may be more basic. These include sex-role orientations (Fischer & Narus, 1981; Williams, 1985), nonconventional versus conventional personal orientations (Bell, 1981b), and friendship motivation (McAdams, Healy, & Kraus, 1984). A detailed discussion of this problem is available elsewhere (Wright, 1988).

Summary. Research reveals a modal pattern of gender differences in same-gender friendships that is impressively consistent. The overall differences are usually not extremely large, nor are their effects observed ubiquitously within gender groups. The manner in which gender-related dispositions influence this pattern is not clear, and gender effects are sometimes attenuated or overridden by other variables. Even so, the pattern exists across a variety of samples and settings, and in spite of several conceptual and methodological difficulties.

GENDER DIFFERENCES IN CROSS-GENDER FRIENDSHIPS

Do Cross-Gender Friendships Really Exist?

A concern with gender differences in cross-gender friendships assumes that such friendships do exist, and that they are sufficiently common to warrant serious attention. Two questions challenge this assumption: Do individuals often admit to having cross-gender friendships? If so, are they really friendships or are they incipient sexual or romantic relationships? Reports on the incidence of cross-gender friendships have varied. Averaging across noncollege samples (Bell, 1981a; Block, 1980; Booth & Hess, 1974; Rubin, 1985), roughly 40% of the men and 30% of the women reported close cross-gender friendships. In Rose's (1985) sample of college undergraduates, 67% of the married men and 53% of the married women named a close opposite-sex friend, whereas all of the single men and 73% of the single women did so. Overall, it appears that cross-gender friendships are not uncommon, and men report then somewhat more consistently than women. Later life is an exception. Cross-gender friendships among the elderly appear to be rare (Chown, 1981).

But are these reported friendships really friendships? Investigators have discussed both structural and dispositional barriers to the formation of cross-gender friendships. Bell (1981a) and Block (1980), noting the importance of similar interests and orientations, suggested that women and men lack the commonality to make cross-gender friendships workable. Also, along with Rubin (1985), they proposed that sexual implications are usually present in close cross-gender relationships, even if not always overtly.

On the other hand, many friendship researchers have indicated, by their lack of explicit attention, that such issues are not a major concern. Along with this lack of concern, our comparative studies of personal relationships (Wright, 1985; Wright & Bergloff, 1984) show that cross-gender friendships clearly differ from any romantic heterosexual relationship on four characteristics, that is, permanence, exclusiveness, degree of social regulation, and salience of emotional expression. Furman (1986) found similarly low scores on these variables for cross-gender friendships among departmental colleagues on several university faculties. Furman's interviews revealed that cross-gender friends generally recognized sexual attraction as a possibility and sometimes experienced it at low levels. They did not take it seriously, however, and managed it easily. Thus people may acknowledge possible sexual implications in some, perhaps most, cross-gender friendships, but they usually do not preclude the possibility that such relationships may be truly platonic.

The Modal Pattern

Although researchers have studied cross-gender friendships far less extensively than same-gender friendships, the modal pattern of gender differences is equally clear and more consistently found. The figures cited above (and others) indicate that men are more likely than women to name members of the opposite sex as close friends. In fact, according to some studies, men very often prefer a woman over a man as a close friend whereas women are much more likely to prefer another woman (Rose, 1985; Rubin, 1986).

In terms of the quality or characteristics of cross-gender friendships, men tend to be more open, more self-disclosing, and more intimate with their women friends than with their men friends. Women tend to be less open, less self-disclosing, and less intimate with their men friends than with their women friends. This point was evident in the interview-based data of Block (1980) and Rubin (1985). In addition, Rose (1985) reported that men's cross-gender friendships were characterized by high levels of acceptance and intimacy, especially the latter, whereas women's cross-gender friendships were characterized by very low levels of both. Narus and Fischer (1982) found that masculine men were more expressive in their cross-gender than in their same-gender friendships. Androgynous men were equally expressive in both. This latter point, considered along with some of the findings reported by Fischer and Narus (1981), suggests that sex-role orientation may attenuate gender differences in cross-gender as well as in same-gender friendships.

Researchers have conducted further studies supporting the modal pattern within the context of adult age differences that I can review more conveniently in later portions of this chapter. For now, note that findings departing from the modal pattern appear to be rare. One of these rare exceptions was reported by Argyle and Furnham (1983) who found that both women and men expressed lower overall satisfaction with their cross-gender than with their same-gender friendships.

Friendships and Other Relationships: Dispositional Implications

One can gain a clearer perspective on gender differences in cross-gender—and, for that matter, same-gender—friendships by considering those differences in light of data about a broader range of relationships. Referring once more to our comparative studies of personal relationships (Wright, 1985; Wright & Bergloff, 1984), we found several differences between women's friendships and their close heterosexual relationships. Most important for present purposes, women regarded their friendships with other women as less intense and lower in salience of emotional expression than their heterosexual relationships. In contrast, they regarded their female friends and their heterosexual partners as equally self-affirming and as equally helpful in a direct utilitarian sense. Women saw their male friends as generally less likely to provide interpersonal rewards than either their female friends or their heterosexual partners. Men made a clearer distinction between their heterosexual relationships and their friendships, regarding their heterosexual relationships as stronger on almost all of the relationship variables. Although the men did not make a clear distinction between their female and male friends, they had a tendency to regard their friendships with women as more secure and supportive. In broad terms, women regard their same-gender friendships as important, but at least slightly less so than their heterosexual relationships. Women's friendships with men are relatively unimportant. Men regard their heterosexual relationships as important and their friendships with either sex as relatively unimportant.

The foregoing conclusion is supported by other findings. As I shall point out presently, men are likely to turn to female kin, especially their wives, for intimacy, emotional support, and the sharing of confidences. Women are likely to include a nonkin friend, almost always a female friend, as such a confidant. As Tognoli (1980, p. 277) noted, perhaps a bit too strongly, "there is evidence that [men] over-invest themselves emotionally in a close relationship with one woman." In a possible exception, Hess (1979) cited studies revealing that working-class men tend not to be emotionally expressive, even with their wives.

Because such findings persist over the adult life cycle, they lend themselves, at least in part, to a dispositional interpretation. But the precise nature of those dispositions and how they operate is uncertain. It appears that both women and men either want or need interpersonal intimacy, supportiveness, and contexts in which they can express themselves emotionally. Women tend to find this in a variety of relationships, including—perhaps especially—same-gender friendships. Men tend to find it in relationships with women, particularly their heterosexual partners. Some researchers have proposed that dispositions relevant to such findings function negatively, that is, as inhibitions to intimacy between males (Lewis, 1978; Tognoli, 1980). Others have proposed that they function positively, that is, as preferences or definitions of appropriateness for both genders (Fischer & Narus, 1981; Reis, Senchak, & Solomon, 1985).

In any case, we have a great deal to learn and clarify about the ways in which dispositional differences affect gender differences in friendships, whether by socialized capacity, socialized compulsion, socialized preference, or some combination of the three. As Winstead (1986, p. 85) pointed out, "A sex difference in preference requires as much of an explanation as a sex difference in capacity."

GENDER DIFFERENCES IN FRIENDSHIP AND THE ADULT LIFE CYCLE

In proposing explanations for changes in the numbers and kinds of friendships that women and men develop over the adult life cycle, researchers have relied heavily on structural assumptions. They have typically attributed gender differences to changing opportunities and restrictions associated with factors such as employment and career development, marriage, parenthood and family responsibilities, the empty nest, retirement, and widowhood. When they have proposed such structural variables, they usually have set aside dispositional differences. The work of Fischer and Oliker (1983) is an exception; they concluded that differing patterns of friendship participation for women and men at middle versus old age could not be explained apart from the interplay of structural and dispositional influences.

I organized the remainder of this review around a tentative conceptual model combining structural and dispositional factors. Relevant research is limited in both amount and appropriate kinds. For example, longitudinal studies are lacking, as are those in which investigators directly explored interacting structural and dispositional variables. Furthermore, researchers have examined some variables at only one or two levels that may operate differentially at many levels. Therefore, developing the model entailed a considerable amount of speculation and extrapolation. It is not whimsical, however. It is consistent with a variety of findings and should prove useful in setting some potentially productive directions for further research.

The Interplay of Structural and Dispositional Factors: A Tentative Model

Some time ago, Beth Hess (1972) proposed an analytic framework recognizing that friendships are heavily dependent upon an individual's total cluster of roles at any given stage of life. I cannot here do justice to the depth and detail of her essay. Most important for my purposes, she specified four types of connections that may exist between friendship and other social roles: (a) fusion, in which friendship is contingent upon the performance of one or more other roles; (b) substitution, in which friendship allows a person to actualize certain functions at periods when she or he lacks the opportunity to actualize those functions through major social roles; (c) complementarity, in which friendship, although not directly related, enhances the performance of other roles; and (d) competition, in which friendship and other roles make conflicting demands upon the individual's time or value allegiances or upon both.

Development through adulthood is marked by characteristic changes in clusters of roles. Therefore, it is reasonable to expect corresponding changes in the kinds of connections that exist between friendship and

other roles. These connections entail structural factors that will
sometimes work in harmony with and sometimes in opposition to
developing differing kinds of friendships based on gender-related
dispositions.

Scholars often claim that social expectations and role demands differ
for women and men at various stages of adult development. From the
present perspective, these different stages cannot readily be marked off
by age-related time periods apart from significant changes in role
configurations. Thus, with respect to clusters of roles that have an
impact upon friendships, we may be in error to think of women and men
as progressing in a parallel fashion into and out of a given stage. Such
changes for women and men are not well synchronized. For purposes of
understanding the interaction of structural and dispositional factors in
friendships, research has suggested a separate demarcation of stages.
For women, the typical demarcation is as follows: single adulthood,
preparenthood or nonparenthood marriage, parenthood, postparenthood (the empty nest), and, usually, widowhood. For men, the typical
demarcation is single adulthood, marriage, retirement, and, sometimes,
widowhood.

The foregoing demarcations are admittedly broad and simplistic. For
purposes of conceptualizing the important details and nuances of adult
development as a whole, they may not be useful. For the limited purpose
of understanding gender differences in friendships over the adult life
course, they seem promising, at least as a starting point. They culminate
in what appears to be a particularly helpful way of organizing what we
know about gender differences in the friendships—or nonfriendships—
of old age. Therefore, our discussion of single adulthood, marriage, and
parenthood in the younger and middle years will serve primarily as a
backdrop for a treatment of gender differences in the friendships of old
age.

Gender Differences in the Friendships
of Young and Middle Adulthood

Single adulthood. Single young adults have relatively uncrystallized
role obligations and a great deal of flexibility. Persons in this situation
experience little competition between friendship and other roles, and
numerous opportunities for the fusion of friendship with work- and
school-related roles. Both women and men should be free to form and
maintain friendships consistent with their individual and gender-related
dispositions.

Young adults are consistently among groups of subjects reporting relatively large numbers of friends (Fischer, 1982; Fisher & Oliker, 1983; Huston & Levinger, 1978; Reisman, 1981; Verbrugge, 1983). The modal differences between women's communal and men's agentic friendships are as strong at this period as any other. In fact, much of the research showing such differences is based on young adults in general and college undergraduates in particular.

Studies to date have indicated that cross-gender friendships occur more frequently among single adults than any other group (Rose, 1985; Rubin, 1985). Even Block (1980), whose data showed an overall low level of cross-gender friendships, found an appreciably higher incidence of such friendships among single than married subjects. Studies that I consider below have suggested that two structural factors are especially important in facilitating cross-gender friendships, that is, opportunities for contact in work- or school-related settings, and definitions of appropriateness—or, perhaps more accurately, the lack of definitions of inappropriateness. Gender-related dispositions do play a part, however. Men usually claim more cross-gender friendships than women. I noted previously that men are likely to consider their cross-gender friendships more communal than their same-gender friendships, whereas women are likely to consider their cross-gender friendships as considerably less so. Apparently the male tendency to seek out women rather than men as confidants begins before marriage, perhaps even in adolescence (see, e.g., Wright & Keple, 1981). Moreover, some data suggest that single college men, but not women, often treat their cross-gender friendships as low-level or incipient romantic relationships (Guinsburg, 1973; Wright & Bergloff, 1984).

According to my typical demarcation, this stage ends with marriage. There are, however, appreciable numbers of people who never marry. Little research is available on never-married women in later life, and apparently even less is available on never-married men. It would be reasonable to suppose that never-married individuals tend to develop friendships to fill this family void. It is not unusual to hear that friends often become the family of persons lacking kinship ties (Brenton, 1974; Pogrebin, 1987). Nevertheless, studies (this volume) have suggested that never-married women more often increase their contact with relatives rather than developing more or different kinds of friendships. Even so, it might prove interesting to study the "friends-as-family" phenomenon in terms of both its frequency and the qualitative aspects of the friendships involved. For the purposes of this chapter, the crucial questions are the following: Is this phenomenon either more or less common among women than men and are there qualitative differences related to gender?

Marriage and cross-gender friendships. Marriage in and of itself seems to have the effect of reducing the number of cross-gender friendships of both women and men. Married people have reported appreciably fewer cross-gender friendships than single subjects (Block, 1980; Rose, 1985; Rubin, 1985). The specific reason for this is a matter of considerable conjecture. There are several possibilities. Perhaps the most obvious is that norms or expectations often define close cross-gender friendships between nonkin as inappropriate, at least implicitly. This may take the form of the assumption that cross-gender friendships almost always involve an erotic element (Bell, 1981a; Block 1980; Rubin, 1985). Another possibility for males is that a man, having found a live-in female confidant, is less inclined to maintain a cross-gender friendship. For women, marriage has traditionally meant quitting work or curtailing professional activities, reducing the number of cross-gender friendships fused with work-related roles.

Marriage does not always lead to an immediate reduction in the number of cross-gender friendships claimed. Weiss and Lowenthal (1975) found that 66% of the newlyweds in their sample named someone of the opposite sex as one of their top three friends. A scant 12% of these subjects, however, named a person of the opposite sex as a closest friend. This suggests that a cross-gender friend named by a newlywed is most often part of a couples friendship held in common with her or his spouse. Findings extrapolated from a study of subjects aged 45 years and older (Booth & Hess, 1974) supported this possibility. Women who reported cross-gender friendships were likely to name persons met either at work or through their husbands as participants in couples friendships. Men claiming cross-gender friendships were likely to name persons met on the job, but not through their wives. Such friendships are likely to be circumscribed and casual. In Furman's (1986) study, cross-gender friendships in the work place were very low in strength or intensity. These findings, along with those related to dispositional differences, suggest that most cross-gender friendships could more aptly be considered what Kurth (1970) defined as "friendly relations."

In sum, structural factors associated with work or marital roles strongly affect cross-gender friendships. As such, they are largely a matter of the fusion of friendship with other roles. Thus it would be reasonable to expect the incidence of cross-gender friendship to vary rather widely from one stage or condition of adulthood to another. As we shall see, available evidence suggests that this is indeed the case.

Men's friendships through the preretirement years. Traditionally, men in our society have been occupied, if not preoccupied, with an activity-centered, relatively impersonal way of life with respect to both jobs or professions and avocational and recreational pursuits. For the most part, their friendships have been fused with the roles involved in these activities, and their social interactions have understandably been task oriented and goal directed. Thus for a long period of time structural factors have worked in harmony with dispositional factors in supporting the agentic kinds of same-gender friendships the average man is inclined to form and maintain.

For communal interaction, men are more inclined to turn to female friends (Block, 1980; Rubin, 1985) or to romantic partners, especially wives (Tognoli, 1980; Wright, 1985; Wright & Bergloff, 1984). Hess (1979) cited evidence, however, suggesting that working-class men may be reluctant to behave in clearly communal ways, even with their wives (see also Rubin, 1985).

Competitive connections may develop between men's friendships and other roles in middle age. Researchers have often found that men at this period often have fewer friends and less frequency of contact than those at younger ages (Huston & Levinger, 1978; Fischer, 1982; Fischer & Oliker, 1983; Reisman, 1981; Shulman, 1975; Verbrugge, 1983). Reisman (1981) suggested that the decreased number of friends and frequency of contact or both result from middle-aged men's greater attention to career development. In any case, the drop is not precipitous and, whatever else may be the cause, it does not appear to be the presence or absence of children in the family. Fischer and Oliker (1983) found that the total number of friends for married men under 36 was somewhat larger than that for married men from 36 through 64. Within these two groups, however, they found no difference for those who did and did not have children. Thus, with respect to the interaction of structural and dispositional factors, the friendship situation does not appear to change dramatically for men between early marriage and retirement.

Women's friendships in the preparenthood and parenthood years. The interplay of structural and dispositional factors in the friendships of most women from early marriage through middle age is more complex than that of men—and less harmonious. I have already discussed women's disposition to form communal friendships. This disposition apparently persists throughout the adult life cycle (Candy, Troll, & Levy, 1981; Goldman, Cooper, Aherne, & Corsini, 1981; Richardson, 1984; Weiss & Lowenthal, 1975). Communal friendships are characterized by confiding, supportiveness, and a highly personalized mutual concern. Therefore, unlike most agentic friendships, they are formed and maintained as ends in themselves. As such, women's communal friendships are not ordinarily fused with other roles and are very often competitive with them. Nevertheless, they sometimes facilitate the performance of presumably unrelated roles and can therefore be considered complementary to them.

Married women's traditionally greater responsibility for maintenance of the home and family probably has considerably less impact on their friendships in the preparenthood than in the parenthood years. In preparenthood, their preferred communal friendships would not be enhanced through fusion with other roles, but neither would they be hampered by competition. With parenthood, this situation changes. Popular and semiprofessional writings, as well as anecdotal observations, often contend that child-rearing responsibilities severely limit women's friendships (see, e.g., Brenton, 1974; Pogrebin, 1987). The findings of Fischer and Oliker (1983) supported this contention.

Although women's responsibilities, especially to their families, result in competitive connections between friendship and other roles, the communal friendships they do manage to maintain often provide complementary connections. The value of women's friendships in facilitating their performance of other roles is practically legendary. It is implicit in the content of much of women's talk (e.g., Aries & Johnson, 1983). It is explicit in the data of Rubin (1986) indicating that women are often able to interact more effectively with their husbands because of the support and advice of women friends. Hess (1979) observed that female friends commonly reinforce one another in carrying out their child-rearing responsibilities. Complementary connections figure significantly in the way friendships between women facilitate their performances in professional roles, especially in male-dominated settings (Hunter, Saleebey, & Shannon, 1983).

Women often form friendships that are fused with vocational, parental, and any number of other roles. These friendships are not, however, the communal kind that women are dispositionally inclined to develop. Furman's (1986) data indicated that women's same-gender friendships with workmates in academic departments were lacking with respect to both voluntary contact apart from the work setting and a personalized interest and concern. Gouldner and Strong (1987) found that a sample of upper-middle-class women aged 30 to 65 years identified some of their female associates as work friends and activity friends. The subjects generally regarded such associations as circumscribed and superficial. Sometimes, but not often, these associations developed into "real" (i.e., communal) friendships. In contrast, men are likely to regard such work friends and activity friends as real friends who, in fact, constitute the majority of their real friends.

Summary. In the years that researchers typically identify as young and middle adulthood, structural and dispositional factors operate harmoniously in the friendship situation of men. The fusion of friendship with work- and activity-related roles supports the development and maintenance of the agentic friendships men are dispositionally inclined to establish. For women, this is not the case. Roles associated with activities such as employment, home management, and child rearing often form a competitive connection with the communal friendships women are dispositionally inclined to develop. Even so, the communal friendships they are able to maintain appear to be related to other roles in a complementary way. Women do form friendships that are fused with work- and activity-related roles. Unlike men, however, they are not inclined to regard such associations as real friendships.

Gender Differences in the Friendships of Later Life

There is no question that changes in friendship accompany changes that occur with increasing old age per se. These age-related changes—including such factors as reduced resources, reduced mobility, declining energy, and increasing ill health—are explored in other chapters in this volume (Allan & Adams, this volume; Blieszner, this volume). My concern in the present chapter, however, is with the impact of structural and dispositional factors on gender differences in friendship. From this perspective, the onset of relevant structural changes does not necessarily coincide with the onset of old age, and it does not usually occur within the same age span for women and men.

For women, the crucial change is marked by the beginning of the empty nest or postparenthood years. Thus the age of onset could vary widely from one woman to the next (e.g., from early 40s to the late 50s) depending upon the number and timing of their children. Whatever the age of onset, postparenthood normally is accompanied by an appreciable reduction in obligations related to the parental role and correspondingly less competition between parental and other roles. Women in this situation should find themselves freer to follow their friendship disposition and devote more of their time and resources to existing communal friendships, and to forming new ones.

For men, the crucial change is marked by retirement and ordinarily occurs within an age range spanning the early 60s through the early 70s. For most men, retirement means flexibility and entails less competition between friendship and other roles. More important, however, retirement means the loss or weakening of friendships fused with work and associated activities. Given the overall predisposition of men to form agentic friendships, men are not likely to replace these lost friendships unless fresh pursuits bring new opportunities for fused friendships to fill the void left by retirement. Several studies cited by Dickens and Perlman (1981) and by Chown (1981) indicated that, as people age, they are not especially inclined to form new friendships. As old friendships are lost, for whatever reason, they are usually not replaced (see, e.g., Shulman, 1975). The findings of Fischer and Oliker (1983), however, suggested that this overall pattern is true for men but is not true, or at least is less true, for women.

In short, structural factors in later life work in harmony with, or at least not in competition with, women's dispositions to form communal friendships. In contrast, they work against men's dispositions to form agentic friendships that are fused with work and other activities. Next I consider some overall comparisons as a backdrop for developing capsule friendship scenarios for older women and men.

Gender differences in the number and kinds of friendships. Findings have been inconsistent concerning gender differences in the number of friendships and the frequency of contact with friends during old age. Studies finding more friends or more frequent contact for men were reported by Ferraro, Mutran, and Barresi (1984), Pihlblad and Adams (1972), and Powers and Bultena (1976). In contrast, Booth (1972) found a slightly greater number of friends for women than men aged 45 years and older. Fischer and Oliker (1983) reported that the number of friendships for men tended to shrink with age relative to the number for women. The relative increase for women began with postparenthood. In the oldest age group (65 years and older) women had more friends than men.

Researchers commonly have suggested that these inconsistent findings may result from varying criteria for friendship from one study to the next and especially to the possibility that women are often more restrictive about the kinds of acquaintances they will identify as friends (see, e.g., Dickens & Perlman, 1981). Another possibility is that researchers typically mark off later life in terms of years rather than status changes. From the present point of view, this could make a great deal of difference, especially considering the wide range of ages during which relevant changes might occur.

One point of high consensus is that older women are more likely than older men to have friends who are confidants, and their friendships are more likely to be close and intimate (Booth, 1972; Lowenthal & Haven, 1968; Powers & Bultena, 1976). I noted earlier that men in general tend to confine such close and emotionally supportive interaction to their wives or romantic partners. Available evidence indicates that this tendency continues into old age; men are likely to name their wives as their primary, and often their only, confidant (Lowenthal & Haven, 1968; Keith, Hill, Goudy, & Powers, 1984).

Another point of high consensus is that cross-gender friendships among the elderly are rare (see, e.g., Chown, 1981). There appear to be several reasons for this. First, as we have seen, cross-gender friendships are largely a matter of fusion with other roles, especially those related to employment. With retirement as well as generally curtailed activities, such fused friendships would be lost or weakened. Second, women tend to live longer than men, so there are relatively few older men available for cross-gender friendships (Adams, 1985; Chown, 1981). Third, older women may face normative restraints against pursuing friendships with men, primarily because they assume such relationships to be romantic (Adams, 1985). Fourth, attesting to the possible validity of the foregoing assumption, older widowed men are likely to remarry, but not to form cross-gender friendships (Cleveland & Gianturco, 1976).

The modal friendship scenario for older women. Closeness and intimacy in same-gender friendships appear to be as important for women in later life as ever, and perhaps more so (Richardson, 1984). In addition, older women find their same-gender friendships a source of feelings of prestige and power (Candy et al., 1981) and of mutual admiration (Goldman et al., 1981). In short, old age appears to be a period in which women's disposition to form and maintain communal friendships is continued and often intensified. At least one set of structural factors—those related to reduced competition of friendship with other roles—work in harmony with this disposition.

Another structural factor enhancing the importance of communal friendships for older women is that they, more often than men, face the prospect of widowhood. Partly because of the relative lack of older men and partly because of normative restraints, it is unlikely that a cross-gender friendship will fill whatever companionship void widowhood leaves. It is easy to agree with Hess (1979), who suggested that a virtually lifelong disposition to form communal relationships with a variety of significant others, including friends, leaves most older women with both the interpersonal skills and social adaptability to create friendship opportunities and make the most of them. Thus structural and dispositional factors interact in a way that make the modal friendship scenario for older women not only psychologically important, but personally satisfying.

The modal friendship scenario for older men. When retirement and the curtailed activities of later life lead to the reduction and loosening of friendship ties for men, most of them still have their primary confidant—their wives. They lose, however, the camaraderie that goes along with agentic friendships. This may be an especially telling loss for working-class men who tend not to have emotionally close and confiding relationships, even with their wives (Hess, 1979), and for whom camaraderie appears to constitute much of the essence of a friendship (Argyle & Furnham, 1983). It is probably the reduction, not the absence, of men's friendships in old age that is related to their psychological adjustment and subjective well-being. According to Tesch, Whitbourne, and Nehrke (1981), available evidence indicates that men without close friendships in their earlier years, unlike those who have them, are not adversely affected by their lack in old age.

Because women usually outlive their husbands, most older men continue the dispositional pattern of relying on their wives for communal interaction. As Hess (1979, p. 505) noted, however, this is an "all the eggs in one basket proposition." The minority of older men who become widowers are especially disadvantaged. Not only have they lost their primary confidant, they often do not have other interpersonal resources. They are not overly likely to have communal friendships, and their background of agentic relationships has typically failed to leave them with either the inclination or the social skills to develop them. It must be remembered that this is the modal pattern. Because it is modal, some widowers have close, supportive friendships. Others have the disposition and the ability to acquire them. Furthermore, as I have noted, an appreciable number of widowers will fill the relationship void by remarrying. All things considered, however, structural and dispositional factors interact in a way that makes the modal friendship scenario considerably less favorable for older men than for older women (see Allan & Adams, this volume).

SUGGESTIONS FOR FURTHER RESEARCH

With respect to research on aging and gender differences in adult friendships, a list of substantive problems in need of further study would probably not be endless, but it would be unmanageably long. Trying to identify the specific issues crying out for clarification through additional research might be futile; there are no specific issues not crying out for additional research. In any case, I am convinced that the problems demanding the lion's share of our creative effort are methodological rather than substantive. One might be well advised to carefully reread Adams's chapter (this volume) on conceptual and methodological issues. Her remarks concerning the importance of longitudinal studies are especially important. Any number of the age-related changes suggested by studies reviewed in the present chapter will remain at the level of sheer conjecture until either confirming or disconfirming longitudinal data are available. Is it really true, for example, that older men are adversely affected by the lack of friendships only if this lack represents a change from earlier years? Cross-sectional data cannot answer such questions, and retrospective data are suspect. As expensive, time consuming, and administratively difficult as they are, researchers need to give longitudinal studies very high priority in studies of aging and friendship.

As the present review attests, Adams's comments about the criterion problem are extremely pertinent. Until researchers give more painstaking attention to how they define or delimit friendships from one study to the next, it will be difficult to compare and integrate, and inconsistencies are bound to occur. Frankly, and perhaps immodestly, I have dealt with the criterion of friendship to my own satisfaction both conceptually (Wright, 1978) and methodologically (Wright, 1985). At least one investigator (Candy-Gibbs, 1982) has found this approach useful in exploring friendships in old age. My criterion is, however, embedded in a broader theoretical structure that many others may not find helpful. Thus it suffers from the possibility of restricted applicability as Adams discussed. The point is not, however, that we should strive for uniformity. The point is that each investigator should devote serious attention to deciding what her or his criterion is. I strongly recommend abandoning the common practice of using subjects' self-identified friendships or self-defined criteria as the sole, or even the major, relationship variable.

Finally, and more specifically, it may be instructive to study the psychological consequences and correlates of plain, unvarnished camaraderie—the joking, griping, teasing, story-swapping, interest-sharing, hobby-sharing, note-comparing kind of interaction that is part and parcel of many agentic friendships. This specific element of friendship has apparently been absorbed into our undifferentiated focus on activity centeredness. In our zeal to demonstrate the importance of personalism and emotional supportiveness in communal friendships, we seem to have overlooked the possibility that camaraderie may very often provide a functionally similar component in agentic friendships. If this is the case, then men who lose their agentic friendships in later life lose a great deal more than we have previously believed.

NOTE

1. I will gladly honor requests for an unpublished discussion of several facets of this problem.

REFERENCES

Adams, R. G. (1985). Normative barriers to cross-sex friendships for elderly women. *The Gerontologist*, *25*, 605-611.

Argyle, M., & Furnham, A. (1983). Sources of satisfaction and conflict in long-term relationships. *Journal of Marriage and the Family*, *45*, 481-493.

Aries, E. J., & Johnson, F. L. (1983). Close friendships in adulthood: Conversational content between same-sex friends. *Sex Roles*, *9*, 1183-1196.

Ashton, N. L. (1980). Exploratory investigation of perceptions of influences on best-friend relationships. *Perceptual and Motor Skills*, *50*, 379-386.

Bakan, D. (1966). *The duality of human existence*. Boston: Beacon.

Bell, R. R. (1981a). *Worlds of friendship*. Beverly Hills, CA: Sage.

Bell, R. R. (1981b). Friendships of women and men. *Psychology of Women Quarterly*, *5*, 402-417.

Block, J. D. (1980). *Friendship: How to give it, how to get it*. New York: Macmillan.

Booth, A. (1972). Sex and social participation. *American Sociological Review*, *37*, 183-192.

Booth, A., & Hess, E. (1974). Cross-sex friendship. *Journal of Marriage and the Family,* *36,* 38-47.

Brenton, M. (1974). *Friendship.* Briarcliff Manor, NY: Stein & Day.

Caldwell, M. A., & Peplau, L. A. (1982). Sex differences in same-sex friendships. *Sex Roles, 8,* 721-732.

Candy, S. G., Troll, L. E., & Levy, S. G. (1981). A developmental exploration of friendship functions in women. *Psychology of Women Quarterly, 5,* 456-472.

Candy-Gibbs, S. E. (1982). *The alleged inferiority of men's close interpersonal relationships: An examination of sex differences in the elderly widowed.* Paper presented at the Annual Scientific Meeting of the Gerontological Society of America, Boston.

Chown, S. M. (1981). Friendship in old age. In S. Duck & R. Gilmour (Eds.), *Personal relationships, Vol. 2: Developing personal relationships* (pp. 231-246). New York: Academic Press.

Cleveland, W., & Gianturco, D. T. (1976). Remarriage probability after widowhood, a retrospective method. *Journal of Gerontology, 31,* 99-103.

Davidson, S., & Packard, T. (1981). The therapeutic value of friendship between women. *Psychology of Women Quarterly, 5,* 495-510.

Dickens, W. J., & Perlman, D. (1981). Friendship over the life cycle. In S. Duck, & R. Gilmour, (Eds.), *Personal relationships, Vol. 2: Developing personal relationships* (pp. 91-122). London: Academic Press.

Ferraro, K. F., Mutran, E., & Barresi, C. M. (1984). Widowhood, health and friendship support in later life. *Journal of Health and Social Behavior, 25,* 246-259.

Fischer, C. S. (1982). *To dwell among friends: Personal networks in town and city.* Chicago: University of Chicago Press.

Fischer, C. S., & Oliker, S. J. (1983). A research note on friendship, gender and the life cycle. *Social Forces, 62,* 124-133.

Fischer, J. L., & Narus, L. R. (1981). Sex roles and intimacy in same and other sex relationships. *Psychology of Women Quarterly, 5,* 444-455.

Furman, L. G. (1986). *Cross-gender friendships in the workplace: Factors and components.* Unpublished doctoral dissertation, Fielding Institute.

Goldman, J. A., Cooper, P. E., Aherne, K., & Corsini, D. (1981). Continuities and discontinuities in the friendship descriptions of women at six stages of life. *Genetic Psychology Monographs, 103,* 153-167.

Gouldner, H., & Strong, M. S. (1987). *Speaking of friendship: Middle-class women and their friends.* New York: Greenwood.

Guinsburg, P. F. (1973). *An investigation of components of platonic and romantic heterosexual relationships.* Unpublished doctoral dissertation, University of North Dakota.

Hacker, H. M. (1981). Blabbermouths and clams: Sex differences in self disclosures in same-sex and cross-sex dyads. *Psychology of Women Quarterly, 5,* 385-401.

Hess, B. B. (1972). Friendship. In M. W. Riley, M. Johnson, & A. Foner (Eds.), *Aging and society* (pp. 357-393). New York: Russell Sage.

Hess, B. B. (1979). Sex roles, friendship, and the life course. *Research on Aging, 1,* 494-515.

Hill, C. T., & Stull, D. E. (1981). Sex differences in effects of social and value similarity in same-sex friendship. *Journal of Personality and Social Psychology, 41,* 488-502.

Hunter, M. S., Saleebey, D., & Shannon, C. (1983). Female friendships: Joint defense against power inequity. *Psychology: A Quarterly Journal of Human Behavior, 20,* 14-20.

Huston, T. L., & Levinger, G. (1978). Interpersonal attraction and relationships. In M. R. Rosenzweig & L. W. Porter (Eds.), *Annual review of psychology* (Vol. 29, pp. 115-156). Palo Alto, CA: Annual Review.

Johnson, F. L., & Aries, E. J. (1983). The talk of women friends. *Women's Studies International Forum, 6,* 353-361.

Keith, P. M., Hill, K., Goudy, W. J., & Powers, E. A. (1984). Confidants and well-being: A note on male friendship in old age. *The Gerontologist, 24,* 318-320.

Kurth, S. B. (1970). Friendship and friendly relations. In G. J. McCall (Ed.), *Social relationships* (pp. 136-170). Chicago: Aldine.

Lewis, R. W. (1978). Emotional intimacy among men. *Journal of Social Issues, 34,* 108-121.

Lowenthal, M. F., & Haven, C. (1968). Interaction and adaptation: Intimacy as a critical variable. *American Sociological Review, 33,* 20-30.

McAdams, D. P., Healy, S., & Kraus, S. (1984). Social motives and patterns of friendship. *Journal of Personality and Social Psychology, 47,* 828-838.

Narus, L. R., & Fischer, J. L. (1982). Strong but not silent: Reexamination of expressivity of the relationships of men. *Sex Roles, 8,* 159-168.

Pihlblad, C. T., & Adams, D. L. (1972). Widowhood, social participation and life satisfaction. *Aging and Human Development, 3,* 323-330.

Pogrebin, L. C. (1987). *Among friends.* New York: McGraw-Hill.

Powers, E. A., & Bultena, G. L. (1976). Sex differences in the friendships of old age. *Journal of Marriage and the Family, 38,* 739-747.

Reis, H. T., Senchak, M., & Solomon, B. (1985). Sex differences in the intimacy of social interaction: Further examination of potential explanations. *Journal of Personality and Social Psychology, 48,* 1204-1217.

Reisman, J. M. (1981). Adult friendships. In S. Duck & R. Gilmour (Eds.), *Personal relationships, Vol. 2: Developing personal relationships* (pp. 205-230). London: Sage.

Richardson, V. (1984). Clinical historical aspects of friendship deprivation among women. *Social Work Research and Abstracts, 20,* 19-24.

Rose, S. M. (1985). Same- and cross-sex friendships and the psychology of homosociality. *Sex Roles, 12,* 63-74.

Rubin, L. B. (1985). *Just friends.* New York: Harper & Row.

Rubin, L. B. (1986). On men and friendship. *Psychoanalytic Review, 73,* 165-181.

Shulman, N. (1975). Life-cycle variations in patterns of close relationships. *Journal of Marriage and the Family, 37,* 813-921.

Tesch, S. A. (1983). Review of friendship development over the life cycle. *Human Development, 26,* 266-276.

Tesch, S. A., & Martin, R. R. (1983). Friendship concepts of young adults in two age groups. *Journal of Psychology, 115,* 7-12.

Tesch, S. A., Whitbourne, S. K., & Nehrke, M. F. (1981). Social interaction and subjective well being of older men in an institutional setting. *International Journal of Aging and Human Development, 13,* 317-327.

Tognoli, J. (1980). Male friendship and intimacy over the life span. *Family Relations, 29,* 273-279.

Verbrugge, L. M. (1983). A research note on friendship contact: A dyadic perspective. *Social Forces, 62*, 78-83.

Walker, L. S., & Wright, P. H. (1976). Self-disclosure in friendship. *Perceptual and Motor Skills, 42*, 735-742.

Wall, S. M., Pickert, S. M., & Paradise, L. V. (1984). American men's friendships: Self-reports on meanings and changes. *Journal of Psychology, 116*, 179-186.

Weiss, L., & Lowenthal, M. F. (1975). Life-course perspective on friendship. In M. Thurnher & D. Chiraboga (Eds.), *Four stages of life* (pp. 48-61). San Francisco: Jossey-Bass.

Werner, C., & Parmalee, P. (1979). Similarity of activity preferences among friends: Those who play together stay together. *Social Psychology Quarterly, 42*, 62-66.

Williams, D. G. (1985). Gender, masculinity-femininity, and emotional intimacy in same-sex friendship. *Sex Roles, 12*, 587-600.

Winstead, B. A. (1986). Sex differences in same-sex friendships. In V. J. Derlega & B. A. Winstead (Eds.), *Friendship and social interaction* (pp. 81-97). New York: Springer-Verlag.

Winstead, B. A., & Derlega, V. J. (1984). *The therapeutic value of same-sex friendships.* Paper presented at the annual meeting of the Southwestern Psychological Association, New Orleans.

Wright, P. H. (1978). Toward a theory of friendship based on a conception of self. *Human Communication Research, 4*, 196-207.

Wright, P. H. (1982). Men's friendships, women's friendships and the alleged inferiority of the latter. *Sex Roles, 8*, 1-20.

Wright, P. H. (1985). The acquaintance description form. In S. Duck & D. Perlman (Eds.), *Understanding personal relationships: An interdisciplinary approach* (pp. 39-62). London: Sage.

Wright, P. H. (1988). Interpreting research on gender differences in friendship: A case for moderation and a plea for caution. *Journal of Social and Personal Relationships, 5*, 367-373.

Wright, P. H., & Bergloff, P. J. (1984). *The acquaintance description form and the comparative study of personal relationships.* Paper presented at the Second International Conference on Personal Relationships, Madison, WI.

Wright, P. H., & Crawford, A. C. (1971). Agreement and friendship: A close look and some second thoughts. *Representative Research in Social Psychology, 2*, 52-69.

Wright, P. H., & Keple, T. W. (1981). Friends and parents of a sample of high school juniors: An exploratory study of relationship intensity and interpersonal rewards. *Journal of Marriage and the Family, 43*, 559-570.

Yoon, G. H. (1978). The natural history of friendship: Sex differences in best friendship patterns. *Dissertation Abstracts, 39*(3-B), 1553.

10

Social Ties and Friendship
Patterns of Old Homeless Men

CARL I. COHEN

In an earlier chapter, Allan and Adams (this volume) suggested that friendship patterns are commonly governed by structural constraints. In other words, individuals dissimilarly located within a society are likely to generate different configurations and options of friendship. Allan and Adams noted that although people may have more choice about friendships than they do about many other relationships, "they are still nonetheless bound by social conventions that circumscribe their freedom of choice" (p. 46). Following from this structural perspective is the notion that definitions and characterizations of friendship vary greatly between groups as well as within groups. Class, age, race, sex, geography, culture, and individual psychological dispositions can affect the definition of friendship. Consequently, as Adams urged in her introductory chapter (this volume), researchers must become more self-conscious about their conceptual and methodological decisions.

In this chapter, I provide the reader with a concrete case illustration for addressing several of the theoretical and methodological issues raised in earlier chapters. Specifically, I look at older homeless men in order to demonstrate how their particular social and ecological niche

AUTHOR'S NOTE: This study was supported by NIMH Grants nos. ROL-MH37562 and H84-MH42443. I wish to thank Jay Sokolovsky, Jeanne Teresi, Douglas Holmes, Eric Roth, and Carole Lefkowitz for their assistance.

creates unique patterns of social interaction. In so doing, I review some of the methodological strategies that must be employed in examining marginal populations.

BACKGROUND

Historically, beginning with the development of industrial society, analysts have sought causes of homelessness generally within the individual rather than looking externally to the social arena. People typically viewed the homeless as shiftless, indolent, and morally depraved. The Protestant Reformation, in which the prevailing ethos was that material success in this world was a sign that one would be favored by God in the next, reinforced this notion. By the mid-twentieth century, this position acquired a scientific patina. In post-war America social scientists attempted to explain how in a country of great wealth and prosperity a person could wind up on skid row, an area that had become a receptacle for homeless men. A principal etiological theory that emerged from this period focused on these men's inept social abilities. Theorists contended that the skid row dweller is "under-socialized" (Pittman & Gordon, 1958; Strauss, 1946), "incompletely socialized" (Dunham, 1953), "disaffiliated" (Bahr, 1973; Bahr & Caplow, 1973), "unable to empathize" (Levinson, 1958), "retreatist" (Bendiner, 1961; Merton, 1949), or "lacking a need for attachments" (Vexliard, 1956). The following observation was characteristic of statements from this camp: "Skid Row seems to be composed largely of discontented individuals who live in semi-isolation, who have few if any close friends, and who survive by being suspicious of everybody" (Bogue, 1963, pp. 169-170). More recently, researchers have added a medical component—mental illness—to the list of explanatory factors. Nevertheless, they still portray the homeless of the 1980s as social nomads: "To talk with homeless people is to be struck by how alone most of them are. The isolation is most severe for the mentally ill" (Bassuk, 1984, p. 43).

By contrast, some writers have argued that skid row men replace former relations with new relations as they become progressively enculturated into the "skid row way of life" (Wallace, 1965, p. 141). Rooney (1976), for instance, claimed to confirm this replacement hypothesis, and he concluded that his findings "run counter to Vexliard's postulate of loss of need for meaningful personal relationships with increased exposure to the life of an outcast" (p. 87). Other investigators have observed that the men frequently coalesced into small groups, some permanent, most in flux, whose main focus was the procurement and consumption of alcohol (Jackson & Connor, 1953; Peterson & Maxwell, 1958; Rooney, 1961; Rubington, 1968; Wallace, 1968; Wiseman, 1979). These groups also served as a source of emotional and material support such as money, clothes, food, medical aid, and even intimate support. For example, Wiseman (1979, p. 38) noted that "although many of the studies . . . have referred to the Skid Row man as lonesome and undersocialized, any observer who spends any period of time on Skid Row will be struck by the general air of open conviviality there." Wiseman further reflected:

> In other parts of the city, the sidewalk is used by adults as a pathway between a point of origin and a point of destination so that it presents areas of continual, on-going movement. On Skid Row, however, the sidewalks are used as areas for conversing, drinking, watching traffic, and panhandling. As a result, the purposeful pedestrian gets a feeling of moving through a private outdoor area. . . . It is more comparable to some of the characteristic use of outdoor space that might be found on a college campus. (p. 38)

The origins of these seemingly divergent viewpoints have stemmed in part from the use of nonspecific terminology such as "isolate" or "disaffiliate." Thus, for example, although Bogue (1963) and Rooney (1976) found virtually equivalent levels of friendship among two similar populations of skid row dwellers, the former characterized them as "semi-isolates" whereas the latter asserted that skid row was "clearly . . . not a population of isolates" (p. 85). Most researchers, by failing to provide any non-skid row groups for comparison, have been especially predisposed toward such vague categorizations.

Perhaps more problematic has been the confusion created by the disparate methodological techniques. Nearly all the techniques involve either participant-observation or a limited choice sociometric approach. A major difficulty with sociometrics has been the use of subjective friendship as the sole measure of sociability (e.g., Blumberg, Shipley, & Moor, 1971; Bogue, 1963). Lowenthal and Robinson (1976) suggested that the difficulty with friendship studies is that there exists a wide disparity in percepts of friendship networks and definitions of friends by sex, socioeconomic status, and geographic location. Because investigators frequently have used the category of friend in questionnaires and interviews without adequately determining whether the concept is relevant or how the population under study interprets it, they have viewed individuals or populations who have few friends as "deviants." Nonetheless, members of some populations may reserve the term *friend* for very special individuals or even deem it irrelevant. That is, some people may consider virtually nobody a friend despite the existence of complex social relationships. Moreover, when researchers concentrate on subjectively important linkages, they tend to ignore weak ties that, nevertheless, may be relevant with respect to the provision of sustenance items such as money, food, and the like (Cohen & Rajkowski, 1982; Granovetter, 1973). Indeed, our studies of elderly who inhabit single-room occupancy (SRO) hotels indicated that in some instances the category of friendship was irrelevant in explaining social behavior and the ability to survive in the community (Cohen & Rajkowski, 1982; Sokolovsky & Cohen, 1981). These kinds of methodological concerns led White, Boorman, and Breiger (1976, p. 734) to wonder if "the stuff of social action is, in fact, waiting to be discovered in the network interstices that exist outside the normative constructs and attribute breakdowns of our everyday categories."

A second problem with sociometrics has been that in the examination of social and material exchange, investigators have posed questions in a predetermined manner rather than exploring concrete behaviors. Elsewhere, I have cautioned against asking questions such as, "How many friends do you have?" or "Do you lend money to anyone?" because they tend to produce data that are inconsistent with observed behavior (Sokolovsky & Cohen, 1981). Nash found that only one-third of her sample responded affirmatively to the question of whether they lend anyone money (Nash, cited in Bahr, 1973, p. 164). Other researchers, however, observed that money lending was ubiquitous (e.g., Jackson & Connor, 1953).

Although most investigators who have relied upon participant-observation have reported higher levels of social interaction and affectivity (e.g., Peterson & Maxwell, 1958; Rooney, 1961; Rubington, 1968; Wallace, 1965) than those using a sociometric approach, some have cited diminished levels of interaction (e.g., Bendiner, 1961; Vexliard, 1956). In order to understand the social structure and behavior of the study population, social scientists engaged in field research generally have observed and interviewed a limited number of informants and then have set out to delineate the enduring role relations and norms that guide these role performances. Boissevain (1974, p. 18) argued that this kind of approach creates "rule books about the ideal behaviour of the non-existent generalized 'average man.'" This approach tends to search for essences, that is, abstractions within the individual that can be generalized to all persons. Thus, for example, the essence of friendship is commonly considered to be "free choice and affectivity" (Litwak & Szelenyi, 1969, p. 469).

More specifically, with regard to skid row, often this has meant that investigators attempting to create these "rule books" have used either objective (external) criteria or subjective (internal) criteria of social interaction. The former approach entailed comparing the average skid row dweller with the average citizen; consequently, he was termed *retreatist* or *disaffiliated*. The latter approach relied upon self-reported norms. Unfortunately, as I contended above, self-reports of sociability may fail to correspond to actual behavior.

Another problem plaguing participant-observation has been the tendency to generalize behavior observed in a limited number of situations within a circumscribed community. Thus Vexliard (1956) depicted homeless men as having few emotional or material needs, whereas Jackson and Connor (1953) focused on bottle gangs and consequently found a great deal of emotional and material exchange. In neither study did the investigators systematically look at these men's ties to kin and nonkin living in the outside world.

A limitation of both sociometrics and participant-observation is their inability to capture quantitative and qualitative features of social formations simultaneously. For example, participant-observation provides good qualitative descriptions of human interactions, but does not provide a systematic basis of comparison with regard to quantitative features such as network size, configuration, and density. Conversely, sociometrics is more adept at accumulating quantitative data, but less successful in uncovering more qualitative features such as the content, direction, and meaning of transactions.

NETWORK ANALYSIS

The thesis proffered here is that one can comprehend friendship only on the basis of underlying social relations. One should not view it as inhering within the individual (e.g., a friend is loyal) or see it solely as a dyadic concept (e.g., exchange of items between two persons), although the latter is a marked scientific advance over the former. Because both conceptual views generally focus on the individual or the dyad apart from their surroundings, researchers have tended to consider revealed characteristics as capturing the essences of friendship and thus being universally valid for all friendships. On the contrary, however, researchers must examine friendship within a particular cultural and temporal setting. Friendship is made up of social interactions that are influenced by other social interactions at various levels (e.g., family, social groups, and institutions). Furthermore, those aspects of friendship that seemingly appear to be traits of individuals (e.g., age and education) actually reflect underlying social relationships. One way in which to begin to describe the manifestations of social relations is through the use of network analysis.

Over the past three decades, beginning with the studies by Barnes (1954) of a Norwegian parish and by Bott (1957) of a London neighborhood, the concept of a *social network* has evolved from a metaphorical term into a precisely defined analytic concept. In recent years, gerontologists have become increasingly interested in the heuristic value of network analysis (Cohen & Sokolovsky, 1980; Cohen, Teresi, & Holmes, 1985; Snow & Gordon, 1980). Mitchell (1969, p. 2) provided a good definition of a social network as "a special set of linkages among a set of persons with the . . . property that the characteristics of these linkages as a whole may be used to interpret the social behavior of the persons involved." Researchers can study all social forms, such as institutions and events, in terms of connections among individuals both directly and indirectly involved.

Diagrammatically, a network is similar to a communication circuit: It indicates that certain persons are in touch with one another. More significant in terms of research, investigators must delineate the content as well as the form of network; that is, they must establish empirically the nature of the transactions flowing in these channels. In so doing, they can regard the personal network as a support system involving the "giving and receiving of objects, services, social and emotional supports defined by the receiver and the giver as necessary or at least helpful in maintaining a style of life" (Lopata, 1975, p. 35; see also Crohan & Antonucci, this volume). In the remainder of this chapter, I illustrate how the various methodological and theoretical issues that I have enumerated above can be addressed through the use of network analysis techniques.

OVERVIEW OF STUDY METHODS

The site for the study was the world's most renowned skid row: the Bowery. The Bowery is a two-way street running for 16 blocks in lower Manhattan, bounded by Chinatown on the south and East Greenwich Village on the north. The actual skid row section encompasses a somewhat larger area of side streets and avenues running parallel to the street, the Bowery. At the time of this research (1982-1983), approximately 3,500 persons lived on the Bowery, of whom 2,500 were in the flophouses. Each flophouse sheltered between 34 and 554 men on a given night. Within the flophouses, the men were encased in 4' by 7' cubicles with a bed, a locker, a night table, and whatever personal possessions the occupant could squeeze into his space. Each cubicle was separated from the adjoining one by a thin wall that extended only part way to the ceiling, the resultant space filled with a 2-foot wide strip of chicken wire. In the ticket hotels (hotels used by the Men's Shelter) there were usually several large dormitories on various floors. The dormitories were dimly lit, foul-smelling, squalid, crowded hovels consisting of several dozen cots, frequently covered with soiled sheets and infested with lice or chiggers.

The objective of this research was to interview a cross section of men aged 50 and over living on the Bowery. In the United States, most people do not consider 50 to be very old but on skid row by age 50 many of the men look and act like men 10 to 20 years older (Bogue, 1963). Roscoe (1969) recommended the use of a sample size that is about one-tenth as large as the parent population. Therefore, the goal was to interview a minimum of 10% of the men aged 50 or over. Our research team consisted of a geriatric psychiatrist, an anthropologist, the administrator of a senior lunch program in a local service agency, and four college educated interviewers. Based on data from the New York City Human Resource Administration, interviews of service providers, and surveys of all flophouse managers or clerks, we estimated that there were 3,500 men living in the flophouses, in apartments, and on the surrounding streets, of whom 2,700 were aged 50 and over.

The final sample consisted of 281 men, of whom 195 were not street dwellers (177 lived in flophouses, 18 in apartments) and 86 were. This sample was not statistically different from our estimates of the overall Bowery population, although it did have a slight overrepresentation of street men and slight underrepresentation of flophouse men. The sample included men living in all 12 flophouses and the three missions that still remained on the Bowery. The mean age of the respondents was 62 years (range 50-80 years) and 69% were white. The men who did not live on the street were somewhat older and were proportionately more likely to be whites than the street men (63 years versus 59 years of age; 73% versus 59% white), which reflected the estimates of the demography of the area.

We used two methodological approaches: (a) a traditional anthropological technique of participant observation and intensive interviewing of several representative Bowery men and (b) semistructured questionnaires. The latter consisted of two instruments: the Comprehensive Assessment and Referral Evaluation (CARE) and the Network Analysis Profile (NAP). The CARE assesses levels of physical and psychiatric health and the socioeconomic needs of geriatric populations (Gurland et al., 1977). The NAP, also relevant for geriatric populations (Sokolovsky & Cohen, 1981), is a semistructured instrument that examines several fields of social interaction: respondent-hotel linkages, respondent-outside nonkin linkages, respondent-kin linkages, respondent-hotel staff linkages, and respondent-agency staff linkages. The social network included persons if they were in contact with the respondent during the previous 3 months (the past 12 months for outside nonkin and kin). The NAP generated 20 social network variables, and these were factor analyzed into two social network scales made up of 14 of the variables. Among the network variables that we examined were structural measures, for example, size (informal and formal linkages), number of clusters (groups of three or more persons in contact with each other), number of large clusters (cluster of five or more members), and network degree (average number of linkages per network member). We also addressed interactional measures, for example, mean exchanges per network member, sustenance aid (exchanges of food, money, medical aid), number of informal linkages involving two or more exchanges, number of formal linkages involving two or more exchanges, importance, intimacy, understanding, availability for help, and length of linkage. In addition, we constructed a scale based on contact with various institutions/agencies (e.g., stores, missions, churches). The interrater reliability of the NAP was .77.

Based on earlier unpublished research we were able to create a comparison group of 12 community-residing men aged 55 and over who had completed the Network Analysis Profile. Their mean age was 67 years, they were all white, they had completed nearly 16 years of education, and two-thirds were still married.

RESULTS OF THE ANALYSIS

Overall Contacts

Virtually all of the earlier estimates of skid row sociability have been based on personal observation of the men, and many observers have tended to use an ideal societal type as a comparison group (e.g., a steadily employed married man with several children in frequent contact with parents, siblings, and others). Thus, in 1946, Strauss described skid rowers as lonely, undersocialized men with no close friends. In the mid-fifties, Levinson (1958) wrote that social contacts were on a "very low level," and Dunham (1953) described skid row dwellers as "incompletely socialized" men who exhibited a "high degree of social isolation." Beginning in the 1960s researchers used more quantitative measures of social interaction, but in general, these were gross measures that focused on "friends" (Bogue, 1963) or "persons they conversed with" (e.g., Bahr & Caplow, 1973).

As noted above, however, investigators have interpreted the data according to different normative criteria. With the exception of Bahr and Caplow (1973), none of the investigators had community samples available for comparison. Depending on the sampling technique and phraseology that the researchers used, they found the percentage of men having friends to range from 33% (Nash, cited in Bahr, 1973) to 67% (Bahr & Caplow, 1973). Bahr and Caplow also found that 53% of the men had conversed with six or more persons on the previous day and that 49% of the men knew the names of more than five neighbors. Importantly, when the authors compared these findings with other low-income men, they were compelled to modify their earlier assumptions: "The Bowery man's history is less distinctive than formerly supposed with respect, for example, to marginality, or undersocialization" (Bahr & Caplow, 1973, p. 312).

Our research using social network techniques has further dispelled the notion that these men are total isolates or loners. Although Bowery men were not total isolates, they were somewhat isolated relative to the comparison group of elderly community men. The Bowery men had 8.5 overall contacts versus 11.1 among the community men. Although the difference in the total number of contacts was not statistically significant, the difference between the two populations in the number of informal linkages (kin and nonkin) was significant. Bowery men had 6.4 informal ties versus 10.8 among the community men. Also, the street men had one-third fewer overall contacts than did those who lived in hotels and shelters (9.6 versus 6.0 linkages); street men also had one-third fewer informal contacts (7.2 versus 4.8 linkages). These differences were statistically significant. Although small, the Bowery man's social world was a highly active one, and was a product of his ecological niche. The Bowery men tended to see their contacts about two-thirds more frequently than did the community men (i.e., the Bowery men saw their contacts 3.6 times per week). The flophouse men were especially apt to interact regularly, perhaps because the lodging house with its communal spaces served as a focal point of interaction. Nonetheless, street men also saw their contacts quite often as well.

Despite the modest degree of socializing found among the Bowery men, a few were nearly complete loners: 5% had only one linkage and an additional 7% had only two ties. Perhaps because the flophouses tended to foster interaction, relative isolation was more common on the street: 9% of the street men had only one linkage and an additional 11% had only two linkages. Among those who were most isolated, their stated reasons for their social withdrawal came from negative experiences in the past such as failed loan repayments or theft of one's belongings: "People are more trouble than they're worth. Ya think they're your friends then next thing ya know your shoes are gone. Living on the street is easier because you can stay away from everyone if ya want to." Another man remarked, "I stay alone because other men are trouble. They could be your friend one minute and your enemy the next." Given the frequency of untoward social encounters it is surprising that more of the men were not isolates.

For some men their isolation was a result of psychological problems. One interviewer described such a man:

> "Mr. Thomas" was an obviously depressed man struggling with his alcoholism and his slowly descending life. He is on welfare and has a hard time meeting necessary expenses. He has a bad arthritic back that causes him pain and discomfort and prevents him from working. He was rather somber and introverted during the interview. He hasn't had a drink for two weeks and is in the AA program at the Bowery Residents' Committee. He is an isolated man who, when he drinks, drinks alone in his room "until the walls start to close in" and he has to get out no matter what. In his depressions he often spends days at a time in his room eating out of cans and sleeping. It doesn't seem that he has anyone he can count on and he is pessimistic about the future.

Paradoxically, although we found several depressed alcoholics such as Mr. Thomas who drank alone and tended to be loners, those men who didn't drink at all were also apt to be more isolated. As one respondent remarked, "I think I have trouble making friends because I don't drink."

Earlier studies asserted that homeless men lacked ability to share with others (Strauss, 1946). Yet of those researchers who have acknowledged the existence of skid row social formations, most have been impressed by the key role that sharing plays in the maintenance of social ties. Peterson and Maxwell (1958) declared that reciprocity and sharing were the norms of skid row life. Men commonly helped each other with money, avoiding the police, finding places to sleep, caring for physical infirmities, and obtaining a drink. Spradley (1970) pointed out that friends are defined not only as persons one travels with, flops with, or shares a jug with, but also in terms of the kind of reciprocity that is involved in doing favors rather than hustling.

We found reciprocity to be especially keen among the Bowery street men who had a mean directionality score of 2.06 (reciprocal = 2; dependency = 3; helping = 1); Bowery men who did not live on the street showed a slight tendency toward increased dependency on others with a mean directionality score of 2.13. General community elderly men had mean scores of 2.17. By contrast, older men living in SRO hotels evidenced the most dependency with their mean directionality score being 2.31 (Cohen, Sokolovsky, Teresi, & Holmes, 1988), which was significantly different from the scores of the Bowery men.

For men who were drinkers, a common element of an important social relation was counting on that person to watch out for them when they were drunk. Many men knew they would drink themselves into senselessness and sometimes end up sprawled out in the street. Consequently, they tried to find someone whom they trusted and would not take advantage of such a situation. "Ken" and "Ed" had such a relationship; it had developed slowly over the last few years. Ed remembered several episodes when he "literally carried Kenny back to his room when he was too drunk." He explained, "I'd take him home and put him to bed. Then I'd take his pants off, hang them up." Ed would tell him, "Here's your wallet and your money. It's in your pants. Make sure you lock that damn door when I leave." And he'd stand there to make sure he'd click the lock. And then Ed would say, "Okay, Kenny. I'm goin' downstairs." "Good-night Ed," he'd whisper.

Group formations were a common part of Bowery life; five out of six men were enmeshed in at least one group formation (i.e., three or more men who knew each other). During our interviews, we encountered various structures and functions of group activities. Some were small groupings of two, three, or four men who might sleep together. In recent years with the escalation of violence perpetrated on older skid row men more groups were forming initially as a protective unit and coming together largely at night. For example, we encountered one group of men who slept together—two on one bench, two on the adjacent bench. There also were larger groups of five or six men who panhandled together, drank together, fed and cared for each other.

Although "bottle gangs" are usually transient, many street groups were composed of men who had known each other for many years. Although relationships oscillated over the years, the overall mean length of acquaintance among street men was nearly eight years. Such groups often provided the men with some emotional and material support in addition to alcohol. In a few instances, group formation revolved around father figures who provided assistance to street men. For example, "Roscoe" was a 75-year-old former street person who had acquired his own apartment and served as the superintendent of the building. He allowed men to sleep in the building's basement in inclement weather.

We employed several empirical measures of group formation. First, we looked at the number of clusters (i.e., respondent plus two other men) that each man was engaged in. Bowery men averaged 1.4 clusters; 83% of the men were enmeshed in at least one cluster and 44% were engaged in two or more clusters. Moreover, nearly half of the men were engaged in clusters of five or more men, which reflected the large groups formed around drinking, food programs, and hotel lobbies. By contrast, community men were engaged in twice as many clusters, but only one-third were engaged in large clusters of five or more men. Thus we found that the community men's social world consisted of two to three small clusters, whereas the Bowery men's social world consisted of one to two clusters, with one cluster usually being quite large and involving a substantial portion of their social network. This finding was also evident in our empirical measures of overall network interconnectivity: Bowery men had approximately twice the number of interconnections among their network members as the community men.

The lodging house setting, bottle gangs, communal lunches, and other activities tended to promote considerable group behavior among men that apparently endured into longer lasting associations. The Bowery men reported that 68% of their linkages could be "counted on for help"; this illustrates the importance of informal social supports. Moreover, a substantial percentage of Bowery men indicated that they would initially go to their informal network system (e.g., hotel nonkin, outside nonkin, kin) if they needed help with cash (54%), food (25%), shopping (49%), or they were sick (35%).

The Bowery man's social world reflected an adaptation to the needs of his environment. Thus in comparing Bowery men with elderly community men among whom only 17% had any formal agency ties and only 5% had any regular personal relationships that involved exchange of sustenance items (food, money, medical aid), we found that more than three-fifths of the Bowery men's relationships involved exchange of sustenance items and two-thirds of them used formal agencies; therefore, instrumentality in social relations was indeed high.

Friendships and Intimacy

One of the most controversial issues in the study of homeless men's social relations concerns the degree of intimacy in them. Theorists have had three opinions. One group of theorists viewed these men as socially inept and therefore unable to establish any social ties, either instrumental or affective (e.g., Bogue, 1963; Dunham, 1953; Levinson, 1958; Strauss, 1946; Vexliard, 1956). A second group of theorists recognized the presence of skid row social ties, but asserted that they are essentially devoid of intimacy (Bahr, 1973; Blumberg et al., 1971; Jackson & Connor, 1953; Rooney, 1961). The last group of theorists claimed that homeless men are capable of forming intimate as well as instrumental relationships (Peterson & Maxwell, 1958; Rooney, 1976).

We found a considerably more complex social world than most writers have depicted. The men generally had a hierarchy of categorizations of relationships. For example, men described the difference between *acquaintance, associate,* and *friend*: An associate is someone who is more that just a casual acquaintance. It is someone with whom one sits and talks. A casual acquaintance is someone one says "hello" to and then may not see for another week. A friend goes out of his way to help a person, and one is more intimate with him. As one older man encapsulated it, "There's limitations to what you'd say and do with an associate where you'd go all out to help a friend."

Another man based friendship on how he was treated when he was sick:

Well they are the only ones who ever come to the hospital and ever done anythin' for me. They came twice. They gave me two packs of cigarettes, some money, and a small bottle of gin. If people come and see ya I figure they must like ya 'cause why waste your time going to the hospital to see somebody if you don't like 'em? So I got some good friends that's all.

Often men denied the possibility of real friends existing on the Bowery and encompassed all relationships with the term *associate*, differentiating the importance of a linkage with phrases such as "casual associate" versus "strong associate." It is as if those who were no longer capable of having friends but only of having associates perceived themselves as living outside of the normal world of regular human relationships and communities. For the most part, older Bowery men represent a classic case of "spoiled identity." They are regarded by the public as worthless bums and to a large extent they have internalized this societal evaluation. In this respect many see themselves as socially terminal. This was expressed clearly by a 71-year-old retired painter who stated an axiom of the street:

Here, you can't have friends when you're old, old people don't have friends, you only have real friends from your childhood. If they are lost, friends are gone, and you just have some associates.

The cultural idiosyncrasies of skid row are most apparent in some of the men's notions of friendship and intimacy. For example, they did not share intimate thoughts with approximately two-fifths of persons in their informal nonkin network whom they had rated as good and best friends. On the other hand, they claimed to share such intimate thoughts with 10% of nonkin contacts whom they did not consider to be friends. Moreover, they stated that 55% of these nonfriends understood their problems, that one-third were persons who could be "counted on," and that one-fourth were important to them. Likewise, with respect to material assistance, friendship classification did not necessarily adumbrate expected behavior. Hence, among informal nonkin contacts considered good and best friends, 43% and 37% did not help with financial aid or food, respectively. Conversely, 25% of nonfriends had provided them with money or loans, and 24% had offered assistance with food.

In contrasting the Bowery men with aging community men, we found that 44% of the Bowery men categorized their contacts as "very good" or "best" friends whereas 64% of the community men did. Similarly, two-fifths of the Bowery men regarded relationships as intimate, whereas the community men similarly rated four-fifths of their linkages. And though 77% of the Bowery men claimed to have at least one intimate, they were not necessarily persons to whom one could unburden their problems; 47% of the men claimed to have no one to talk to about their problems. Two-thirds said that they usually kept problems to themselves. By contrast, only one in eight community men lacked someone to unburden his problems or reported keeping problems to himself. One elderly Bowery hotel man described his interaction with his "best friend":

> We rarely talk about deep stuff or confide in each other. Most is just run-of-the-mill conversation in the flophouse. We really never have anything that's really intelligent. I don't go to anybody to talk about deep things. I solve my own problems. I solve my problems myself or live with 'em.

On the other hand, the men felt that nearly three-fourths of their contacts "understood their problems." Therefore, I propose that Bowery men had an intermediate level of intimacy. In other words, their levels of intimacy were not as intense as community men, but their relationships were not devoid of feeling and empathy.

The resistance to forming very close human relationships belies a seemingly easy conviviality that many writers have commented on and that is still easy to observe. As members of our research team discovered, someone arriving on the Bowery with a week's growth of facial hair, and wearing old jeans and a tee shirt is readily accepted as a member of the society of "down and outers." This instant comraderie, however, is very shallow with regard to the degree of interpersonal exchange that it readily permits. Buying a bottle of Thunderbird wine for a group of three men one has just met might entitle one to share in the next bottle bought by someone else but it will not mean you can inquire as to their actual names or what they were doing before landing on the Bowery. The men here accept the idea of skid row being a refuge area where normative expectations of the outside society toward family and work obligations do not obtain. Having failed in their non-Bowery lives, any probing into this other part of their past involves a violation of a sacred cultural norm. It usually evokes an angry response that assures the ostracism of the transgressor. In *Ironweed*, William Kennedy (1984), pp. 23-24) vividly depicted the ambiguity of these men's relationships:

By their talk to each other they understood that they shared a belief in the brotherhood of the desolate; yet in the scars of their eyes they confirmed that no such fraternity had ever existed, that the only brotherhood they belonged to was the one that asked that enduring question: How do I get through the next twenty minutes?

Interestingly, neither intimacy nor being rated as a "very important" contact were related statistically to length of acquaintance. Length of acquaintance and mean proportion of sustenance ties (food, money, medical exchange) were modestly, significantly associated. Therefore, long-term linkages may help with material support, but they may not necessarily engender trust or intimacy. Although the overall length of the informal linkages that Bowery men had was somewhat longer than might be expected (7 years), it was substantially shorter than the community men had who had mean length of acquaintance of 29 years. The transience of relationships was reflected by the fact that nearly one-fifth of the men reported that a close friend had died or moved away in the past year. Nonetheless, as with most our findings, there were numerous exceptions. One 61-year-old man had two men with whom he had been friendly for over 40 years, and it was these men to whom he turned after he had been robbed of all of his money.

Kin Versus Nonkin Support

Whereas earlier investigators such as Wallace (1968, p. 146) went so far as to argue that homeless men are kinless "by definition," our research and work by Bahr (1973) in Philadelphia and Bahr and Caplow (1973) in New York City have indicated that these men are relatively kinless rather than totally kinless. In our Bowery research we found that approximately one-fourth of the social networks of men who lived on and off the street were composed of kin contacts; 65% of the men who did not live on the street and 55% of the street men had at least one kin contact. In absolute numbers, the men who lived off the street had approximately one more kin contact. Perhaps living in a hotel fostered a stability that allowed for more contact (e.g., letters, telephone in lobby, and so on). For example, one older man wrote to his brother "about every second week, and his brother calls the other week." Of course, 62% of Bowery men who reported having at least one current kin contact is far below the 92% of community men having such contacts. Moreover, in absolute numbers, community men had more than twice the number of kin contacts (4.5 versus 2.0).

For skid row men, there was little expectation that relatives would provide any material support. Roughly half of the community men indicated that they would go to kin if they needed cash, food, medication, or were ill, or needed shopping done. In contrast, fewer than 1 in 30 Bowery men would rely on kin for addressing these problems. The one exception was needing cash, where one in eight Bowery men indicated that they would contact kin. As noted above, for most of these problems, Bowery men would be much more apt to contact nonkin.

Despite the lack of material assistance from kin, Bowery men still reserved the most intense emotional feelings for family members, leading some observers to suggest that for many men, "family still comes first." The following excerpt from an interviewer's notes illustrated this phenomenon.

> "Mr. Daniels" is a very depressed and tearful 63-year-old black man who is currently homeless and sleeping on the streets. His wife died in May and the situation with his step-daughter and step-grandson is so bad that he would rather be on the street than with them. He is currently very depressed and occasionally hears the voice of his dead wife.

SUMMARY AND IMPLICATIONS

Previous research on homeless men has (a) used nonspecific terminology, (b) lacked comparison groups, (c) used limited-choice and predetermined response items, (d) relied excessively on external norms, (e) relied excessively on self-report, (f) generalized behavior from a few situations, and (g) sacrificed qualitative for quantitative data or vice versa. In this chapter, I have illustrated how researchers can profitably employ network analysis to overcome the methodological difficulties outlined above. Utilizing a network method, I have been able to address a variety of questions concerning the breadth and depth of these men's sociability, friendship, and intimacy.

Specifically, many older homeless men subdivided their relationships into friend, associate, and acquaintance, unlike the general population, which tends to dichotomize relationships into friends and acquaintances. Moreover, friends within the skid row culture did radically different things (e.g., providing food, money, and other material supports) than friends of older men in the general community. Among the skid row men the correlation between friendship and intimacy was relatively low, suggesting that friendship was often not a matter of choice but of availability. Perhaps, among those friends considered intimates, choice played more of a role.

Using external norms of friendship would have overlooked many of the key interactions of these men, and using only their self-reported categorizations of friendship also would have missed important interactions. For example, Bowery men considered one in ten nonfriends to be intimates and one-fourth of nonfriends to be important. By not imposing any prior assumptions about friendships, the network approach made it possible to uncover important behaviors that cut across traditional boundaries or that did not fit the modal patterns of the population under study.

The network method, by avoiding the imposition of fixed, a priori categories, provides three levels of analysis. First, through statistical analysis, it can describe general (modal) patterns of friendship for the population. Second, it can describe those patterns of social interaction that do not fit the general patterns (e.g., intimates who are not friends). Finally, it can move from the general to the particular. It enables investigators to examine the interactions of specific individuals and to determine the role that network members play in their material and emotional life. It further allows for the exploration of how general sociocultural patterns mix with personal biographies to generate the unique social matrix of each individual. Also, work at the individual network level can have important clinical significance. Elsewhere, my colleagues and I have shown that support networks significantly influence mental and physical well-being (Cohen et al., 1985).

The network approach also enables an examination of individuals across life situations. Much of today's literature and mass media depict street persons within a limited perspective (e.g., on a park bench, on a street corner) and assume that they must be total isolates. Network assessment, however, in tandem with observations on these men's daily routines, has helped refine this perspective. Elsewhere, my colleagues and I have shown that even those older homeless men who have psychotic symptoms or histories of psychiatric hospitalization are rarely isolated (Cohen, Teresi, & Holmes, 1988). In fact, they had nearly identical scores a nonpsychotic homeless men on various social network measures.

Use of the Network Analysis Profile enabled us to work with a large sample, to obtain detailed information about the respondents and their interactions within their networks, and to develop a broad range of social indices. Thus we were able to establish meaningful generalizations about the sample as well as being able to identify exceptions to these general trends. Traditional anthropological network techniques have been successful at providing detailed descriptions, but sample sizes have been small. For example, working in Malta, Boissevain (1974) identified social networks of up to 1,751 persons. Nonetheless, this level of elaboration limited him to a sample of only two subjects. Conversely, sociologists have generated considerably larger samples but have often sacrificed detail. The NAP seemingly offers a good alternative to the antipodal positions of the anthropological and sociological techniques.

Finally, having used a network approach we can more easily resolve the debate among researchers as to whether homeless men are sociable or not. Clearly, our investigative methods have demonstrated that these men are not complete isolates nor incapable of intimacy and complex social formations. Moreover, they are able to enlist the support of their compeers to help fulfill their daily needs. On the other hand, skid row dwellers have fewer social ties and fewer intimates than their aged counterparts in the general population. Hence the contradictory statements in the literature regarding skid row sociability may have depended on the perspective of the investigator. Because the skid row inhabitant is not inept at manipulating his social world, researchers who have studied skid row from a process or situational perspective were able to discern a panoply of interactive phenomena. On the other hand, by standards of the general population, the skid row man's social world is relatively small and constricted. It is not difficult to see how writers who have tried to portray the skid row resident from a more normative perspective would be apt to view him as isolated and as having a detached need for others. As Wiseman (1979) suggested, normative theories tend to view these men as pathological because they are being compared with middle-class living arrangements. Thus the present analysis lends strong support for a structural perspective on friendship (see Allan & Adams's chapter, this volume).

Although this chapter has focused primarily on older homeless men, the methods have broad implications. Because our work and the work of others (e.g., Allan, 1977; Blau, 1961; Bott, 1957) tend to affirm a structural perspective on friendship, it follows that investigators cannot easily generalize notions of friendship across populations. I have proposed a minimum of seven items that must be considered before attempting to characterize the social matrix of a particular population, especially those on the margin. By addressing these items, researchers can use network analysis to induce percepts of friendship and to delineate other important social patterns within a population.

REFERENCES

Allan, G. (1977). Class variations in friendship patterns. *British Journal of Sociology, 28,* 389-393.
Bahr, H. (1973). *Skid row: An introduction to disaffiliation.* New York: Oxford University Press.
Bahr, H. M., & Caplow, T. (1973). *Old men drunk and sober.* New York: New York University Press.
Barnes, J. A. (1954). Class and committees in Norwegian island parish. *Human Relations, 7,* 39-58.
Bassuk, E. L. (1984). The homelessness problem. *Scientific American, 251,* 40-45.
Bendiner, E. (1961). *The Bowery man.* New York: Thomas Nelson.
Blau, Z. S. (1961). Structural constraints on friendship in old age. *American Sociological Review, 26,* 429-439.
Blumberg, L. M., Shipley, T. E., & Moor, J. O. (1971). The skid row man and the skid row status community. *Quarterly Journal of Studies on Alcohol, 32,* 909-941.
Bogue, D. J. (1963). *Skid row in American cities.* Chicago: University of Chicago Press.
Boissevain, J. (1974). *Friends of friends.* New York: St. Martin's.
Bott, E. (1957). *Family and social networks.* London: Tavistock.
Cohen, C. I., & Rajkowski, H. (1982). What's in a friend? Substantive and theoretical issues. *The Gerontologist, 22,* 261-266.
Cohen, C. I., & Sokolovsky, J. (1980). Social engagements versus isolation: The case of the aged in SRO hotels. *The Gerontologist, 20,* 36-44.
Cohen, C. I., & Sokolovsky, J. (1983). Toward a concept of homelessness among aged men. *Journal of Gerontology, 38,* 81-89.
Cohen, C. I., Sokolovsky, J., Teresi, J., & Holmes, D. (1988). Gender, networks, and adaptation among an inner-city population. *Journal of Aging Studies, 2,* 45-56.
Cohen, C. I., Teresi, J., & Holmes, D. (1985). Social networks, stress, adaptation, and health. *Research on Aging, 7,* 409-431.
Cohen, C. I., Teresi, J., & Holmes, D. (1988). The mental health of old homeless men. *Journal of the American Geriatrics Society, 36,* 492-501.
Dunham, H. (1953). *Homeless men and their habitats: A research planning report.* Detroit: Wayne State University.
Granovetter, M. S. (1973). The strength of weak ties. *American Journal of Sociology, 78,* 1360-1380.
Gurland, B. J., Kuriansky, J. B., Sharpe, L., Simon, R., Stiller, P., & Birkett, P. (1977). The Comprehensive Assessment and Referral Evaluation (CARE): Rationale, development, and reliability. *International Journal of Aging and Human Development, 8,* 9-42.
Jackson, J. D., & Connor, R. (1953). The skid row alcoholic. *Quarterly Journal of Studies on Alcohol, 14,* 468-486.

Kennedy, W. (1984). *Ironweed*. New York: Penguin.

Levinson, B. M. (1958). Some aspects of the personality of the native-born white homeless man as revealed by the Rorschach. *Psychiatric Quarterly Supplement, 32*, 278-286.

Litwak, E., & Szelenyi, I. (1969). Primary group structures and their functions: Kin, neighbors, and friends. *American Sociological Review, 34*, 465-481.

Lopata, H. (1975). Support systems of the elderly: Chicago of the 1970's. *The Gerontologist, 15*, 34-41.

Lowenthal, M. F., & Robinson, B. (1976). Social networks and isolation. In R. H. Binstock & E. Shanas (Eds.), *Handbook of aging and the social sciences* (pp. 432-456). New York: Van Nostrand Reinhold.

Merton, R. K. (1949). *Social theory and social structure*. Glencoe, IL: Free Press.

Mitchell, J. (1969). *Social networks in urban situations*. Manchester: University of Manchester Press.

Peterson, W. J., & Maxwell, M. A. (1958). The skid road "wino." *Social Problems, 5*, 308-316.

Pittman, D. J., & Gordon, T. W. (1958). *Revolving door: A study of the chronic police case inebriate*. Glencoe, IL: Free Press.

Rooney, J. (1961). Group processes among skid row winos: A reevaluation of the undersocialization hypothesis. *Quarterly Journal of Studies on Alcohol, 22*, 444-460.

Rooney, J. (1976). Friendship and disaffiliation among the skid row population. *Journal of Gerontology, 31*, 82-88.

Roscoe, J. T. (1969). *Fundamental research statistics*. New York: Holt, Rinehart, & Winston.

Rubington, E. (1968). The bottle gang. *Quarterly Journal of Studies on Alcohol, 29*, 943-955.

Sokolovsky, J., & Cohen, C. I. (1981). Toward a resolution of methodological dilemmas in network mapping. *Schizophrenia Bulletin, 7*, 109-116.

Snow, D. L., & Gordon, J. B. (1980). Social networks analysis and intervention with the elderly. *The Gerontologist, 20*, 463-467.

Spradley, J. P. (1970). *You owe yourself a drunk. An ethnography of urban nomads*. Boston: Little, Brown.

Strauss, R. (1946). Alcohol and the homeless man. *Quarterly Journal of Studies on Alcohol, 7*, 360-404.

Vexliard, A. (1956). The hobo: Myths and realities. *Diogenes, 16*, 59-67.

Wallace, S. (1965). *Skid row as a way of life*. Totawa: Bedminister.

Wallace, S. E. (1968). The road to skid row. *Social Problems, 16*, 92-105.

White, H. C., Boorman, S. A., & Breiger, R. L. (1976). Social structure from multiple networks. I. Block-models of roles and positions. *American Journal of Sociology, 81*, 730-780.

Wiseman, J. P. (1979). *Stations of the lost*. Chicago: University of Chicago Press.

PART V

Epilogue

11

An Agenda for Future Research on Friendships of Older Adults

ROSEMARY BLIESZNER

Despite the numerous published reports on friendship in the later years summarized by Adams (this volume) and cited by the other authors (this volume), many gaps remain in the literature on this topic. Each essay in this collection includes suggestions for additional study of friendship in the later years. Table 11.1 charts the major points made by the various authors. (Often several authors made the same suggestion in their various contexts; this duplication does not appear in the table.) Besides these substantive recommendations associated with the content of the chapters, the contributors to this volume mentioned the need for

- theoretically-based
- multivariate analyses of
- diverse subgroups of adults, using
- innovative data collection strategies and
- longitudinal designs.

Descriptive, correlational studies are appropriate for establishing the basic contexts and parameters of friendship. Beyond that, it is essential that analysts frame their research in conceptual approaches that provide

TABLE 11.1
Summary of Authors' Suggestions for Future Research

Authors	Research Needs
Adams	Investigation of types of friendship and factors that influence definitions of friendship; open-ended questions; data on all friends in the network; probability samples
Allan & Adams	Studies that integrate more than one structural feature and examine friendship within the social context; how structural characteristics of early life friendship explain later patterns
Litwak	Longitudinal studies of differences among short-, intermediate-, and long-term friends
Tesch	Influence of friends on individual development and adaptation across the life cycle; differences in friend behavior based on attachment experiences; role of personality in friendship patterns
Blieszner	Circumstances and processes of initiating, sustaining, and dissolving friendships across the adult years; cyclical nature of friend relations and processes
Crohan & Antonucci	Mechanisms by which social support operates; norms for social support from friends and consequences of violating them; distinctions among types of nonkin; influence of social support on quality of life
Roberto	Stability and change in patterns of exchange across adulthood; extent and quality of exchanges; influences on exchange patterns over time; how people assess balance of exchanges; application of mathematical formulae to calculations of equity
Rook	Types, causes, and consequences of friendship strain across adulthood; influence of self-disclosure, personality, deficient social skills, and the larger network on friendship strain; techniques of conflict management
Wright	Connection between dispositional differences and gender differences in friendship; gender differences in friendships of never-married persons; correlates and consequences of comaraderie versus intimacy in friendships
Cohen	Application of network analysis techniques in friendship research; recognition of the cultural and temporal contexts of investigations

the basis for developing testable hypotheses about the relationships among variables. Moreover, these empirical efforts should incorporate multiple predictors of friendship interaction and outcomes. This will facilitate examination of key variables within a realistic context, rather than studying them in isolation from each other. Because the literature contains studies of only selected samples of older adults, the authors called for expanded attention to many subgroups of this heterogeneous age group. One-shot surveys and questionnaires have yielded some useful data, but now it is time for researchers to recognize the benefits of expanding the designs and methods they use and the types of data they gather. Later sections of this chapter elaborate on these points.

The authors in this volume further advised adopting a research perspective that acknowledges the reciprocal influences of

- structural features of the individual's social world,
- dispositional characteristics of the persons involved in friendships,
- processes of friend interaction, and
- functions of friendship in older adults' lives.

Friendship is a dynamic, multidimensional relationship. Friendships change over time yet remain stable in many respects. They differ according to numerous aspects of the individuals involved. The methods people use to make and retain friends, the ways they incorporate friends in daily activities and special occasions, and their reasons for having friends all vary across people and situations and time. Further advances in the field of late-life friendship will occur when researchers begin to take these interacting features into account.

THE CONCEPTUAL AGENDA

Taking a broad view of the gerontological friendship literature, one finds a focus that is rather limited in analysis of the effects of cohort, class, and culture. Existing studies describe friendships of the current cohort of older adults, with little regard for the potential effect of sociohistorical change on this personal relationship in the later years. In future studies, researchers should acknowledge the effects of demographic trends, technological advances, and historical events on the nature of older adult friendships. At the same time, the field could also benefit from a more explicit life course perspective. Developmental changes and role transitions may affect friendship patterns in ways that researchers have not yet explored fully. Long-term friends may be more helpful than newer friends for buffering the effects of developmental transitions (Stoller, 1987), but the literature does not contain a clear picture of this potentiality. Gerontologists could learn much more about age differences in expectations concerning friendship, both across the adult years and within the final stage of life.

Current studies of friendship have involved fairly homogeneous samples of elderly participants with respect to class and culture. Investigators should provide more empirical analyses of friendship patterns among many subgroups. Ethnic minorities, rural residents, frail and institutionalized aged, recent immigrants, and individuals who have relocated are but a few examples of the groups of older adults whose friendships remain understudied. Gerontologists with a socio-logical or psychological inclination should team with those possessing an anthropological perspective to gain assistance in separating the effects of aging on friendship from the effects of culture (Stoller, 1987). Scholars should explore the influence of health and utilization of community services in conjunction with the friend role. The field also needs more information on the lives of older adults who do not maintain close friendships. Then, gerontologists should analyze all of these topics in international settings, to determine the effects on friendship of culture more broadly defined.

The phenomenology of friendship is not well represented in the body of older adult friendship literature. Direct questions as to people's desires for friendship interactions, and satisfaction with various styles of friendship, are all too rare. Connections between dimensions of personality and aspects of friendship are still unexplored. Examination of older adults' motives for developing, maintaining, and dissolving friendships would be useful both theoretically and practically speaking. Although the literature contains evidence about support and social exchange among older adults' friends, relatively less information exists on concepts such as self-disclosure or attribution processes in late-life friendship and on the contributions of friendship to self-identity and self-esteem in old age. Whereas some general information exists on frequency of friend interaction, researchers should gather more specific data on what friends actually do together on a day-to-day basis and on perceptions of the quality of those activities and their overall significance to older adults.

A more explicit grounding of research questions in sociological and psychological theory would lend conceptual and predictive power to research efforts. Investigators have conducted numerous descriptive and exploratory studies, yet advancement of the gerontological friend-ship field is contingent upon theory-based research. Examples of theoretical frameworks that researchers might employ include role theory, symbolic interactionism, a conflict perspective, structural-functionalism, a labeling perspective, a life span developmental approach, and various personality theories.

THE METHODOLOGICAL AGENDA

Issues of research design, sampling, and data collection also need attention (see Adams, this volume). Short-term and long-term longitudinal studies of friendship could address many unanswered questions. A more thorough understanding of friendship would result from increased study of the specific ways that friendships either change or remain stable over time, and of the correlates, causes, and consequences of such stability or change. Investigators might consider alternatives such as age simulation techniques (Baltes & Goulet, 1971) or self-perceptions about change (see Ryff & Heincke, 1983) when longitudinal designs are not possible.

Comparisons of results across studies would also advance understanding about late-life friendship. Researchers should attempt to use consistent definitions and operationalizations of key constructs and variables. Those who seek to improve upon previous work by introducing new variables or measures might consider including constructs from previous studies in their work as well. This way, they could evaluate new approaches against old and accomplish more the building of a coherent body of knowledge than the proliferation of disjointed fragments. Along these same lines it is important that investigators replicate the same research questions across similar and different subgroups of older adults.

Convenience samples have dominated the friend studies in gerontology. The time has come for researchers to find support for larger, representative samples of older adults so they can examine the generalizability of their findings. Beyond the typical focus on each respondent describing one or more friendships, it is also time to employ network strategies that involved circles of friends in the study.

Scholars must think carefully about how they obtain information about friendship from aged adults. Gouldner and Strong (1987) used only open-ended interviews with their young adult and middle-aged respondents. They justified this decision on the basis that people so idealize friendship in the United States that they may be unable to give accurate answers to structured questions about it. Stoller (1987) cautioned that respondents' emotional well-being in old age may color their memories of friendships in the past. In our study of friendship development among residents of a new retirement community (Blieszner, this volume) we asked about exchanges of affection, assistance, and other resources. The overall rates of exchange were quite low on the structured questions, even among friends who were very close. We discovered why during the open-ended part of the interviews. Respondents considered their compliments, favors, and other activities to be so commonplace as to be trivial and assumed we had no interest in them. In fact, it was those everyday friend behaviors that were precisely the data we were trying to capture. These examples of factors that can influence the results of studies—self-deception about the quality of one's friendships, current feelings affecting retrospective accounts, and discounting the importance of various behaviors—are but three possibilities. Scholars must continue the pursuit of sensitive indicators to validly and reliably measure friendship characteristics.

The recommendations in this chapter and elsewhere in the volume pertain most directly to researchers who seek to explicate specific aspects of older adults' friendships. The authors recognize, however, that friend is often a category of relationship that emerges in studies of other topics in elderly persons' lives. Even when findings about friendship are of only peripheral importance to the main study at hand, researchers should define and measure friendship constructs carefully, and be sensitive in the interpretation of results to the issues discussed herein, so as to obtain the most accurate results possible.

Table 11.2 provides a summary of these suggestions for future research. It should be helpful to friendship researchers and to scholars who employ friendship concepts in other studies as well.

THE INTERPLAY OF STRUCTURE AND PROCESS

A key question in the study of older adult friendships is the following: What is the effect of different structural contexts and positions on aged persons' experiences of friendship and on the processes by which they engage in friendship? Structure and process interact to affect friendship in several ways. Individual characteristics such as gender, ethnicity, residential location, health, and so on supply opportunities or con-

TABLE 11.2

A Conceptual and Methodological Agenda for the Analysis of
Structure and Process in Older Adults' Friendships

Topic	Recommendations
	Conceptual Issues
Structure	Definition of friend Effects on friendship of gender, birth cohort, race, ethnicity, health, residential location, employment status, class, religion, marital status, social network participation Cross-generation and cross-gender friendships Life course perspective: effects of changes in roles Norms and individual expectations for friendship
Process	Identification of stages and cycles of friendship Strategies for accomplishing friendship goals, motives, influence of personality characteristics, meaning of friendship, effect on psychological well-being, everyday friendship interaction patterns
General Theory	Role theory, symbolic interactionism, conflict perspective, structural-functionalism, labeling perspective, life span developmental approach, various personality theories
	Methodological Issues
Design	Cross-sectional comparisons of diverse groups of elderly adults Longitudinal studies to assess change over time Quasi experiments, time series, ethnographic interviews, participant observation Replications
Sampling	Diverse subgroups, representative national samples, random selection Multiple members of networks, sociometric techniques
Data Collection	Daily interaction records, telephone calls by interviewer, interview transcriptions, observation notes, responses to quasi-experimental conditions

straints in forming and enjoying friendships. Personality characteristics affect perceptions of self and others, emotional closeness and satisfaction with friendships, and other dimensions that impinge on one's subjective assessment of friendship. Network characteristics such as number of friends, types of people in the friend circle, frequency and location of getting together, and so on influence the nature of the interactions that take place among friends. A more comprehensive understanding of older adult friendship awaits research projects that integrate such multiple aspects of this relationship.

Gerontologists can learn much about aging by studying it in the context of friendship. Friends typically are age peers, and thus share common experiences and similar resources. Older adults may express personality characteristics and social patterns differently with friends than with kin and other associates. Friendship provides a focal context for separating cohort effects from aging effects when investigators examine it for members of the same and different cohorts. Because friendship is a voluntary arrangement, expressions of personality traits and lifelong social patterns may be most veridical in the context of friendship as opposed to other forms of association. Even though other important adult roles may end in late life, friendships endure. Gerontologists can explore patterns of coping with aging and role loss by examining how aged friends assist each other to maintain or regain psychological well-being over the years. They can examine the place of friends in the lives of elderly adults whose kin are few and widely scattered. This information becomes increasingly important as families' childbearing and employment patterns affect the kin available to assist their elderly members. All of these examples imply that friendship is a fruitful domain for important advances in gerontological research.

REFERENCES

Baltes, P. B., & Goulet, L. R. (1971). Exploration of developmental variables by manipulation and simulation of age differences in behavior. *Human Development, 14*, 149-170.

Gouldner, H., & Strong, M. S. (1987). *Speaking of friendship.* New York: Greenwood.

Ryff, C. D., & Heincke, S. G. (1983). Subjective organization of personality in adulthood and aging. *Journal of Personality and Social Psychology, 44*, 807-816.

Stoller, E. P. (1987, November). *Discussion for the paper session, friends and isolates.* Comments presented at the 40th Annual Scientific Meeting of the Gerontological Society of America, Washington, DC.

Author Index

Subject Index

About the Authors

REBECCA G. ADAMS is Associate Professor in the Department of Sociology and Chair of the Interdepartmental Studies Gerontology Program at the University of North Carolina at Greensboro. She received the Ph.D. from the University of Chicago, with an emphasis on the sociology of aging. Her major research interest is friendship, especially in later adulthood. She has also recently published on adult day care and the support provided to older people by religious institutions.

GRAHAM A. ALLAN, Ph.D., has taught in the Department of Sociology and Social Policy at the University of Southampton, England, since 1975. Most of his research has been concerned with the sociology of friendship, sociability, and domestic life. His publications include *A Sociology of Friendship and Kinship* (1979) and *Family Life* (1985).

TONI C. ANTONUCCI, Ph.D., is Associate Research Scientist at the Institute for Social Research, Associate Professor of Psychology in the Department of Family Practice, and Adjunct Associate Professor in the Department of Psychology at the University of Michigan. A developmental psychologist by training, her research has focused on social relationships over the life span. She is currently the recipient of a Research Career Development Award from the National Institute of Aging.

ROSEMARY BLIESZNER is Associate Professor in the Department of Family and Child Development and Associate Director of the Center for Gerontology at Virginia Polytechnic Institute and State University. She received the Ph.D. from Pennsylvania State University in Human

Development-Family Studies with a concentration in Adult Development and Aging. Her research focuses on family and friend relationships and life events in adulthood and old age, with an emphasis on the contributions of close relationships to psychological well-being.

CARL I. COHEN, M.D., has been working with homeless populations since 1973, when he was a resident in psychiatry at New York University/Bellevue Medical Center. He has published widely in the areas of social psychiatry and gerontology. He is currently Professor of Psychiatry and Director of the Geriatric Psychiatry Program at the State University of New York Health Science Center at Brooklyn.

SUSAN E. CROHAN is a candidate for a doctoral degree in social psychology at the University of Michigan. Her research focuses on the social and psychological contributors to well-being over the life cycle, with a particular interest in interpersonal relationships.

EUGENE LITWAK, Ph.D., has a joint appointment as Head of the Division of Sociomedical Sciences in the School of Public Health and Professor in the Department of Sociology at Columbia University. His major fields of interest are the study of optimal patterns that formal and informal groups can take in a modern society and the nature of tasks they can best manage. He is currently applying these interests in the study of helping patterns among older people and the reduction of mortality and morbidity in the general public.

KAREN A. ROBERTO is Assistant Professor and Coordinator of the Gerontology Program at the University of Northern Colorado. She received the Ph.D. in Human Development from Texas Tech University. Her research interests include friendship patterns of older men and women, psychosocial changes in the lives of older women due to chronic illness, interaction patterns of older adults and their informal networks, and older caregivers of developmentally disabled adults.

KAREN S. ROOK is Associate Professor at the University of California at Irvine. Her research focuses broadly on psychosocial factors that affect older adults' physical and mental health. Since receiving the Ph.D. from UCLA in 1980, she has published widely in social psychological and gerontological journals.

STEPHANIE A. TESCH received the Ph.D. in human development from the University of Rochester in 1980, after receiving a B.A. in psychology from Macalester College in 1975. Her research interests are the development of friendship, intimacy, and ego identity. She is currently an adjunct lecturer in the University of Wisconsin system.

PAUL H. WRIGHT received the Ph.D. in social psychology from the University of Kansas in 1963 and is now Professor of Psychology at the University of North Dakota. Most of his research and writing have been in the area of interpersonal relationships. He has been particularly concerned to develop a model and coordinated technique for studying personal relationships with an emphasis on friendship.

NOTES

NOTES

NOTES

NOTES